A FOREIGN CAPITAL
INVESTMENT AND ITS LAW

Efforts to Establish a Learning Institution
within a Campus of International Character

ASPR SURD

Order this book online at www.trafford.com
or email orders@trafford.com

Most Trafford titles are also available at major online book retailers.

Printed in the United States of America.

ISBN: 978-1-4269-9559-0 (sc)
ISBN: 978-1-4269-9560-6 (hc)
ISBN: 978-1-4269-9561-3 (e)

Library of Congress Control Number: 2011916967

Trafford rev. 10/06/2011

 www.trafford.com

North America & international
toll-free: 1 888 232 4444 (USA & Canada)
phone: 250 383 6864 ♦ fax: 812 355 4082

to Establish a
**Learning Institution Within
a Campus of International Character
(To Pursue Educational, Health, Environment,
and Community Project Objectives)**

This work is dedicated to
my grandchildren
and to all grandchildren
around the world

Preface

FOREIGN CAPITAL INVESTMENT INTO ITALY, A TREATY
BETWEEN ITALY AND UNITED STATES; IMPROVEMENT
OF THE LAW #43/56 IS A MUST IN ORDER TO PREVENT
FURTHER FRAUD AND CORRUPTION.

Researched material on the Law#43/56, investment of foreign capital
in Italy, a treaty between Italy and United States, the whole can help
to understand much better the free and not too free local and global
financial devices implications. Past, present and future scandals in Italy
and other places show clearly that improvement of this specific law is not
only required but also urgent for its enforcement to prevent other financial
disasters. Besides the source and legal authority of this law's and its various
implications on connected R/D undertaken project activities, there seems
to exist an apparent desire to discuss the need to revisit the entire matter.
Without any doubts, there never was contemplated to discuss this with
concerned parties, although a much greater sensitivity of the issue exists at
present time. It is very important that many areas of this law are revisited
and taken into consideration in lieu of the several financial scandals and
community affairs.

In Italy and other countries around the globe, particularly at Avezzano
(Aq) as reference, financial operators may engage in wide cases of alleged
fraud and corruption of all kinds. The researched material in connection
with the projected CAMPUS OF INTERNATIONAL CHARACTER
AND THE LAW #43/56 could be a business school textbook on public
and private governance. It is certain that such researched material in

itself might have an important impact on urging a better enforcement of this law. The researched material is a product of years of meetings and discussions with private and public leaders from Italy and United States. The numerous pages are presented, at priori, as a proposed guideline for a foreign capital investment, which is based mainly upon recommendation of the mentioned law and its agreement. It is the failure of this law that must protect and encourage specific investment from relevant discrepancy and identified wrongdoing. A much greater transparency is needed to protect the investment of foreign capital into Italy, especially when there is a conflict of interest.

Within the frame of the law #43/56, it is time to ask: Who should pay the legal bills when there is an alleged criminal conspiracy to defraud an undertaking capital investment on behalf of the projected "CAMPUS" development activities? Is the City Hall of Avezzano that must be forced to pay as stated in related courts' sentence or somebody else, as lawyers often demand? Is the time for sentencing taken into account for all kind legal fees determination? Is the same time relevant and to be used also for costs re-evaluation of occurred expenses and out-of-pocket cash advances? The court determines legal fees, but who should calculate properly other related projects' costs that are used for collateral development activities? The amount of money, which has been paid for these specific projects' activities, must be accounted as legal expenses or as an investment according to the mentioned law and its treaty between Italy and United States? Information and researched materials derived from the "CAMPUS" could help scholars and students to understand much better how to invest not only foreign capitals in Italy and other countries, but first of all how to use their own human resources and personal efforts.

Though the court and legal experts have ignored the need to tackle such an important issue, the majority of capital investment firms often claim to recover certain accounts by means of insurance policy. However, if there is no insurance coverage, then it is very difficult to collect paid projects' expenses and legal fees. Also, from a capital investment perspective, foreign or not, the whole is an ultimate financial tragedy within the framework of the law #43/56 in substitution of a "Letter of Intent" which Italy seems to avoid. Insurance coverage within the spirit of this law is very important, at least when there is an interpretation or an anticipation that all this might have triggered fallout in such projects' activities coverage, especially where and when fraud and time are main factors for a court decision. Insurance companies, now seeking to stop payouts to wrongdoers, are proposing new insurance policies to be written differently than in the past. Again, the researched material and information derived by investigating the "Campus of International Character" at Avezzano, Italy, the entire matter can help to re-write the new insurance policy rules.

This and other laws, in Italy especially, give an image of a system in which does not want to pursue wrongdoing. It is not really the government that is affected, it is the system of Italy and above all the credibility and reliability. If there are foreign capitals to be invested and opportunities to do business in Italy, then it is important to ask before anything else: Is Italy a reliable country?

By Aspr Surd

Introduction

Motives and Methods:

The goal of this project is to establish an American school of physical education, health, recreation, camping, and outdoor activity. The investigation and research into strategy and organizational structure began as a result of writing comparative physical education programs. The initial thought was that an examination of the way different schools of physical education carried out the same programs would have as much value as a study of how an American university campus program carried out all these activities. Such a comparative analysis could have permitted deeper probes into the nature of the functions studied.

Of the several activities besides the physical education and athletics core that will be offered by this projected American university campus, administration and organization appear to be among the most promising for the projected institution.

If changing developments in organization and administration of this university present a challenging area for comparative analysis, the study of innovation in the matter of academic curricula seems to furnish the proper focus for such an investigation. Historically, Italian schools have rarely changed their daily routines and their positions of power except under the strongest pressures. Therefore, a study of the forms and methods implemented in the creation of a new school should point to urgent needs and compelling opportunities both within and without the university campus. For a study of such forms, the organizational structure used to administer the most complex of American colleges and universities seem to offer the wildest possibilities.

What, then, has been the structure used to administer such colleges and universities? And what were its innovators?

A preliminary survey of some American colleges and universities in the East and Midwest helped to answer these questions. This survey showed that in recent years what may be called the multi-divisional type of "educational" organization has generally become used by most of the leading higher learning institutions in the country, which carry on the most diverse economic, financial, and educational activities.

In this type of organization, a general office plans, coordinates, and appraises the work of a number of operating divisions or colleges and allocates the necessary personnel, facilities, funds, and other resources. The executives in charge of these divisions, in turn, have under their command most of the functions necessary for handling one major line of programs and services in a specific area. Each of these top executives is responsible for the financial results of the division or college and for its success in the specific area.

As my investigation of educational-organizational innovation in these colleges and universities progressed, several important facts became clear. First, a meaningful analysis of the creation of a new educational administrative form called for accurate knowledge about the institution's previous organization and, in fact, about its entire administrative history. Second, changes in organizational structure should be intimately related to the ways in which the institution had expanded. An evaluation of any administrative change, therefore, demanded a detailed understanding of the justifications and methods of growth. Third, these patterns of growth, in turn, should have reflected changes in the overall community economy, particularly those affecting the areas, or fields, in demand for the institution's programs and services. Finally, the reorganizations were influenced by the state of administrative art in the United States at the time activities were being carried out. The first two points have required further investigation into the history, philosophy, and implications at these institutions. The third and fourth call for broader awareness of the history of American colleges and universities and their related businesses and economies.

A need to enlarge the scope of the study of the American University of Avezzano made possible a broadening of its objectives. One way to ascertain the impact of the more general economic and administrative developments on the growth and organization of these educational institutions was to compare the experience of the four institutions studied with similar Italian institutions (Instituto Superiore di Educazione Fisica; Universita per Stranieri di Perugia; Center of Studies; and other local universities). Such an expanded comparison not only could make the process of innovation in areas of the projected university more comprehensible but could also provide information on which generalizations might be based about the history of these colleges and universities as institutions—one of the most critically important aspects of modern institutions. In this way, what began as an attempt to compare physical education programs was broadened to encompass the writing of a physical education philosophy and its implications for the projected Campus of International Character.

To carry out these broader objectives, the administrative and organizational histories of other American educational institutions were briefly examined.

The information on several educational institutions came primarily from readily available materials, such as manuals and educational reports, agencies' publications, articles in periodicals, and occasionally via educational institutions' business bulletins. Using these data, I have attempted to lay the foundation for the American University of Avezzano as a basic, modern, liberal, independent, international institution.

Propositions

If useful comparisons are to be made among educational institutions and then fourscore more, and if decisions and actions in this projected American university are to indicate something about the history of other educational institutions, the terms and concepts used in these comparisons and analyses must be carefully and precisely defined. Otherwise, comparisons and findings could be more misleading than instructive. The following set of general or theoretical propositions attempts to provide some sort of conceptual precision. Without reference to the historical reality of this project foundation, it proposes to explain in fairly clear-cut, simplified terms how the "decentralized" structure of the American University of Avezzano comes into being.

Before developing these propositions, the term *American University of Avezzano* needs to be defined. In a broad sense, it means a private, nonprofit-oriented incorporation, involved in the handling of services in some or all of the successive educational processes, from the procurement of the educational materials to the promotion of exchange programs among students and faculty, as well as educational tourism. In other words, the American University of Avezzano is conceived as an independent economic-educational organism which is created over and above the individuals who constitute it. This entity appears then as the agent in each of these transactions and leads, as it were, a life of its own, which often exceeds the length of its human members.

While the American University of Avezzano may have a life of its own, its present and future health and growth surely depend on the individuals who guide its activities. What, then, are the functions of the executives responsible for the fortunes of the American University of Avezzano?

Executives will coordinate, appraise, and plan activities. Activities may include actual teaching, promotion, accounting, or research, but in the advance phases of this projected university, the execution or carrying out of these functions is usually left to such individuals as specialized staff and specific professionals. Typically, the executive president of this university should not personally supervise the workforce but rather administer the duties of other executives. In planning and coordinating the work of subordinate supervisors or directors, the president's office allocates tasks and makes available the necessary equipment, materials, and other physical resources necessary to carry out the various jobs. In appraising these activities, it must decide whether the employees or subordinate supervisor and director are handling their tasks satisfactorily. If not, actions can be taken by changing or bringing in new physical equipment and supplies, by transferring or shifting the personnel, or by expanding or cutting down on available funds. Thus, the term *administration*, as used here, includes executive action and orders, as well as the decisions taken in coordinating, appraising, and planning the work of the enterprise and in allocating specific resources.

Administration

The initial proposition for the American University of Avezzano is that administration is an identifiable activity, that it differs from actual buying, selling, or service-processing. In other educational institutions, the concern of the executives is more focused on administration than the performance of functional teaching and learning work. In large educational institutions, administration usually becomes a specialized full-time job. A second proposition is that the administrator must handle two types of administrative tasks when coordinating and planning the activities of the American University of Avezzano. At times, it must be concerned with the long-term health of this university and at other times with its smooth and efficient day-to-day operation. The first type of activity calls for concentrating on long-term planning and appraisal; the second on meeting immediate problems and needs and handling unexpected contingencies or legal matters, though in the actual life of the American University of Avezzano the distinction between these two types of activities or decisions are often not clear-cut. Yet some decisions will clearly deal largely with defining basic goals, while other decisions have more to do with the day-to-day operations carried out within the broader framework of goals, policies, and procedures.

The next few propositions deal with the content of administrative activities handled through the different types of posts or positions in the administrative structure of this university. The executive in this "decentralized" educational institution carries out administrative activities from four different types of positions. Each of these types of positions within the university organization has a different range of administrative activities. Normally, each is on a different level of authority.

At the top is the general office (president and supervisor-coordinator). These top executives and related staff specialists coordinate, appraise, and plan goals and policies and allocate resources for a number of Quasi-autonomous, fairly self-contained divisions or colleges. Each division handles their own program of studies or carries on the educational activities in one of the specific service areas. Each division's central office, in turn, administers a number of departments. Each of these departments is responsible for the administration of a major function: courses of studies, instruction, extra-curricular activities, services, purchasing, research, and finance proposals. The departmental headquarters, in turn, coordinate, appraise, and plan for a number of field units. At the lowest level, each field unit runs a program or service, a branch or sales office, a purchasing office, restaurant, swimming pool, or dormitory, et cetera.

The four types of administrative positions in this multi-divisional university are: the field unit, the departmental headquarters, the division's central office, and the general office. These terms are used throughout this project to designate a specific set of administrative activities. They do not, it must be stressed, refer to the university campus office buildings or rooms. One office building could house executives responsible for any one of the positions or conceivably those responsible for all four. Conversely, the executives in any one of the posts could be housed in different rooms or buildings.

Only in the first, the field unit, are the directors or managers primarily involved in carrying on or personally supervising day-to-day activities. Even there, if the volume of activity supposes to be large, they spend much of their time on administrative duties. But many duties must be largely operational, carried out within the framework of policies and procedures set by departmental headquarters and the higher offices. The departmental and divisional offices may make some long-term decisions, but their executives work within a comparable framework as determined by the general office. The primary administrative activities should also tend to be tactical or operational. The general office makes the broad strategic or educational or entrepreneurial decisions as to policy and procedures and can do so largely because it has the final say in the allocation of the American University of Avezzano's resources—staff, money, and materials—necessary to carry out administrative decisions and actions and others made with its approval, at any level

Policies and Procedures

It seems wise to emphasize the distinction between the formulation of policies and procedures and their implementation at the American University of Avezzano. The formulation of policies and procedures can either be strategic or tactical. Strategic decisions are concerned with the long-term health of the entire projected university. Tactical decisions deal more with the day-to-day activities necessary for efficient and smooth operations. But decisions, either tactical or strategic, usually require implementation by an allocation or reallocation of resources: funds, equipment, or personnel. Strategic plans can be formulated from below, but normally the implementation of such proposals requires the resources that only the higher office of the American University of Avezzano can provide. Within the broad policy lines set down by that office and with the resources it allocates, at the lower levels the executives of the university carry out tactical decisions.

The executives who actually allocate available resources at the American University of Avezzano are the key persons here. Because of their critical and difficult role in establishing the university economy, they will be defined in this organization as trustees. In contrast, those who coordinate, appraise, and plan within the means allocated to them will be termed president, vice-presidents, supervisor-coordinator (provost), director or deans, chairman, or manager. So trustees' board decisions and actions will refer to those persons who affect the allocation or reallocation of resources for the American University as a whole. Operating decisions and actions will refer to those carried out using already allocated resources.

Just because the board of trustees will make some of the most significant decisions in the American University of Avezzano economy, they should not all necessarily imbued with a long-term strategic outlook. In this justification, the executives responsible for resource allocation may very well concentrate on day-to-day operational affairs, giving little or no attention to changing educational programs, technology, sources of service supply, and other factors affecting the long-term health of the American University of Avezzano. Their decisions may be made without forward planning or analysis, but rather by meeting every new situation, problem, or crisis in an ad-hoc way as it arises. They accept the goals of their enterprise as given or inherited. Clearly, wherever the board of trustees act like directors or managers, wherever they concentrate on short-term activities to the exclusion or to the detriment of long-range planning, appraisal, and coordination, they have failed to effectively carry out their role in the economy, as well as in their American University. This effectiveness must provide a useful criterion for evaluating the performance of an executive of the American University of Avezzano.

As already pointed out, the executives in the American University work in four types of offices, each with his own administrative duties, problems, and needs. These four types operate on different scales, and their officers have different business horizons. The head and managers in the field unit are concerned with one function—educational program, marketing, service, recreational program, tourism services, and so forth—in one specific area. The chairman or directors of the department plan, administer, and coordinate the activities of one function on a broad area of studies or services and often are large-scale rather than just specific. Their professional-academic activities and their outside sources of information concern persons and programs operating in the same specialized function. The divisional or college deans, on the other hand, deal with more complex institution business rather than a function. They are concerned with all the functions involved in the overall processes of handling a line of academic activities, service, and curricula. Their professional horizons and contacts are determined by the American University of Avezzano rather than functional interests. Finally, the president, the supervisor-coordinator, and the director in the higher office have to deal with several collateral businesses, schools, services, and programs, or one program division in several broad and specific areas of studies or services. They set policies and procedures and allocate resources for divisions or colleges carrying out all types of functions, either in various specific areas or in quite different services and programs. Their responsibilities and business horizons and interests are broadened to range over the university campus jurisdiction and even the international economies affairs of the American University of Avezzano.

While all four types of offices may exist on the university campus, each can, of course, exist separately. The American University of Avezzano, as here conceived, can include one, two, three, or all four of these offices. At the beginning, project phases of this university may have only a simple office managing a single aspect: promotion, organization, planning, finance, structure, curriculum, committees, or coordination. Advanced phases of the project, with an already established number of operating units, will carry out a single function, such as courses for liberal arts, physical education, languages, sports programs, recreational, swimming, et cetera.

The overall administrative structure comprises a headquarters and field or campus offices. Here, also, are integrated educational and services programs that handle several economic functions rather than just one. Finally, diversified projects (business enterprises, endowments, et cetera), carry on different functions and produce a variety of activities and services in all aspects of the American University of Avezzano's objectives.

As each type of position handles a different range of administrative activities, each will result from a different type of growth. Until the volume or technological complexity of the American University of Avezzano's economic-financial-academic activities grows to demand increasing division of labor within the institution, little time is needed to be spent on administrative work. The resulting specialization requires one or more of the university's executives to concentrate on coordinating, appraising, and planning these specialized activities. As soon as the American University of Avezzano expands by setting up or acquiring facilities and personnel to fulfill its needs, it has to create an organization at a central headquarters to administer the units in the campus and off the campus. Soon, as it grows and moves into new functions, a central office will evolve to administer the departments carrying on the different functions. Such a central administrative unit will prove necessary when, in following the policy of vertical integration, the division or college begins to do its own study programs and services, procuring students, tourists, visitors, and producing new ideas and projects. Finally, when the integrated university becomes diversified through purchasing or creating new facilities and entering new programs and lines of business, or when it expands its several functional departments over a still larger specific area, it will fashion a number of integrated divisional colleges units administered by a general office.

Strategy is defined as the determination of the basic long-term goals and objectives of the American University of Avezzano's projects, the adoption of courses of action, and the allocation of resources necessary for carrying out those goals. Decisions to expand the volume of activities, to set up remote activities through branches and offices, to move into new educational-economical functions, or to become diversified along many lines of business involve defining basic new goals. New courses of action must be devised and resources allocated and reallocated in order to achieve those goals and to maintain and expand the university's activities in the new areas in response to shifting social and economical demands, changing sources of supply, fluctuating economic and political conditions, new technological developments, and actions of concerned persons. The adoption of a new strategy may add new types of personnel and facilities and alter the business horizons of the person responsible for the American University; thus it can have a profound effect on the form of the organization and future development.

Structure is here defined as the organizational design through which the American University of Avezzano is administered. The design, whether formal or informal by definition, has two aspects. It includes, first, the lines of authority and communication between the different administrative offices and officers and, second, the information and data that flow through those lines of communication and authority. Such lines and data are essential to assure the effective coordination, appraisal, and planning necessary to carrying out the basic goals and policies and in knitting together the total resources of this university. These resources include educational philosophy; financial capital; physical equipment, such as buildings, offices, facilities, and other educational-recreational programs, and purchasing facilities; sources of original educational-recreational materials; research and laboratories; and, most important of all, the technical marketing and administrative skills of the personnel involved.

The results that will be deduced from these several propositions include that structures follow strategy and that this type of structure is the outcome of the concatenation of several basic strategies. Expansion of volume leads to the creation of an administrative office to handle one function in one local area. Growth through geographical dispersion brings the need for a departmental structure and headquarters to administer several local field units. The decision to expand into new types of functions calls for building a central office and a multi-departmental structure, while developing new lines of services and programs or continued growth on a local, national, or international scale brings the formation of a multi-divisional structure, with a general office to administer the different divisions. The move into new functions will be referred to as a *strategy of vertical integration* and that of the development of new educational programs and services as a *strategy of diversification* (see: a bridge with three double lanes and traffic problems).

At this point, this theoretical or practical discussion must be carried a step further by asking two questions:

1. If structure does follow strategy, why should there be a delay in developing the new organization needed to meet the administrative demands of the new strategy?
2. Why did the new strategy, which called for a change in structure, come in the first place?

There are at least two plausible answers to the first query: either the new organization-administrative needs that will be created by the new strategy are not positive or strong enough to require structural change, or the executives involved are not unaware of the new needs. There seems to be no question that a new strategy can create positive new organizational administrative needs. Nevertheless, executives of this university could still continue to administer both old and new activities with the same personnel, using the same channels of communication and authority and the same types of information. Such an organization and administration, however, must become increasingly efficient.

This proposition should be true, however, for the relatively initial phases of the university's project, which structure consists of informal arrangements between a few supporters and executives, as well as for advanced activities whose size and numerous administrative personnel require a more formal definition of relations between offices and officers. At the time when expansion should create the need for new organizational-administrative offices and structures, the reasons for delays in developing the new organization will rest with the executives responsible for the university's longer-range growth and health. Either these administrators will be too involved in day-to-day tactical activities to appreciate or understand the longer-range organizational needs of the university or else their training and education will fail to factor into their perception of organizational problems or their ability to handle them. They may also resist desirable organizational-administratively changes because they feel structural reorganization will threaten their own personal positions, their power, or, most importantly, their psychological security.

In answer to the second question, changes in strategy that call for changes in structure will also refer to the opportunities and needs created by changing student-tourist populations, local-national-international income, and the "campus" educational-technological innovations. Population growth that shifts from nearby areas to the city near the campus, depressions and prosperity, and the increasing pace of equipment and technology changes, will all create new demand or curtail existing activities for the campus project's objectives or services. The prospect of new educational initiatives or the threatened loss of a current program's incentives stimulates geographical consideration, horizontal integration, and programs and service diversification. Moreover, once the university has accumulated large resources, the need to keep its personnel, money, and materials steadily employed provides a constant stimulus to seek new endeavors by moving into new areas, taking on new functions, or developing new project lines. Again, the awareness of the needs and opportunities that will be created by the changing environment seems to depend on the training and personality of individual executives and on their abilities to keep their eyes on the more important university problems, even in the midst of pressing operational needs.

The answers to the two questions can be briefly summarized by restating the general thesis. Strategic growth will result from an awareness of the opportunities and needs created by changing economic, political, and social populations; income; and technology to employ existing facilities' programs or expanding resources more profitably. A new strategy will require at least a refashioned structure if the enlarged American University of Avezzano's activities are going to be efficiently operated.

One important corollary to this proposition is that growth without structural adjustment can only lead to economic inefficiency. Unless new structures are developed to meet new organizational-administrative needs that result from the expansion of the American University of Avezzano's activities into new areas, functions, or parallel endowment project lines, the technological, financial, and personal economies of growth and size cannot be realized. Nor can the enlarged resources be employed as profitably as they otherwise might be. Without administrative offices and program structures, the individual units within the university campus (the field units, the departments, and divisions) could undoubtedly operate as efficiently—even more so in terms of cost per unit and volume of output per student-employee as independent units—as if they are part of a larger enterprise. Whenever the executives of the American University of Avezzano are responsible for the failure to create the offices and structure necessary to effectively bring together various administrative offices into a unified whole, they fail to carry out one of their basic economic financial roles.

The actual patterns of growth and organization-building of the campus complex, as well as other parallel activities of the American University of Avezzano, may not be, as often happens, as clear-cut as they are theoretically defined here. One strategy of expansion could be carried out in many ways; and two or three basic expansions will often be undertaken at the same time. Growth might come through simultaneous building or purchasing of new facilities and equipment and through affiliating or merging with other universities and associations. Occasionally, the American University of Avezzano must simultaneously expand its volume, build new facilities in geographically different areas, move into new functions, and develop different types of activities and endowment projects lines. Structure, as the case studies indicate, is often slow to follow strategy, particularly in periods of rapid political and financial oscillations. As a result, the distinctions between the duties of the different offices and persons remain confused and only vaguely defined. One executive or small group of university personnel should carry out at the same time the functions of a general office, control office, and departmental headquarters. Eventually, however, this institution may come to devise the specific units to handle field or campus facilities, a functional department, an integrated division, or diversified parallel project activities. For this very reason, a clear-cut definition of structure and strategy and a simplified explanation or theory of the relation of one to the other should make it easier to comprehend the complex realities involved in the expansion and management of the projected university and easier to evaluate the achievement of the organization's building structure.

A comparative analysis of organizational innovation demands should be more than an explanation of the terms, concepts, and general properties to be used in assessing comparable experiences of different institutions. It also calls for an understanding of the larger historical educational situation, both within and without the American University of Avezzano, during which strategic expansion and organizational change will take place. The executives and people connected with this university must keep in mind that time does not solve their administrative-organizational problems in a vacuum. Other large or small institutions are meeting the same needs and challenges and seeking to resolve comparable structural problems. Their responses will have an impact on the history of this university, just as the experiences of this one will affect that of many others.

The organizational-administrative story in each of the case studies falls into basic parts:

—The creation of the organizational structure after the university's first major growth or corporate rebirth
—Its reorganization to meet the needs arising from the strategies of further expansion

In developing its early organizational-administrative structures, the American University of Avezzano followed practices accepted in other American universities. Here, the organizational building structure could have benefited from other project activities. In fashioning the modern, multi-divisional structure, these old and new approaches, on the other hand, went beyond existing practices. Here, others will learn from eliminating mistakes. An evaluation of the measures taken by each must improve the development of the activities required.

One way to provide such a historical setting is to present a brief review of the growth and development of this projected university. As the survey is based only on readily available materials and information, supplemented by personal studies and research, its findings must be considered preliminary and tentative. Much more detailed study will be necessary before the history and progress of the American University of Avezzano can be accurately and fully explained. Nevertheless, even such a preliminary study indicates significant trends in the growth and development of this university's projects. An awareness of these trends is essential for understanding the more detailed case studies presented for this projected university and of the subsequent changes in the structure and strategy of the undertaking to promote and develop a Campus of International Character in Avezzano, Italy.

—Memorandum—

In the year 1969, at Avezzano, Italy, the projected Campus of International Character was chartered in the state of Ohio (USA), on March 5, 1970, identification number 23-7100165, as the American College of Avezzano, Inc.; all related project material was submitted to the concerned parties, such as the city hall of Avezzano and the Prefect of L'Aquila Province. Copies of acknowledgement went to governmental agencies in Italy and the United States. Among the various objectives defined, with connected programs to be implemented, health, recreation, and education activities were and remain the basic foundation on which the entire undertaking was developed. A site of seventeen acres, with more land optioned for expansion, was identified for construction of the projected campus facilities, and a check was cashed by the city hall of Avezzano for the land acquisition as negotiated and requested, with the approval of local and provincial government authorities. Unfortunately, litigation then followed, as it was suggested by the local power-of-attorney. Low and high Italian courts have ruled in favor of the American College of Avezzano. However, a petition to the International Court of Justice has been drafted to reevaluate the Italian courts rulings.

In spite of some difficulties, even at the present time, the health-recreation-education aspects of this project are still a major focus of interest. In fact, it is well reported from private and public sources of this specific projected Campus development that providing people with food and shelter is not enough. These sources also admitted that people must be provided with some means to utilize increased leisure time. It is quite evident that the practice of putting health and recreation into one compartment and education and working conditions into another has not been successful. Current events may show that some local situations could be more efficiently eased by new approaches toward specific involvement in community affairs and other kinds of local and regional projects, where the practice of self-persuasion will be used to foster the importance of such health-recreation-education activities.

It must be underlined that some concerns from a review of the present health system at this specific location already are indicated,, including administrative inefficiencies, supply shortages, poor training, conflicts with providers, systemwide inflexibility, and potentially some sacrifice of quality caused by the relatively slow adoption of new technology. Hence, the originally conceived health-recreation-education program for Avezzano (Italy) will contribute a much larger and meaningful role to the creative activity in the training of both youngsters and adults of the community. This will above all be a campus of work in preventive and corrective medicine; prevention is better than cure and vastly cheaper in the long run.

August, 1969

To whom it may concern:

Your comments, criticisms, and additions to the ideas contained in the attached presentation are welcomed. Please send them to the author at the address below. Thank you for your attention and thoughtful consideration of this proposed project.

P.S.—The enclosed "Presentation of the Idea to Establish an American School of Physical Education, Recreation, Health, and Camping with Outdoor Education in Avezzano, Italy" has been submitted and approved by the city hall of Avezzano as of "Verbale delle Deliberazioni della Giunta Municipale," N. 889, dated 8/18/69, and also N. 219, dated 10/1/70.

December 13, 1967

"Mens sana in corpore sano": a healthy mind in a healthy body. This has been the motto of world leaders and sports heroes from the glorious golden days of early Greece to the present time.

In this grand tradition, we propose a new and unique educational institution, located in the heart of Italy, to be known as American University of Avezzano, Italy. The proposed university will consist of schools of liberal arts, science, and physical education, with particular interest and emphasis on the exchange of educational techniques, cultural understanding, and sociological concepts among the United States, Italy, and the world. The school and its curriculum would be accredited in Italy and the United States.

Avezzano, which is set in a region of natural beauty easily accessible from Rome and all parts of Europe, is a perfect location for an international campus. The numerous advantages to students in the establishment of such an educational institution include the fact that they would acquire an education in their chosen field, learn the language of another country, gain an understanding of the country's past and present trends of living and its development in world society. In addition, through physical education and sports, men would be brought together in a competitive and friendly manner. What better way to answer the call of our young people who are seeking to better their lives through increased mutual understanding? The time is *now* to extol the virtues of our rich heritage and stress ethical character, augmented by intercommunication among world populations striving for harmony of ideals and intellectual advancement to achieve the finer sentiments required for a healthy and enduring society for all mankind.

I greatly welcome your comments regarding the ideas set forth in the attached proposal.

Project for Promoting
An American University in Avezzano, Italy

Liberal Arts and Sciences, Fine Arts, Foreign Languages,
Teacher Education, and Leadership Training in Health,
Physical Education, Recreation, and Outdoor Education

Physical education in the United States has a sense of pride and accomplishment; its success has captured the imagination of the people of the world. This educational system greatly impresses foreigners because the American physical education curriculum provides for, and is adapted to, the needs of contemporary society.

The philosophy of American physical education foundations, its implications, and its result in the accomplishment of goals for a better society has spread more confidence among the peoples of the world. As a matter of fact, this physical education curriculum is one of the most effective for helping human beings to better understand the importance and means of achieving high knowledge and friendly relations among peoples.

In contrast to the American physical education curriculum, Italy, as well as many other countries, has its own national program of physical education. The educational standards, courses of study, time allocation, attendance, and even facilities requirements are outlined by a national university of education or other agency, showing what a gap there is among these systems. In these countries, there is a great uniformity in educational programs. This situation sometimes makes it difficult for the people of these countries to comprehend and to pursue the objectives of a physical education curriculum as meanful to life and to master positive values. In order to better transmit the knowledge of advanced American physical education programs to these people, a university carrying out and developing the program should be founded, especially where the needs are evident. These needs must also be related to the social, economic, and geographic conditions of the university location.

A university based on a physical education philosophy of this kind would be very helpful to Italian and other societies. Avezzano, Italy, because of its geographic position, its nearness to a variety of people of different nationalities for the interest of students, the population of this area, as well as its cultural background, is one of the best locations in which this institution could be placed. Being near Rome, it would be without a doubt the best place for carrying out the various kinds of objectives for which the university might aim.

The philosophy of this institution and the policy and objectives for which it is established must be based primarily upon an American curriculum for training leaders and personnel in physical education, health, camping and outdoor education, et cetera. This curriculum should be one that has already been accredited by one of the institutions of higher education in the USA.

The main objectives and purposes of the American University in Avezzano are to contribute to the development of a true value of American physical education philosophy (honesty, generosity, altruism, sincerity, loyalty, courage, et cetera) and to training those students who would be best qualified. Materials of study would be selected carefully; facilities must be the most efficient and the most appropriate for the time and use; and the staff must be one of the best prepared for the job of teaching and carrying out the philosophical intent of this institution. Moreover, the American University will try to pursue other cultural goals and services:

—Encourage exchange of individuals and groups for education or informational purposes

—Project a reasonable appreciation and an enjoyable image of the country, its cultural past, and present trends of living

—Provide language training, since knowledge of a language is considered the key to understanding much about a country

To a large extent, knowledge will spread out of this institution's programs. Students need to learn the latest technological developments. By visiting townspeople, they can learn about local life and absorb impressions of a direct, solid knowledge of a foreign country. The American University of Avezzano would deeply support cultural exchange and cultural cooperation, because cooperation wins friends, and friendship stimulates exports: "Trade follows the book." Here, also, will be room for understanding a country's habits and traditions, fostering an understanding of the reasons for a policy, if not agreement with it. So the American University will be concerned with reasonably ensuring that both the "giving" and "receiving" countries benefit from this project. Nevertheless, there is a great measure of idealism.

The basis of the work of the American University in Avezzano should be bilateral, most of it involving movement of people and materials between Italy and the United States. It is two-way traffic; in the interest of efficiency, cooperation must be close between the promoting members of the American University of these two countries. There is no doubt that this work of promoting the American University based upon the physical education philosophy will help reduce misunderstandings, reduce prejudice, and promote knowledge. "The closer countries move together politically or economically, the more, not the less, important cultural work is likely to become. The national performs its essential function, not in its capacity as a power, but in its capacity as a society." Senator J. W. Fulbright.

The physical structure of this institution must have some original style, tied up somehow with a model of an American university campus. Even if some change in this structure takes place to adapt to the location and conform, more or less, to local construction, the general concept of this university aesthetic must be a prototype of an American university "micro campus". The facilities and equipment employed here must also be of American standards; however, locally manufactured equipment should be taken into consideration.

Given the character of this institution and the objectives for which it works, special facilities and equipment play a big role, and, for that reason, they have a priority. For instance, grounds for recreation and play, a swimming pool, gymnasium, and social hall should receive particular attention and consideration. This complex, carried out and developed accurately for the best purposes, certainly will achieve concrete results.

Besides the use of these facilities for academic purposes, they must be extended for other purposes, such as recreational and resort uses. Athletic facilities for the performances of American, Canadian, and other foreign students enrolled as visitors to the American university campus would result, without any doubt, in intense interest in the university and its benefits to the country.

The swimming pool during the summer could be used for a variety of purposes, from instruction to exhibition and international meetings, and for many other uses, including availability to the youth of the community, under close supervision of the university staff.

The social hall, where shows, musicals, ballets, concerts, et cetera, would be performed with an American-Italian accent, could contain and entertain guests, tourists, students, parents, friends, and the local population. Programs would be selected and prepared specifically for the purpose of satisfying the needs of students and visitors.

An atmosphere of cordiality, of work and relaxation, and the enjoyable and productive values of the social life of the American University must be the main foundations.

American students, as well as transients, must find their own housing.

Personnel working for this university must be the most qualified for the fulfillment of their jobs.

Courses of foreign languages, primarily Romance languages, would be offered for American, Canadian, and other foreign students. Fine arts courses also would be available; these courses would be requirements of the university curriculum. Students enrolled in fine arts courses would directly and deeply appreciate the practical use of academic materials. Some courses would be held in "mobile classrooms" in order to allow visitors to admire personally and practically the materials subjected to study. Science courses, offered adequately, should give balance to the university curriculum and contribute mainly to the needs of the local educational system.

International experiences would be mutually achieved by American students in Italy and by foreign students who wish to be prepared for study in the United States. Vocational efficiency, too, would be paramount, with attention to each field of specialization, as manifested in the individual interests and aptitudes of the students. Courses in the American University should be open to full enrollment toward a baccalaureate or for part-time study abroad with transfer of credit to the native college or university of the transient student.

Camping areas near the university should be developed so that tourists can explore and enjoy one of the most beautiful and primitive locations of Italy. Mountain climbing and ski areas will be natural implications of the program of this university because of the local mountains (Mt. Velino, Gran Sasso d'Italia, Maiella) around the university's location. The extensive history of this location in archaeology and anthropology would satisfy those people for whom these subjects are interesting.

Since this university would be located at the center of Italy, tourists and students would be able to move in any direction, traveling to the best Italian cities such as Rome, Florence, Naples, Perugia, Pescara, and L'Aquila in a very short time and at little cost.

It would be the policy of this University to host and to assist students, tourists, and visitors from the United States, Canada, and other parts of the world in order to create the atmosphere of an American university based essentially on physical education philosophy.

The American University of Avezzano, Italy, within a "campus of international character," would offer liberal arts and sciences, fine arts, and professional arts, with a major emphasis directed toward an American curriculum in physical education, health, recreation, and camping with outdoor education. It must be presented as a nonprofit organization whose objectives are to develop an American curriculum in the above areas of study and train personnel to be qualified for these jobs and, in the meantime, offer services for tourists and exchange students in Italy.

This institution would be governed and directed by its promoting members and founders; however, many functional responsibilities would be delegated.

Meetings at all levels of responsibility should be held in order to maintain and promote a sound democratic philosophy in this institution.

Students, faculty, administration, tourists, visitors, staff, et cetera, should be organized properly, with equal rights and functions for the best cooperation and collaboration in achieving the objectives of the university curriculum.

The curriculum and the university itself should receive accreditation from an American institution of higher learning from national and international accreditation organizations, et cetera. It must be consistent with aspirations of these institutions and organizations.

American University of Avezzano, Italy

A new and distinctive American University will be established in the heart of Italy. Its purpose is to exchange educational techniques and to promote cultural understanding among Italy, the United States, and other countries.

The program of studies, based on the American curriculum, will include liberal arts and sciences, fine arts, foreign languages, teacher education, and leadership training in health, physical education, recreation, and outdoor education. International experience will be achieved by American students in Italy and by foreign students who will be prepared for study in the United States. A two-way exchange will accordingly broaden the scope of higher education. Vocational efficiency, too, will be paramount, with attention to each field of specialization, as manifested in the individual interests and aptitudes of the students.

Avezzano, set in a region of natural beauty and easily accessible from Rome, is a perfect location in which an international campus of distinction can flourish. It is a classic land, where relics of great art, revealing archives of Western civilization, abound in ancient edifices and in museums. Many will be seen in the unfrequented valleys, in sleepy little townships nearby, or on the attractive mountainsides that surround the city. Students of fine arts courses will directly appreciate the practical use of rare academic materials. Some courses will be held in "mobile classrooms" in order to visit and to admire the objects subjected to study.

A picturesque campus, already acquired, consists of sixty acres on the edge of the city amidst woodlands and rolling fields. College buildings will express the architectural harmony of the academic spirit inherent in an ancient setting of natural splendor. There, scholars may assemble to study and work together, or retreat, if they choose, to the comfortable solitude of the environment. For active recreation, the adjacent park with playing fields provided by the town will contribute an unsolicited and welcome adjunct to be enjoyed alike by citizens, students, and faculty. The site is in a good place for a vacation, either in summer or in winter. Youth of today will be especially attracted to the excellent ski resorts in the neighboring mountains.

College curricula tend to evolve from (1) the demands of society, (2) the needs and interests of students, and (3) the nature of the environment. In Avezzano, where landscape and location combine to offer a full range of outdoor activities, a program of leadership training in health and physical education is as logical as are studies in history and classics in Rome. A major emphasis, therefore, will be directed toward an American curriculum in health, outdoor education, physical education, and recreation. Leadership training in those subjects will be particularly welcome in Italy, as certified by the hearty endorsement of the Ministry of Education, which acknowledges the proposed plan as unique to the country, as well as paramount to the improvement of instruction.

"Pimpernels you shall gather on the mountains and starfish on the shore."

Courses in the American University will be open to full enrollment toward a baccalaureate degree or for part-time study abroad, with transfer of credits to the native college of the transient student. The cost, including room, board, and round-trip transportation, will be three-fourths of the cost of comparable private education in the US.

Immediate plans include a campaign for funds to begin construction and to employ personnel for the university. The projected campus will include a library, classrooms, science building, women's dormitory, men's dormitory, a gymnasium with an auditorium, and a swimming pool.

In an era of uncompromising ideologies and radical displays of force among peoples and between nations, the time is now extant to extol the virtues of our heritage and to stress the ethical character that can be augmented by intercommunications among world populations. We are no longer strangers but neighbors who should strive for harmony in ideals and seek intellectual advancement to achieve the finer sentiments required for an enduring society and a satisfying state of affairs for all mankind.

SPONSOR MEMBERSHIPS

The American University of Avezzano, incorporated in the United States, is a nonprofit institution dedicated to higher education in compliance with the foregoing stated principle of cross-cultural influence. The policy of the university will be to assist members with living accommodations and counseling service while touring in Italy.

Funds will be sought through the participation of sponsors in the United States and other countries who may, by their contributions, become founders of a worthwhile project. Sponsors are classified into three categories.

Patrons will be honored with individual name plaques in the foyer of the Library.

The names of all sustaining members will be inscribed on a single plaque, and supporting members and associates will have their names posted in the founders directory.

Remission of tuition in the amount of 50 percent of the contribution will be credited to the families of patrons and sustaining members.

The "Campus of International Character" of the American University of Avezzano, Italy

The American University, like the human mind, will not work at its best in isolation. There are times when the creative thinker, in order to function most perfectly, must seek solitude, but such solitude is valuable only because it is not continuous. Thought may be developed in solitude, but in typical experience, it is not aroused except in community. Though much is spoken of self-reliance, the truth is that we need each other, not only in the application of ideas but in the inception of ideas. Though minds are stimulated in various ways, their chief source of stimulation is other minds. Intellectual life grows in a variety of ways, but its most nourishing soil is that of a fellowship of minds.

It is out of the need for an intellectual community that the idea of the American University should develop. Civilization is a risky business that can move rapidly in different directions. It can go down as easily as it can advance. Indeed, a great deal of recorded human history is the story of the decline of some brilliant civilizations.

What is the chance that the American University of Avezzano will have a different outcome? This is unknown, but at least we are aware that, whether it endures or advances, such endurance and advancement will be achieved only by conscious and imaginative effort. It is intrinsic to the very nature of the human situation that stability is impossible. The lone thinker is a voice crying in the wilderness; he needs students and teachers and colleagues and helpers if he is to be effective. In short, he needs to be part of a thinking community.

The American University of Avezzano may profitably be compared to a pumping station on a pipeline. Nearly all who have traveled near the great pipelines have noticed that in order to keep the oil moving, pumping stations are installed every few miles. This is true even when the line goes downhill, because the natural forces are inadequate. It was necessary to do some thinking about it, and the pumping station was the answer. The American University of Avezzano will be a pumping station on the pipeline of civilization. It is designed to do what cannot be done naturally or easily. It is a conscious effort to avoid civilization's decay and to make that civilization worthy of permanence.

That this university is bound to have an effect upon the outcome of current history is obvious. If the destruction of the races is prevented, that will be partly because of what has been developed in today's universities; and if it will come out into a brighter day, that, too, will be in part because of what some men and women of the American University of Avezzano have thought. Only then can it be said that every "ivory tower" is among the most productive of human structures. Men who are sufficiently advanced in scientific thought to put satellites and artificial planets into orbit should likely think creatively along other lines, including those of social order and moral values. A totalitarian government is, therefore, in a hard predicament. It is forced to encourage higher education if it is to achieve dominance in weapons or in industrial achievement, but the higher education that is encouraged may include, as essentials of the process, the seeds of the destruction of the system that supports it. Knowledge gives power, but it is hard to develop knowledge without freedom as a by-product.

Because the university is a contrived product, it declines rapidly and seriously without constant vigilance. In this regard, it is like hybrid seed corn and other products of human imagination, both flora or fauna, which lose their peculiar excellence whenever conscious effort is relaxed. In some places, academic decay that is truly shocking is already evident.

Because there is so much inequality and confusion, as well as the danger of a general decline of civilization, it is a matter of first importance to reconsider the whole question of what the American University of Avezzano will be and ought to be. The reason for stressing this university is that it has to provide the characteristic and central pattern of higher education. Because this will be so, it is necessary to examine it in regard to both ends and means.

What the American University of Avezzano will be seeking to illuminate has to be in the realm of platonic ideals, naturalism, and pragmatism. Each particular institution has its faults, and faults will certainly be part of this institution; but there has to be a good chance of correcting such faults, provided the standard will be clear and consequently potent. Only by fastening our gaze upon the universal will the particular be altered. In this case, it is necessary to build this new and unique university as a consequence of the growth and exigence of the population; and when this is done, the founders ought to be careful to profit from all the former academic experiences available.

Though a delineation of the ideal is needed when establishing the new American University of Avezzano, it is needed even more in regulating, reviving, and guiding old and existing institutions.

The American University of Avezzano must be a liberal, open institution, providing instruction in liberal arts, science, and health and physical education, which will be its characteristic intellectual product, not duplicated in other parts of the West, besides the USA. The chief reason Europeans have such great difficulty in understanding this type of American university is that they simply do not have its counterpart. They are mystified when they hear about students attending American universities, which are obviously concerned with important studies, and learning many different things at once in settings different from either school or university as these institutions are known to them.

During two hundred and fifty years, the American college (and university) has developed into an institution that stand in contrast to nearly all European patterns of academic life. It is an intellectual society, usually located alone instead of in clusters after the English plan, devoted to the general education of persons usually between the ages of eighteen and twenty-two. Many, and perhaps the majority, of those who attend do not know when they enter what their subject of concentration may be, and they certainly feel uncertain about particular vocation choices. They attend, characteristically, not because they know what they expect to do but in the hope that they may discover the answer under optimum conditions of intelligent choice.

The college pattern as developed in America is substantially similar to that which was elaborated in the fertile imagination of John Milton and described by him in his famous tract on education. In his essay, he not only outlined a course of general studies but indicated something of the nature of the academic society that he believed an advancing civilization required. In his treatise, Milton concerned himself with liberating studies, with exercise, and with diet, all made possible by a setting described as follows:

> "First to find out a spacious house and ground about it fit for an academy, and big enough to lodge a hundred and fifty persons, whereof twenty or thereabouts may be attendants, all under the government of one, who shall be thought of desert sufficient, and ability either to do all, or wisely to direct, and oversee it done. This place should be at once both school and university, not heeding a remove to any other house of scholarship, except it be some peculiar college of Law or Physic, where they mean to be practitioners. After this pattern, as many edifices may be converted to this use, as shall be needful in every city throughout this land, which would tend much to the increase of learning and civility everywhere."

The European university, in contrast to most American institutions, is made up largely of students who enter for a particular purpose, often vocational. Frequently, European students are a little older when they enter than the characteristic American freshman, because secondary school has included some of the studies beyond those ordinarily pursued in an American high school.

The characteristic student of any European university goes to "read" some subject (such as classics or history), and often concentrates on this subject from the beginning. Only a minority of students, however, do this in American universities. Thus, in America the idea of a college is not limited to institutions that happen to be called colleges but is found also in the great universities.

The majority of undergraduate students experience up to four years of general education. The part called "university," which is comparable in mood to its European counterparts, is the professional graduate schools and the departments concerned with advanced degrees. In short, though the term *university* is used widely, the undergraduate college pattern is the chief pattern of academic America.

Since, for better or for worse, this is how American intellectual life has developed, the task is to understand this pattern and glorify it.

The first American colleges were not intended to be essentially different from the English colleges on which they were modeled. Undoubtedly, the small institution on the north bank of the Charles River was expected to become, in the New World, comparable to what John Harvard's college at Cambridge already was. The absence of a cluster of colleges came about not through principle but because of the facts of geography. Colleges as they were founded in succeeding generations were widely separated according to the needs of an expanding nation. The establishment of these many points of potential illumination was actually a fortunate development. Equally fortunate will be the intended construction of the American University of Avezzano, which will be unique, in that it is going to be both school and university in one sense, while in another sense it is neither.

The American University of Avezzano, within a Campus of International Character, will bear a general resemblance to the American colleges from which it springs; not, however, without important modifications, which will bring it into nearer conformity to the genius of other institutions, into closer connection with the wants and wishes of the people—the people who will be building it with their own hands and cherishing it in their own hearts. It will be the selected university of the selected people.

Scarcely anything in the campus of the American University of Avezzano will be more distinctively international than the relation between the university and its people.

In its most characteristic form, the American University of Avezzano will be neither governmental nor private. Though some states and municipal institutions will support and endorse it, somehow these will not represent the major tradition and should not serve the majority of this institution's objectives.

It will not be considered private because it does not exist for the profit of its owners; it does not limit itself to one denomination or party; and it will accept a high degree of responsibility for the cultivation of public taste and the encouragement of public service. The American University will be not of a private character, even though it will not be tax-supported. The service of this institution of learning will not be private but public. It will be plan what the matter or country needs or its affairs will grow more and more complex and its interests should begin to touch the ends of the earth. It will need efficient and enlightened men. There will be many ways of differentiating between the American University of Avezzano and other universities, but the distinction between public and private is perhaps the least valuable. In terms of contribution to the public good, this institution, as other independent institutions, should exhibit a high level of competence. Of the colleges which have, per capita, made the greatest contribution in service, thirty-nine out of the top fifty institutions were those with independent boards and financial support, typically comparatively small, with a Christian emphasis. Excellence will also emerge in unexpected ways at the American University of Avezzano.

A striking difference between this independent university and its tax-supported counterparts will be that the former can be more truly international in character.

This independent university will gain enormously from the fact that it will draw its student sand staff from all parts of the world. This is what the state university cannot normally do, while the municipal one does it practically not at all.

Indeed, it is realized that there can be genuine merit in an independent, open, liberal institution. If this is true, the right answer to the enormous demands involved is not to destroy the already existing universities; rather, the decision comes to starting a new one. This is the plan because it is believed by many that the idea of the American University of Avezzano with international character, far from being a second-rate conception, really will provide the best chance for greatness.

One of the reasons why the American University of Avezzano will represent a best ideal is that it can produce a higher degree of unity than can any alternative academic organization with which it is acquainted. The state university has many advantages, but unity is not one of them.

The old university had two typical characteristics, both of which were expressed in its name.

Universitas may mean: *universitas litterarum* and thus stand for the unity of the sciences in one integrated conception of the world. Or it may mean *universitas magistrorum at scholarum* (the original meaning) and thus stand for an independent community held together by the ideal of common search for truth. But the modern university is neither.

Hence, the American University of Avezzano must and will exhibit intellectual vitality. The best minds should continually stimulate one another, instead of always working in departmental isolation. It will be one of the great merits of this new American University that such a pattern will be intrinsically impossible. The embodiment of this ideal is not always attempted, and in some places, it will not even be recognized as an ideal, but the exciting fact is that in the really high standards of the American University of Avezzano, it is still possible.

The name given to this university, implying an international character in education, is a good name: the American University of Avezzano. This university will be a place of a real sharing of life, in which each person is an individual instead of a number, and in which the worth of each individual will be more than a pious American expression, even if today there are still few universities in which the achievement of this ideal is seriously attempted.

It will still be the standard experience for professor and students to be genuine friends, not ashamed to be seen together, for most teaching will be such that there will be a truly personal relationship between teacher and taught. There will be, on the other hand, a chance that a young person going to the American University of Avezzano will be treated impersonally, but fortunately the chance will be slight.

The American University of Avezzano will exist in order to provide a situation of maximum growth within the whole life of a student. It will be a means of bringing to bear maximum beneficent influence in the hope of producing maximum progress in the lives of the individuals concerned. This is why the American University of Avezzano will be concerned with more than learning, in the narrow sense. Membership at this institution will involve far more than attending classes, and this is as it should be. Ideally, the members of the American University of Avezzano, both teachers and students, work together, think together, play together, and may pray together. It will not allow any of these to act as substitutes for the others. It must not let progress remain separate from thinking or allow playing to become wholly dissociated from working. It will consciously and deliberately seek wholeness of life.

What the American University of Avezzano will hope to produce in those under its care will be not merely a knowledge of facts, which may be evanescent or even illusory, but the ability to judge. The aim will be the kind of mind that can judge among apparent facts which ones are really facts and can do so in a great variety of fields. It is hoped this experience will develop acute and accurate judgment of men and movements of faiths. The goal of education is "knowing a good man when you see him;" and "the most important science of all is the science of choice." Because man is free, in the sense that his actions are not wholly determined by forces outside his own mind and character, nothing is more important than the development of character in such a way that better and better choices are made. This cannot be accomplished in any easy or simple way. That is why the educational process is inevitably a long and a difficult one, if it is to be worth anything.

Because education today is big business and enjoying a boom, this doesn't mean that the American University of Avezzano must make it easy to lose sight of fundamental goals. It will be easy to concentrate upon the construction of buildings and efficiency of administration without seriously searching for the purpose, apart from which these are as nothing. Because attendance at universities today is fashionable, thousands now enroll without any burning desire to learn and without any clear understanding of why they are in the university at all. Students assemble in huge classes and walk from building to building, carrying heavy textbooks that effectively serve to keep them from better quality reading. Often, the whole undertaking seems more like a factory than anything else. It is booming, but to what end? It is developing judgment in regard to literature or art or conduct. It is producing creativity in science such that new discoveries will be made. It is encouraging new imagination concerning the ways in which men can live together in real peace. Do people come out of this community more compassionate and more unified in their lives than they were when they entered? Do they emerge with the desire to go on learning and reading and exploring as long as they live? These are embarrassing questions, but they are the questions it cannot afford not to ask. The right questions for the American University of Avezzano may be more important than anything else.

Projected Campus of International Character and Health Recreation Centers in the Italian Region's Development

The birth and growth of the projected Campus of International Character, American University of Avezzano, and the Health Recreation Center in the Italian region's development shall not be a simple, one-time process but a continuous, direct evolution. In order to wrestle away a share of the local political-bureaucratic government power and win the community battle, what is needed is an alliance, a symbol, a leader, or, more specifically, an awareness of this project's true individuality and objectives, consensus from the members in the community, and, most of all, the inspiration and support of a new political class. However, to win such a battle—that is, the struggle for independent individuality and community autonomy against the centralized political government-bureaucracy—the projected Campus and the Health Recreation Center's developmental approach needs the support of solid organizations, a league made up of consistent teams with creative visions and performances.

Today, no one will openly challenge the objectives and the validity of the projected Campus of International Character and the related Health Recreations Center in the Italian regions, not even those who disputed the philosophical-educational substance on which the project is based. Nevertheless, a lot of enemies of the project were established, who work behind the scenes to drain off all the power that the project may generate and undermine its innovative drive. And, what is more important, this "group" of enemies are those who, in fact, are holding the reins of political-bureaucratic power and responsible to the immediate needs of the community. This means that the existing political-bureaucratic establishments have no intention whatsoever of spontaneously abdicating from the "lethargic" position they have held up to date. And why should they? Having grown up and been thoroughly imbued with the principle of centralism, they cannot fail to be suspicious and hostile toward all that smacks of an innovative and dynamic undertaking. This certainly is nothing new; it is fully expected! What is of concern must be not so much the intensity of the reaction—even if greater than the most pessimistic forecasts—but the shrewdness with which it will be applied.

The American University within a Campus of International Character and its connected Health Recreation Centers' development must take place and be there to stay. Certainly the fact that the major problem facing local communities in specific regions is the nonfunctioning of the public administration must be recognized by any subtle and intelligent politicians, who have an undeniable, profound feeling for the institutions they are fully acquainted with, at least from the administrative standpoint. Since the Health Recreation Centers are of a vital need and must exist, and the public governments are falling apart, and since the entire project could, if all goes well, also represent a reorganization of a community, let's make this project grow and work. However, in order to accomplish such an endeavor, the proper recognition that its objectives and functions are an important contribution to the community must be given. Above all, some of the functions must be of reducing the tension and the destructive potential of both bureaucrats and corrupted politicians, placing the projected campus and the connected Health Recreation Center in a position of moral leader. Naturally, should this be the approach that is followed, the goals and views of this project are not merely the pure and simple rationalization of a community's mechanism but represent the reactivation of other reconstructional phases, leading to the creation of a healthy community. In the mind of this project's conceiver and supporters has been born the concept that either the campus or centers should apply the unifying approach, making it possible for different social and territorial setups to play leading roles in the community democracy. In other words, the idea is to shift power from the isolated "Ivory Tower" into the community, undermining the fortified political position of the few local privileged classes that have always sprung up and clustered around the unitary-centralistic-totalitarian concept of government.

The projected American University, with a Campus of International Character, as well as its connected Health Recreation Centers in Italy's regions, comes about because social forces have raised the problem of social consumption, health reform, urban reform. All those reforms that justified the breakdown of the same old inadequate concepts are no longer capable of carrying solid principles forward, other than through an atmosphere of delusion and deprivation. The possibility of eliminating the old inadequate concepts restoration—based primarily to a political-economical-educational concept formula of the past—is not even considered here. The present one should be considered only as transitory and beneficial! In spite of that, other possibilities for concept consideration should not otherwise be underestimated or rejected, although it is foolishly opposed at its very beginning.

But How Could It Succeed?

It needs a new, different concept based on new people and on a new league made up of valid teams that could defend the autonomy of the project's proper objectives and its structural independence against any challenger who might want to impose full authority from a political-bureaucratic governmental hegemony. In other words, this project in its whole must be identified as the symbol of individual autonomy, independence, and of constructive values of the human society. To make such an endeavor a success, therefore, what is needed is simply a rallying around the idea of a team league and the idealistic and pragmatic facts that will lead to the battle for setting up the project's structures and services in the feasible sites of the proposed regions. Therefore, what's required is a symbol of truth, a trusted leader, and asking a valid question: are the citizens, or the politicians and bureaucrats, truly aware of the contributions that the projected Campus of International Character and the developmental aspects of the Health Recreation Centers could offer to their community? Certainly citizens and politicians and bureaucrats are strongly conscious of the importance of the entire project, even though in different ways, which are distinctly felt by the members of the community. What gives substance to this project, indeed, is the logic of the problems facing the same community—

from schools to housing, from welfare to health, from unemployment to manpower, from infrastructures to industrial sites, and organization of the territory. Most of these problems can be solved by the project's efforts and cooperation, rather than through political manipulation and anticultural-educational traditions generated from emotional sentiments. Thus, the projected Campus of International Character and it connected Health Recreation Centers will come pass just when the deteriorating society and the failed governmental agencies recognize the impossibility of carrying out by themselves a renovation process through the adoption of new reform concepts. As a matter of fact, the project's objectives and managerial know-how could be applied in general to community problems. Furthermore, the Center itself will pay attention to one specific regional problem, which, aside from most dynamic socio-political conditions, will help to take on the leadership of its autonomous battle for the resolution of the community's struggles.

The community's problems during the last decade have "immigrated" mainly to the large cities of the Italian regions; specifically to the Capoluoghi di Regioni. The territory and population of this city have suffered from downgraded environment and infrastructure. While this crucial problem is more likely related to the working class as well as the commuters and immigrants, who are very much in demand for such kinds of projects, similarly the most high-minded business organizations are loudly demanding that this project be established. The projected development of the Campus and the Health Recreation Centers will follow a specific regional planning program, which will offer sound points of reference and consequently benefit the financial-economical-educational development program within the same region. And yet, it must be pointed out that in the past the business world and the political power that it represents had never given support for such projects; rather, it was determined to defend the business of the bureaucracy and the centralization of government.

It was not so long ago when some manipulated opposition gathered to obstruct the efforts of establishing the basics of the entire project. Why? Perhaps some of these opposed factions viewed the projected campus and the connected developmental approach as an upsetting element that would have destroyed the equilibrium that has maintained the community's power relationship. Or perhaps these factions were resentful of the fact that the majority of the people of the community have openly supported the project's concept as an alternative solution of their grievances, often obtained only by the backing of the politicians. Now, however, that the bite of the political-economical and socio-educational crisis is being felt by all, the big, medium, and small people see the water rising over their heads: the local politicians and bureaucrats stand by with the lifeboats ready to rescue only themselves. And because the public government they represent appears totally incapable of readying the necessary defenses due to its paralyzed and antiquated structures, the community's people seem to have no other choice but to place their hopes in a project that will be close to the citizens' needs, becoming more responsive to the actual problems and situation and consequently more prepared to act.

It is accepted that the reorganization of the community's life and its democratization rests with the renewal of local autonomy. This is at the roots of the project's main interest for a local experience in which business-industrial-educational extraction and development is blended with validity and feasibility that seek concrete planning, continually directed at implementing a manageable dimension in order to have the satisfaction of accomplishment. As a matter of fact, such a project's accomplishment will be more directed towards the final result than the manner of procedure; the concern in the last analysis will be more in managerial know-how. In the meantime, the project's developmental approach has promotion commitment at the municipal level, and it has been convinced that the autonomous approach is the right one. From other parallel experience in other communities, the belief must be acquired that many problems are and will be most proper at the regional dimension. Thus, the projected Campus and Health Recreation Centers in Italy's regions will become the correct way of accomplishing the renewal process they are now facing. It must be viewed as an individual who desires democratized citizens, starting from the bottom; however, when the project's power is constructed, then it intends to stress the other crucial problems of the community. The idea of starting the project's developmental approach from a regional level is motivated precisely by the objective of reestablishing the primary position of human relations on the basis of the need to launch a new alliance between power and consensus.

As soon as the project performance will be appeared with lack of power and hazy in objectives, the leaders of the project's programs and services should not hesitate to leave their post of responsibility. This kind of decision should be viewed as perhaps the most fertile of all other matters, as it will demonstrate how taking motivational action without power is possible, provided there is the ability to create it on the basis of consensus and legitimization. At this point, the community's problem solving on a voluntary basis will be approached; in other words, it will attempt to resolve the community's regional problems by keeping together a group of persons animated by a strong drive that arises from the desire to see these problems solved. The project's efforts must unquestionably contribute to the community's awareness of the connection between vital issues and concrete problems. However, a lack of thorough theory and the questions asked today are the fundamental reasons behind the idea of conceiving the American University within a Campus of International character and the connected Health Recreation Centers, seeking a correct relationship between the project and its implication in the community, between its structural elements and superstructural elements, which remain rather confused in many minds! In spite of that, the machine must start up, and a certain minimum of community concern and promotional efforts have already begun. Therefore, it becomes evident that the horizon will be expanded to take on a project of national as well as international dimension.

The conviction has gained ground that the crisis in the political parties may receive some injection of vitality from the projected campus as an inspired institution. On the other side, a dissatisfied consequence of the community's inability to relate to this project's objectives are the real components of its socio-economical and educational problems! It should be pointed out that some bureaucrats and politicians exposed to this project, with the exception of a few, did not have a feeling or vision for such concepts of a national or international dimension. Many of them, in fact, will arrive at that day only when the project is established and efficiently operating in its structural-regional dimension. Even though it must not repudiate the importance and objective of the national and international dimensions, the regional community's approach must be viewed as a synthesis of minor syntheses and not be considered as a monolithic dimension. It is our conviction that the evolution of the local political-social-economical alliances can only come about by jolts, in relation to choices made on the national and international scale.

Another question to be asked: How will it be possible to develop the projected Campus of International Character and the connected Health Recreation Centers; and how can a centralist political-bureaucratic government abdicate from its "status-quo" principles? The key to answering this question shifts to the relationship between the crucial problems and the reform to be tackled; in order to put this endeavor into effect, it is necessary that either the system fall apart or evolution is a possibility at the present time. One main thesis in support of the project has been that it would have come about when it was clear that the ships of local, regional, and national governments were sinking; at that time, the local population, especially, would have to take the lifeboat offered by this project's alternative and watch the sinking from a respectable distance. Up-to-date evidence proves this thesis is correct.

At the time the projected Campus of International Character was proposed, some politicians and bureaucrats, mainly those that were already threatened with dissolution, openly supported this project in order to survive their political careers.

Because of this premise, promotional development efforts were accomplished; but once those accomplishments had shown some positive results, the same politicians and bureaucrats made clear to the supporters of the endeavor that they shouldn't believe the community really wanted this project. As a matter of fact, it was previously supported only for personal political survival, and now that the danger was going to pass, who's to pay the price? Certainly not these politicians and bureaucrats, as the situation has changed. They have forgotten, however, that the hot weather did not go through yet. In effect, the power relationship is going through a profound change; those classes which up until the last few years were left out in the cold have increased their efforts and have led the battle for the establishment of this projected campus. It is another hinge that forces the politicians and bureaucrats to positively support the projected Campus of International Character and the connected Health Recreation Centers in Italy's regions, which previously were accepted to save local government politics, now to be used to accomplish what, for many years, couldn't be accomplished.

October 5, 1970

To Whom it may Concern:

Criticism, additions, and contributions are welcome to the attached Proposed Business Enterprises of the American University of Avezzano.

Please send your suggestions to the author of this proposal, and thanks for your consideraton.

Proposed Business Enterprises

July 10, 1970

Investments in public and private stocks or bonds should be one of the primary operations of the American University of Avezzano in order to ensure itself a fixed income for yearly operation and self-support. Inasmuch as this is one form of investment, it should not be the only one. On the contrary, the university should and must explore other possibilities where evidence of the best profit manifest. Therefore, two business enterprises could be analyzed immediately and considered here:

1. Development of tourism services and assistance programs on both sides of the Atlantic (Abruzzi, Italy with Ohio or Midwest, USA).
2. Construction of parking garages (American types) in different locations in Italy, as well as in the United States.

These two enterprises could function independently or dependently, because of their affinity. The possibility of the second proposal could be extended, with due consideration for traffic safety regulations.

Because of the ever-increasing national tourism activities in Italy, and with specific consideration of those of the Abruzzi region, it is logical to see the implication of the American University of Avezzano. Travel agencies with proper permits already exist in Italy. However, they do not require any technical qualifications other than a license to operate. A study should be made of this situation in order to guarantee better quality and proficiency of operation. At present, anyone in possession of a license can operate reception facilities, regardless of background training, interest, or ability.

Inadequate technical preparations for the management of hotels, restaurants, stores, and public services in general can cause disturbing consequences, such as:

1. Dissatisfaction of foreign students, visitors, and their families because of poor services, lack of manners and courtesy, ignorance of foreign languages, lack of vision, and lack of cooperative spirit
2. Economic damage to the locality because of missed revenues
3. Administrative problems for the American University, such as decreasing budget, fewer guests, and fewer enrollments

In order to ensure quality of service along these lines, courses in leadership and management of the tourism trade should be offered by the University. Collaboration with Italian-American authorities, both private and public, will help to ensure the achievement of the university's objectives and will provide the necessary financial assistance.

With regard to parking garages, the Italian government as well as local agencies should provide wide legislation and solid support. The parking business should be incorporated separately from the University. This will avoid direct and indirect interference with the educational objectives of the University but still remain its main support. This project could be handled in several ways:

1. The American University could be the sole owner of the enterprise.
2. The American University could participate as a member promoter and share the risks and benefits with other persons.
3. The American University, as a promoter and owner, could subcontract such activity.

Initial capital could be raised either by loans or by issuing stock. Members of the board of trustees of the American University and other persons who are working closely together on behalf of the university must have the option to buy shares and have priority in being consulted.

This project's physical structure should resemble parking garages in the USA. Another possibility could be the incorporation of adjacent services such as a bar, restaurant, hotel, gasoline station, and stores for automobile parts. Maybe connecting the parking facility with a car wash and gas station could give it a better start.

Parking space in Italy is very much a necessity. The problem has become more alarming because of automobile accidents, traffic congestion, and car thefts. From a practical and aesthetic viewpoint, the American University of Avezzano should help men to restore order and to safeguard environmental beauty.

As a counterpart, the Italian citizens and the public authorities will give full support and cooperation to a beneficial endeavor that will reflect their efforts.

Economic-Financial Plan

Without a doubt, establishment expenses must be given considerable thought. For instance, the kinds of expenses to be incurred include:

    A. Construction and equipment costs
    B Operation and maintenance expenses
    C. Interest on borrowed capital

A typical characteristic of the costs of establishment is that services derived from it are going to be fixed (automatic counter, elimination of personnel tickets). The speculative capacity of this enterprise will be constant but will also be exploited to the maximum. The cost of the service will be high, but it will tend to decrease and reach the minimum when all the capacity of production is exploited. Therefore, the best system for the above speculation is to obtain in a short time all the amortization costs of its establishment and of its structure and to obtain the maximum profit through its global implementation. Even if it is possible to obtain a major profit, so as to permit a more rapid amortization of its expenses of establishment, structure, et cetera, it is certain that intensity in exploitation will also determine a major increase in maintenance expenses.

In spite of such oscillation (which should not be considered relevant), it is possible to conclude that the costs related to establishment will be high. So, the best solution for this enterprise, on the basis of the mentioned premises, will be productive activity that is characterized by a stable and constant process. With well-determined plans, this enterprise will reach the amortization of its costs in a precise and predetermined period of time.

All of the above considerations were surveyed analytically on my last trips to Italy on behalf of the projected American University of Avezzano. Other considerations, studies, contacts, and analysis are more than vital to the practical realization of this goal.

It is suggested that we address ourselves to the following questions with respect to securing a license and/or franchise from the Italian government to operate a parking garage facility in major Italian cities:

1. Would the license and/or franchise prohibit any other agency from participating in the same type of venture?
2. If the operation of the garage, including construction, could be subcontracted, would the American University of Avezzano be permitted to collect a fee or percentage of the total operation?
3. What agency would establish the criteria in respect to location, size, and architectural design? Under this heading, all aspects of construction standards would have to be considered.
4. Who would control the sale of gas, food, beverages, and other types of services on the premises controlled by the parking garage?
5. Would the employees operating the parking garage and/or concessions within the facility be employees of the University of Avezzano or would they be employed by some other firm or sub-contractor (or lessor)?

Aspr Surd

August 16, 1989.

To Whom It May Concern:

    The attached presentation, Health-Recreation-Education Programs within a Campus of International Character, was submitted to the city hall of Avezzano, Italy, and other related Government Agencies during the project phases implementation in the years between 1969 and 1972.

    Additional materials and activities have been developed and acknowledged according with agreements and legal understanding among the concerned parties in Italy, the United States, and Canada. Also, an abstract of the same program concepts connected educational material were introduced to Project P.E.A.C.E. in Cleveland, Ohio, in the year 1974.

    Information pertinent to the development of the entire program are available upon request.

Enclosures

Health and Recreational Education Program within a Campus of International Character

Providing people with food and shelter is not enough. They must also be provided with something to do, something they feel to be worthwhile, as a means to utilize the enforced leisure with which they find themselves. One of the reasons so many people do not know what to do with their leisure time and so spend it in all kinds of dull folly is that the creative part of them has not been awakened.

Health And Recreational Education Programs within a Campus of International Character At Avezzano (L'Aquila), Italy, will not be an escape from the toil of education into the emptiness of leisure time but a vitalizing element in the process of education itself. The problems of leisure will exist only so long as leisure is thought as a vacation or a vacuum separate from the rest of life, needing to be filled with activities especially designed for filling it. In the life of a correctly educated man, there should not be such vacuums or such boring vacation time.

The proposal for putting Health and Recreation into one specific compartment and Education into another has generated some difficulties encountered in presenting the proposition of their indissoluble unity. This situation would be eased at the Campus of International Character, where the practice of self-persuasion will be used to foster the importance of health and recreation activities.

Health and recreation programs at this specific campus must include the re-creation of things that get damaged in human beings, the repair of human damage where it is repairable, and the prevention of it in the rising generation within a greater human community. Human damage and threat of further damage is abundant in this contemporary world. This enormous problem affects the population of the same community in which a health-recreation-education program is feasible and relevant.

-**Nature of Program Feasibility**: Health and recreation programs are formulated as an art of living that is one and indivisible. It is not a composite art made up by adding the art of play to the art of work, the art of leisure to the art of labor, the art of the body to the art of mind, or the art of recreation to the art of education. When life is divided into these or any other compartments, it can never become an art but at best a medly or, at worst, a mess. It becomes an art when work and play, labor and leisure, mind and body, education and recreation are governed by a single vision of excellence and a continuous passion for achieving it.

The art of living and related program activities so conceived should not draw sharp distinctions between work and play, labor and leisure, mind and body, and education and recreation. It simply pursues the vision of excellence through whatever an individual is doing and leaves others to determine whether he or she is working or playing. The programs are planned to essentially unite the things that have become separated in contemporary society: health-recreation and education.

These health recreation programs will make the health and recreation of people, both children and adults, much more educational than similar programs are at present time; the innovative "Campus" concepts should give education some of the interest and joy that belong properly to health-recreation as a way of living. Hence, two results should positively result: first, health-recreation life will become far more enjoyable than is now; and secondly, work in education will become far more effective in building up a fine, noble generation of citizenry.

-**Program Expectations**: It is quite possible to anticipate that a vast increase in human joy can be brought about by uniting education, health and recreation. And if it gives more joy, then other things are wanted; clean conduct, good fellowship, community spirit, beautiful neighborhoods, and more value in social life will occur. With this increase of joy in community life, a great revival of trade, economy, and human relations will occur.

Health-recreation programs will include more than the playing of games. They will include skills, crafts, and the arts that all human beings are capable of acquiring in one form or another, if they are educated correctly. These arts, crafts, and skills provide the most enjoyable kind of health-recreation for the concerned community. All human beings are hungry for skills, for some kind of creative activity in which they can express themselves, and they are never happy and contented until the hunger is appeased. Health-recreation programs will give a much larger role to creative activity in the training of both youngsters and adults. These groups have a vast amount of undeveloped skills waiting for the health-recreation programs to bring into fruition, followed by an immense increase in joy and the value of life.

Another important result that will follow from uniting health and recreation with education is the reduction of crime. Criminologists are now agreed that crime is largely the result of thwarting the natural play instincts of young human beings. It begins as juvenile delinquency and develops later into adult crime. There is an interesting fact to be pointed out in many areas of industrial cities. I found that the figures for juvenile delinquency tend to be lowest in those parts of the city nearest to a well-organized and efficient health-recreation program, where opportunities for practicing arts and crafts, as well as physical education activities, were provided. Juvenile delinquency tended to be highest in other parts of cities that were deprived of similar health-recreation programs. If juvenile crime can be prevented in this way, all crime will be proportionately diminished. The health-recreation programs at the Campus of International Character will be a source of preventive medicine. The social evils to be prevented are: disease, crime, vices, folly, and bad citizenship in general. Prevention is better than cure and vastly cheaper in the long run. The priority of the health-recreation programs will be to overcome many of the inadequacies that exist when a participant leaves his or her home, his or her place of work, his or her school, or when she or he completes day-to-day tasks.

-**Program Objectives:** The Health Recreation Program will pursue the following objectives: improved community relations; knowledge of the community culture; and development of physical fitness activities; satisfaction of the basic human needs for creative self-expression to promote total physical, emotional, mental and social health; to provide an antidote to the strains and tensions of contemporary living; to provide an avenue for abundant personal and family living; to aid development of good citizenship; character development to aid crime prevention, to foster community solidarity, morale, safety, economy, and better friendship for the entire community population.

-**Health Development**: The Health Program is related to activity during leisure hours, as well as during work hours. The manner in which a person spends his or her free time determines in great measure the quality of his/her physical, mental, emotional, and spiritual health. The cultural, recreational, and adaptive physical activities specifically available at the Campus of International Character facilities will be conductive to organic health as a whole. A wide range of activities will implement opportunities for every individual to promote his or her organic health. These activities must provide relaxation, an alternative to the tension of work, and a chance to reflect on one's problems; thereby they will contribute to emotional health. Activities at the Campus facilities will attract the participation of many persons, which is conducive to better social relations and will promote spiritual health.

-**Human Relations**: The human relations aspect of this program will represent one of the major valid contributions in efforts to enrich community living and to develop basic individual qualities. Such attributes as tolerance, justice, patience, courage, fairness, and honesty will be a few that will be developed while people are playing together and joining in the many activities that comprise the total program.

Wholesome attitudes of social cooperation, loyalty to the group, recognition of the rights of others, and the belief that a person receives from the group in direct proportion to what he or she gives makes for better relations and enables the accomplishment of worthy goals. In addition, the growth of family recreation will also help to make a more unified home life. This is essential, since the family group in the community should represent the foundation on which good human relations are built. Furthermore, to develop good social traits, it will be necessary to bring people together in a situation where there is a feeling of belonging and where each individual will be recognized. The successful hosting of this program, with a very positive welcoming spirit, good attitude towards visitors, courtesy, friendliness, sincere interest, willingness to serve and to get better acquainted, and other manifestations of warmth and friendliness, will help the plans for the Campus facilities bear fruit.

-**Civic Development**: The program of the Campus of International Character, with its unique structural organization, will contribute in many ways to the development of the community. It will increase community solidarity by uniting people in common projects, regardless of class, creed, economic status, or other discriminatory factors. It will help to build the morale of the members of the community. In addition, it will provide a setting and activities in which youth and other individuals may engage in constructive, worthwhile activities rather than in destructive, antisocial activities. It will help to make the community more prosperous by maintaining good individual health, cutting down crime, and increasing the total work output of an individual.

It will help the growth and development of the individual so that he/she becomes a more valuable citizen in the community and has more to contribute in its behalf. Moreover, the Campus contributions and successes are not simply matters of having better programs or services or facilities, but of adding a particular human flavor in keeping with traditional ways of life and in projecting a favorable image of the benefits to visitors and travelers and others in such organizational structures and services.

-**Cultural Development**: Cultural development at the Campus of International Character will cover programs of travel in and out of community locations, with contacts whereby people will learn about each other's ways of life and thought. Personal contacts have always been an important way of spreading ideas about other cultures. In fact, this health-recreation-education program will be an important aspect of promoting cultural relations within the concerned community.

This particular aspect of the entire program will be used, furthermore, as one of the basic approaches of promoting not only knowledge and understanding but a favorable image of the community among foreign students, visitors, tourists, travelers, and any other guests of the Campus facilities. It will provide and assist modern travelers and visitors in becoming intelligent interpreters and observers of this and other related communities, instead of repeaters of often erroneous and irrelevant generalizations.

-**Self-Development Aspect**: The potential for developing the individual to his/her fullest capacity in the Campus programs will be achieved through a variety of activities that contribute to the balanced growth of a person. The designed activities will allow for growth in ways other than through the antiquated production of material things for utilitarian purposes without reference to the community needs. It will satisfy the human desire for such things as creative arts and sciences, as well as literature, sports, and other relevant projects activities that are connected and related to Campus program objectives.

It will allow and involve a person in creating things not only for their material value but for the joy, satisfaction, and happiness that occur when producing something through one's own efforts. It will allow for development of skills and human abilities that are often latent and dormant until they are aroused by inspired leisure hours spent in proper settings and, as a matter of fact, these skills will help to make a better-integrated person. especially in this chaotic world of sorrow and heartbreaks; it is essential for humans to revitalize themselves through the medium of health-recreation activities that provide a release from the tensions associated with their day-to-day routines. Such activities certainly will afford a place for many to excel. Such an urge is oftten unsatisfied in one's regular job or profession.

-**Program Summary**: This health-recreation-education program will provide an opportunity to satisfy cultural needs, and it will contribute to educational experiences most of all. New skills and new techniques, new knowledge and new abilities will be developed from the various activities. Participants will file away new and different experiences that will be helpful in facing those situations encountered from day to day. Besides using the Campus programs and facilities for community purposes, they will be extended to serve immigrants and students from the area, as well as visitors, guests, tourists, and others.

To accomplish the program objectives, other tasks include:

-Development and carrying out of the community program of health and physical fitness activities involving all local and other government agencies and organizations that share similar interests

-Utilization of available leadership in promoting and supporting the enactment of government-enabling legislation to authorize and facilitate the health-recreation-education programs endeavors

-Providing financial or moral support from persons and other public and private institutions which believe in these Campus programs and objectives.

Because in the community at large there is an increasing human need to be satisfied, it is quite certain that these Campus goals will be reached and translated into reality.

Submitted by:

August 1969.

Aspr Surd

An Inquiry at Avezzano

(Politicians, Bureaucrats, and Lawyers In a Mess of Their Own Making)

. . . . oo0$0oo . . . .

It is pretty sad that someone who has learned certain things from his own region is often been regarded as naive by unscrupulous individuals to chuckle over and over again during specific illegal political-administrative city hall maneuvers, all in connection with the promotion of the projected American University of Avezzano, within a Campus of International Character. It must be said deductively that certain people connected with this matter, especially some local "famous and concerned citizens," are usually strangers to human humility. The mess in which they are now is largely of their own making. The urge to point the finger of accusation is very strong among these kinds of local politicians, bureaucrats, and lawyers, within and outside their jealous community's circle at large.

Accusations or blaming should be resisted, particularly when the city hall of Avezzano, together with others, smaller and larger, from the same vicious circle, have already run into several cases of wrongdoings. They have overcommitted themselves politically and are now financially and morally undersubsidized. Unfortunately, some particular individuals, the ones who had claimed the Campus facilities on this city's land, have been playing a kind of game that certainly will lead to inevitable political and financial bankruptcy. What makes these particular individuals different from others from the same kind of circle is that their representative politicians, their servant bureaucrats, and their "prominent" lawyers educated for their own close personal gains have tried foolishly to play much faster and for higher stakes.

For many years, these Avezzano City Hal political vassals have demanded and got more subsequent community services projects than they were willing or able to fulfill due to their related political bosses' commitments. Traditionally in this city, only these kinds of "fabulous politicians" and "petulant bureaucrats" could have said no to attractive ideas and sound projects, such as the Campus of International Character. Often in this specific city hall, when politicians and their related bureaucrats are faced with some request by privileged groups or close family friends, after sufficient time for illegal maneuvers, they have customarily figured out some new way to direct or undermine projects' expectations. They have already supported and understood the proper plans and objectives, certainly with obscurity in their mind, to *essentially* benefit further developments of *their* city's *economy future.* They have done this hoping that a miracle would have happen and the treasury of their city hall could be filled up overnight with gold coins or that the same politicians and bureaucrats won't be around when the day of reckoning comes.

But mortgaging this city hall's future by issuing illegal political maneuvers or through other unscrupulous strategies has meant that certain obligations are jagged down while legal troubles remain subject to the local political machine of the time. Nevertheless, the same politicians and bureaucrats' incomes largely depend, directly or indirectly, on the income of their city hall. They seemed to have forgotten that their city government can't get money out of people who have limited earnings or assets. They have had little respect for the theory that all loans, or any other obligations, must be repaid out of future gains. As the cost of borrowing has gone up and the city of Avezzano's commitment have gone down, prospective lenders and investors for a specific project have backed away. They mainly feared economic and financial stagnation and plain bad management from the conduct of the people connected with illegalities, especially, when considering Avezzano's financial possibilities. Unlike a State government, city hall cannot print its own money to pay off its obligations. And furthermore, a specific city hall government, was unable to conduct its business as any public or private enterprise should have been handled, with prudence.

Obviously, all the wrong-doings would not have been possible unless some of those first "concerned citizens" were also willing to stop pressing their elected officials about some questionable deals with their community projects (including the case of the projected AUA Campus development): specifically when certain dubious individuals attached to some questionable interest group have asked for more personal conveniences, more handouts than the poor taxpayers within the "trampled community" are willing or forced to pay for. It was ignored, also, that to enjoy the abundant life, certain "privileged people" of this community had first to learn how to save and be productive. And, one thing seemed to be forgotten, which is old but basic, was manipulating and discrediting an already undertaken project, and forced people policies cannot do the job. The particular city hall of Avezzano should be bailed out, even if temporarily, by a cumbersome political-financial arrangement, but there could be no permanent solution until some prominent citizens also cut back on nice but costly life extravagances and political luxuries that many more honest and reliable people cannot afford.

This problem has popped up in connection with the projected AUA, but it is happened also in many other nearby communities, for almost the same reasons. At this point, given the many reasons implied, the questions to be raised are the following: Should the principals of the projected American University of Avezzano be ruled out of order, so that there is every man for himself before trying an appeal in Avezzano's court room? Is this move to protect someone already exposed, even by hiring a lawyer in the same community that will be hidden in a law book, which is already an insult to justice? How can one who claims an exception for someone that has committed abuses and various crimes in this community's law statutes weigh the fate of others who are deceived and rubbed? Another puzzle, obviously, is how a judicial system in this same community can manage to encourage respect for and trust in the processes of law, as it is supposed to do? If a judge or a lawyer, or the entire judicial system, believes it necessary to defend someone for self-protection or for a specific cover-up, who else will succumb to fear and follow that example? Lawyers? Judges, plaintiffs, prosecutors, witnesses? Who, then, in this community will be the first to be involved in defining the right course of law and justice? Has order and decency in Avezzano's court also evaporated in puffs of smoke? Maybe some judge in Avezzano's court room, and also some lawyers, worry about hostile interest group pressures outside and inside the same courtroom? They might already admit, silently or not, that their efforts have been threatened. Or, maybe, they complain of an inadequate retainer or some protection of one and another kind, or poor "money" evidence available for a case, thus to let someone know to look for himself?

This questioning, however, is not all that unusual in Avezzano's communities. Every day countless persons in this specific location, in public and private life, because of their concern, feel intimidated by different kinds of pressures. They are exposed to all manners of peril, including sometimes assault, mockery, discredit, and outrages. But among these countless persons, there is still someone who is able to accept risks and take precautions without going so far as to reach for a kind of "false compromise."

In this community, maybe it's time that some lawyers and judges, in the name of justice and common sense, start to disarm themselves. If they cannot do so, if they consider their work too hazardous, then they might be happier and feel more secure dedicating themselves to different jobs where other people's interests and plans are not in jeopardy.
Thanks very much for the attention.

July 1976.

Memorandum: The Lawsuit Filed Against the City Hall Of Avezzano
                 and Facts Based on the Historical Background of the
                 Projected AUA And Colleteral Activities

Myself, author and promoter of the projected American University of Avezzano, within a Campus of International Character, as well as principal of the related nonprofit corporation registered in the state of Ohio (USA), after many thoughtful considerations had to arrive at the conclusion to sue the city hall of Avezzano for damages derived from breach of negotiation with the same city's representatives, and possibly charging at the same time the newspaper *Il Tempo, Pagina Marsicana*, all conspired illegalities, which have forced the plaintiff to claim with hardship the connected projected AUA's legal rights and privileges. Therefore, the author and promoter, the plaintiff, already for some time has claimed specific wrongs allegedly committed against myself personally and against the projected AUA. It was previously asked and demanded at the proper time clarifications of agreements and documentation, open meetings, and discussions be made available, before and until the legal case was introduced to the Tribunal of Avezzano.

In all my complaints as to what is stated in my summons submitted to the office of the court, I have always claimed that the wrongful, illegal, and malicious actions by the city hall of Avezzano's various administrations have mainly damaged my personal reputation, have cost me personally large sums of money and seriously hampered my future in my chosen professional career. Furthermore, I have said in some of my petitions, directed to proper authorities and governmental agencies, I have been victimized by the city hall political machinery, through discriminatory business and illegal practices of correspondences, defamation of character in furtherance of a planned conspiracy among the city hall of Avezzano corrupted politicians and associates, and denial of due hearing in regard to the charges presented against the city hall of Avezzano on February 1975 (See letter and Trip-Memo of February 1975).

At subsequent meetings and court hearings, I informed my representative lawyers of the complaint already charged that the city hall of Avezzano's cover-up attitude, and the alleged discriminatory practice against myself, by the malicious and wrongful statements published by the newspaper *Il*

Tempo, Pagina Marsicana in repeated articles has impugned my professional character. There have been also charges that the city hall of Avezzano, in its attitude and in furtherance of a pre-planned conspiracy, would have caused enormous damages to the projected AUA's developmental objectives and caused, also, to the projected AUA's collateral activities those rights and privileges which would have been lost without affording the due process of law. Hence, I must claim that the above-mentioned alleged acts by the city hall of Avezzano and the newspaper *Il Tempo, Pagina Marsieana* have caused permanent and continuing injury and damages to my professional reputation and to my general business and project activities.

At this point, in order to make understand the grievances of my claims, a summary of the historical background and events of the projected AUA should be presented fully, to be supported by facts and evidence. As a matter of fact, the idea to develop a school of physical education within a Campus of International Character in Avezzano, Italy, was conceived and grew from a series of trips, meetings, and discussions with academic people that began between 1966 and 1967. It was first supported and sponsored by myself only, and then included the support and encouragement of some friends, to most of whom I have presented information papers and formal presentations that covered a variety of topics, mainly studies and proposals, and obviously discussions and suggestions related to a development approach, with a specific number of projects' members and guests. (See Proposals Projected AUA—exhibit N. 1.)

When the concept of the Campus was first proposed in 1966, at that time, I wrote a collection of papers for a feasibility study of the location and a supportive analysis of the validity of the objectives set forth. This suggested a more ambitious project, which would have provided scholars and laymen with a systematic analysis of recent trends in the fields of physical education, health education, and recreation activities. It led to a decision to devote more efforts to the larger community issue of change, which at the time seemed to be more propitious than was anticipated. Just as the first promotional meetings for the project organization and preparation were underway, the news of the project plans was announced, heralding several turning points in the projected AUA's history, often raising the question of its validity and positivity for further development. (See city hall of Avezzano—exhibit N. 2.)

Myself, as author and promoter of the project, together with a specific number of other persons who believed and were interested in the projected AUA's development, met officially in some first meeting sessions during 1969, mainly to plan the undertaking and to talk over the negotiations and contacts made with government officials and concerned citizens. It was during this year that the first projected Campus draft was presented, and meetings followed to assess results. Some of the project's presentations and revisions were completed early in 1970, and most of the collective source materials were edited, assembled, and brought up to date by the beginning of that summer, to be submitted to the proper office of the city hall of Avezzano. This offered an unusual opportunity to consult among the project's concerned parties in order to assess critical stages for its future development. It was the hope and understanding from the very beginning of the negotiations with the city hall of Avezzano's officials to be able to turn out something more than an assortment of papers. It was aimed as a genuinely collaborative work with support from all the concerned parties, which would have reflected the facts that the author and promoter of the projected AUA was listening very carefully and all was properly documented. (See city hall of Avezzano's deliberations and Decree of Public domain by local and provincial government.)

As a matter of fact, the city hall of Avezzano's interest in the project provided the point of departure for the organization and promotion of the same. It was the contention that a sound assessment, on behalf of the city hall itself and other government organizations and agencies, established the necessity of understanding the international character and behavior toward the project and its principals in the years ahead. Accordingly, emphasis was given to the domestic location of the regional area where the Campus was planned, although in many other proposals and studies other areas of project's implication were discussed.* Several individuals have contributed separate suggestions for the project's setting. But no one involved in the project's development has yet devised dependable techniques for the prediction of some of the human aspects, let alone the fate of the entire project. At this point, there is no claim to have accomplished any miracles of fortune-telling, nor it has been the purpose of the encyclopedic of to

---

*   *Light weight materials (microballoons) and ultra-light such as Polyacrylonitrile Enhancement for the campus structural facilities because of seismic zone.

be established super colossal structure. One thing has been accomplished, however; efforts have been made to employ an array of specialized scholars and executives, full of talents, to the analysis of the past and present project's conditions, from which the future of the project has flowed from one area to the next. In fact, topics of studies and proposals of the project, such as those in relation to the community activities and other implications, lend themselves to quantitative measures and were inherently limited with respect to rates and magnitude of changes, which have extended forecasts in the area of finance and economics. Political trends, for obvious reasons, are also subject to rapid, frequent, and unforeseen shifts.

Generally speaking, it has taken a span of approximately a decade for a working guideline and planning, but there have been also variations from one proposal to the next, from one study to another, according to how well the proposals of feasible projects would have lend themselves to long-range treatment, depending on the willingness of individual supporter to combine a certain boldness with the traditional caution of professional businessmen and scholar. (See Letters of Suggestions and Proposals: exhibit N. 4).

My contribution, as author and promoter of the project, in addition to the overall organization and editing of my own writing, has included forming the conditions for the project's presentations; brief introductions to the project's meetings and business sessions; and above all, the concluding documentations file, which has brought together the material from the project sources. I've tried to avoid imposing a merely mechanical uniformity upon my technical contributions, preferring to offer the widest scope to every individual adviser in treating or discussing specific matters. In conclusion, the resulting differences in many of the project areas approaches, including the detail of the documentation, as well as in the level of discussions from related memos, are welcomed not so much as stylistic forms of the work accomplished but as substantive strengths from the projected AUA-connected presentations and endorsement. It is believed a genuinely organic unity in the content of the various presentations has been achieved, easy to identify, especially if the materials are read in sequence, as in the projected AUA specific areas of concern. (See Specific Area of Concern as properly organized.)

P.S. The above was summarized to represent the Plaintiff in the case brought against the city hall of Avezzano at the Tribunal of Avezzano (AQ), Italy.

Avezzano, June 1977.

Re: Project AUA's Litigation (Case N. #336/86).

The litigation against the city hall of Avezzano for breach of contract continues at the end of a second decade. In times when high technology instructions are transmitted in and out of private and public offices almost instantaneously by means of computers and other kind of devices, the litigation concerning the projected American University of Avezzano (AUA) has broken all records for delays and legal procedures. The basic question to be asked is: "Who must pay the price for these legal performances that take so long, that cost very much in terms of time and money, and above all, have diverted resources from an individual finance program?" It is recognized that somebody has taken much of the work and litigation burdens, as evidenced from the submitted legal documentation. Although it seems appropriate to point to these litigation time delays as an example of a country's judicial system failure, even more insidious are the many contrived excuses and particular manipulations vis-a-vis the high financial responsibilities tied to this unique and specific litigation, which is very much dormant at the Court of Appeals of L'Aquila.

According to documentation submitted to the Court and competent government agencies in Italy and USA, the time and money spent for legal expenses are already especially excessive in the entire project activities. To put it in another way, this project's legal expenditures amount almost to the project's final anticipated financial budget. This lengthy litigation has imposed other significant burdens upon an individual who has been forced through this and other related legal procedures. Anyone who has been aware of these specific legal procedures can attest firsthand to the allocation of time and energies. In addition, potential business opportunities have been lost during all these years of litigation, especially because highly advanced project results are at stake. The uncertainties of these specific judicial decisions have delayed the implementation of some important business plans. Above all, this litigation has also effectively destroyed longstanding business and personal relationships. It should be more than evident that high costs and time delays in a competitive international business project's activities can no longer be tolerated. A prompt resolution to this case could make a solid effort to reduce other costs and to benefit potential business activities survival.

To Whom This May Concern:

This letter is tendered in testimony of dilatory and inconsistent replies to letters and telephone conversations on the part of the city administration of Avezzano in completing contractual agreements with the American University of Avezzano.

The American University is a nonprofit organization, incorporated in the State of Ohio, United States, to establish a university in accordance with action of the City Council of Avezzano on Oct. 18, 1969.

In November of that year, the board of trustees delegated the author and promoter to visit Avezzano in the company of an architect, to appraise the site that had been designated by the Council and to report on the suitability of the area for the erection of educational buildings. The architect's report was very favorable. Based on his appraisal and the assurance of Council's deliberation, the newly organized board of trustees agreed to proceed with the project.

Periodic meetings of the board continued in hopes of raising funds to begin construction of the campus. Progress has been slow and is now encumbered by the unwillingness of campaign professionals to proceed without assurance in the form of a certificate of title to the property. Our experience as mentioned in the foregoing has been one of repeated letters to the city administration, followed by weeks, months, and even longer delays until we again requested replies. Some of those experiences, however, may have been the result of changes in city administration, although we are of the opinion that succeeding regimes have not been as receptive to the project as their predecessors. A brief summary of our experiences will clarify our viewpoint.

A letter from the Mayor of Avezzano, of Jan. 14th, 1970, enclosed a map of the designated land and stated, "I will propose to the council that the land be ceded gratuitously to the American Institution."

Nothing further was received from the administration until the succeeding mayor replied to our inquiries with a letter dated Nov. 21st, 1971. I should mention that this letter was a reply to earlier letters from me and arrived a very long time after he had talked with us on the telephone on June 8th, 1971. He repeated his telephone promise, writing that "The Administration would accomplish the initiative." Our treasurer then, in response to administrative specifications from the Mayor, sent payment of the token price in the amount of $300.00. This Mayor acknowledged payment on Mar. 20, 1972.

Our letters after Mar. 20, 1972 were not answered.

On Jan. 30, 1973, Project AUA concerns, in a three-way telephone conversation with the mayor, received his assurance that conveyance of a certificate of title would be soon forthcoming. Finally, the mayor sent his letter of Oct. 31, 1973, sending a copy to our attorney. In that letter he outlined a revised proposal whereby the portion of the land covered with pine trees would be retained by the City, although leased to the university at a token price. He also suggested that the university deposit money in escrow to show good faith. I replied that we would accept the revised terms but would not deposit money as a forfeiture should we not complete the first building in the specified period of five years.

On Nov. 22, 1973, I informed our attorney again of our intentions and wrote to the mayor, requesting that the certificate be conveyed to our attorney, in the name of the university and that our representative had power of attorney to complete the contract (Dec. 18, 1973).

Our next letter was from the new mayor, written on Feb. 23, 1974, reasserting the previous mayor's revised proposal. With agreement of our board of trustees, we accepted the proposal. I should state that this letter specified a final date for reply as of one month from the date of the letter, dated Feb. 23rd. We received that letter on April 6, 1974.

On Nov. 27, 1974, I again wrote to this mayor requesting the certificate of title. I also asked for a provisional contract for the pine tree area. At this point, our correspondence has been without definite reply, and the project is still pending an affirmative response from the City Administration.

In rebuttal to the latest mayor's contention that the university is not now and never has been financially sound, I hasten to refute his remarks. In the years between 1969 and 1973 our promotion committee raised an ample amount of money through banquets, fashion shows, and private subscription to undertake the campus and to further raise money for commercial enterprise to support the university. Large sums were promised, although not encouraged, because we could give no assurance that the city of Avezzano would confirm its commitment by issuing a certificate of title as promised by the original Mayor and as inferred in subsequent letters attendant to our payment of the stipulated price in December of 1971 and acknowledged by the mayor in March of 1972.

MEMORANDUM

Background

Files in both the Italian Embassy in Washington, DC and the American Embassy in Rome, Italy, contain certain essential memoranda and documents indicating progressive steps and problems of the inter-cultural educational project, AUA, jointly developed by this board of trustees and the city of Avezzano, Italy, at all times promoted and implemented by our intermediary, an Italian citizen. Embassy files will include many notes generated during visits of our intermediary.

The key decision or transaction flowed from acceptance of the American and Avezzano dual campus connected by a transfer "bridge." The Case Western Reserve campus and physical health sciences program were "in place," and the city of Avezzano acted through lawful enactments of the council to allot land for its campus; in due course this board of trustees sent the check in payment for the land, which check was accepted and endorsed by the mayor. Concurrently the American planning group promoted AUA to the extent of raising substantial development (so-called "front end") funds and applied this money to many approved planning projects. One project was a trip to Avezzano by the first group of enrolled students, for which there was not yet a campus. Substantial persons expressed interest in funding when the campus in Avezzano was established; i.e., with title delivered to this board of trustees.

The title to the Avezzano campus site was never delivered, and the undersigned chairman of the board of AUA has a file drawer full of the endless flow of letters imploring action or reasons for not acting. Certain powers of attorney were delegated to lawyers to seek answers and provide new positions for discussion, but these efforts also came to nothing. The author and promoter made a number of trips at his own expense, facing wholly unexplainable campaigns to discredit and avoid him. This board was brought to the reluctant conclusion that, for completely unknown reasons, the city of Avezzano had elected to block the project. Meanwhile, substantial work has been done on programs and connections relevant to general citizen health maintenance, presently a modern educational resource of great interest to employers, who, similar to present American employer action, will want to consider a special educational center for seminars, workshops, short courses, library access, et cetera. Since our

Italian cities have contacted us for availability of the AUA program, we have every reason to believe that substantial public welfare is involved here.

Decision and Action

The board of trustees harbors a (perhaps) remote hope of an equitable solution to the campus site controversy. The author and promoter was forced by his own financial disaster over some ten (10) years to initiate litigation against the city of Avezzano and the local newspaper to recover his own damages. While the board is not a party to this action, it realistically recognizes that a settlement will probably involve disposition of the land title claims. Since delay tactics and postponements have exhausted all funds for paying legal fees, the eminent disaster is possible dismissal of the action on April 16, 1977, Avezzano Court, for simple inability to appear with counsel.

The board has learned of the availability of the Italian Senior Council of Magistrates, purporting to hear petitions in the public interest to prevent obstructions of justice, and we now enclose such a petition: one copy for Embassy files and one copy to be forwarded by the Embassy to the council. We lack information as to how to reach the council and respectfully appeal to the American Embassy to forward our petition to the council.

Petition

In the Matter of the Litigation

The author and promoter versus city of Avezzano, et al

(next scheduled hearing is set for April 26, 1977, Avezzano)

From the board of trustees of

American University of Avezzano, Inc. Nonprofit, Ohio, USA (hereinafter AUA)

To The Italian (constitutional) *Senior Council of Magistrates*

This is a petition for timely intervention in the captioned matter to hold further proceedings open for review by this council of procedural tactics and the principal merits to evaluate the grossly inequitable consequences of further postponements and delays as they work to obstruct justice.

The constitutional basis for this board's petition is the belief and documented history of a public service mission, now threatened with disaster, reasons for which belief are set forth in our memorandum to the respective embassies, intended to provide a current status report. A copy of this memorandum is attached and made a part of this petition and will be sworn testimony at the appropriate session by the council.

In plain language, the last hope of this board and its representative, to save the original AUA jointly approved plan and some ten (10) years of dedicated work and many thousands of dollars of expenses is for this council to intervene to stop the delays now threatening to end in dismissal simply for lack of means to continue, and to require and schedule a hearing session without right of postponement or continuance for the purpose of negotiating a good faith and equitable plan for going forward or liquidating the original project with a fair and reasonable settlement in behalf of Project AUA.

Accordingly, this board of trustees now comes forward to request said action by your Honorable Council (senior) of Magistrates, and while engaged in deliberations on said ruling to give notice to the Avezzano Court to hold up further action on the matter until further notice from the Senior Council of Magistrates.

This petition is respectfully submitted by signatures and dates below:

Memorandum

Your mission involves several objectives, personal and for the university. First, your personal mission is to resolve by settlement or agreement upon a time scheduled for litigation, the issue of personal damage incurred by the acts of one or more defendants. Definite action is vital to unclouded forward progress with development of the university; all should understand this.

Your first act upon arrival should be telephone contact with counsel to set times(s) for working conferences. Such conferences should be restricted to the record and merits of the one personal damage matter.

In the event certain discussions of settlement take place in which the university's vital interest in the land deed are thrust into consideration, you are empowered by the board of trustee president's letter and my approval, herewith, to weigh the merits of any proposal. Please be informed that any settlement in which the delivery of the land deed incurs or appears to incur obligation by the university, such settlement must be cleared with the board of trustee president and may not take effect without his concurring signature.

As our director of projects, you are to make the personal contacts we have discussed, and with whom we have had exchanges of correspondence, to investigate the proposed sites, programs, and resources available for consideration to develop the essential network to facilitate our "open university" concept. This relates to our development of field work programming and the appropriate sites for cooperation with industry to implement the plan of international exchange-of-information sessions.

You are aware of and may mention the fact of the series of working sessions of industrial medical directors with Case Western Reserve University's Health Center Library to expand and implement the presently active information network, to embrace industry health delivery experience and data, and to add an additional component of public health-physical fitness research and experience. This network is available for international cooperation and will be a resource to our university project.

The new project work and forward planning must take second place to your primary mission of resolving litigation. Once your primary work sessions are scheduled, however, the open times should be utilized for other contacts.

With reference to your request for information on my time involvement in university affairs, the first dated document in the files goes back three (3) years; I have worked a minimum of ten (10) hours per month, on average, and my senior consulting rate (management engineering, corporate lawyer) is $60/hour, reduced to $40/hour for long-term contracts. My contract fee would have been about $14,000 for the entire period, had it been charged pursuant to contract.

You are, of course, to telephone the board of trustee president should you need further information. We are hopeful you succeed in all missions. We extend greetings to all with whom you confer on our mutual problems.

My strong commitment to write *"Fight the City Hall"* and to disclose related documented material developed in the projected American University of Avezzano, Italy, within a Campus of International Character are the result of several years of personal struggle and efforts. This undertaking is also an attempt to assemble the various aspects of knowledge of the project activities: the dealing with bureaucrats and politicians, lawyers, and their local courts, and the effect of financial laws in substitution of a Letter of Intent."

Present and past events in connection with these undertaken activities, researched and analyzed, certainly help to provide a better understand of how to deal with similar situations now evidenced more often in a growing global cultural behavior amid alarming human relations. However, one of the major tasks in this publication is the pursuit of the truth behind the many difficulties and wrongdoings against personal endeavor to reach specific project objectives. An inquiry in searching for the truth becomes almost imperative, and necessary to differentiate between the moral truth and a predominant public official culture full of deceit.

Writing English and Italian versions ought to be taken into consideration to avoid the reoccurrence of the same events and deception used in contractual dealings. Suggestions and/or support to publish this book are more than welcome. Please contact the author at the above address.

There Are No Other Alternatives But To Write and
To Publish the Inquired Evidence, Such As:

A Campus of International Character:
    Project American University Of Avezzano, Italy

    —Learning How To Deal and Cope with Crooks,
    Thieves, Liars, Scoundrels, Cowards, Bureaucratics,
    and Corrupt Politicians—and Also with Some Decent
    Individuals—in Thirty Years of Work, Study, Research,
    and Development.

The title of this publication speaks for itself. The time and current events
are very appropriate to disclose what has happened in one city hall; it may
happen to many others, and it does not matter where, when, and why.
Prevalent cultural and social symptoms were and are basically the same
in the political arena. The motives are basically also the same when a few
irresponsible politicians, bureaucrats, and crooks of any kind get into the
deal. Dealing with a very important matter has taken almost thirty years of
intensive and extensive battle against the most pernicious political behavior
from the city hall of Avezzano, Italy. It must be said that since the early
days of pursuing specific written agreement in negotiations related to the
Campus of International Character with city officials and other concerns,
my personal affairs have been damaged and my professional working career
has also been effectively destroyed. One of the main reasons is that the
efforts in specific dealing and undertaken activities might have collided
with some kind of Obscure Forces that attracted interest at highest levels
of government agencies in Italy and United States.

While I started to question fundamental agreement verifications and
validations connected with strange Avezzano city hall behavior, numerous
evidences of emerging wrongdoing had to be brought to the attention
of competent authorities. The overwhelming evidence was ignored and
avoided, and they often refused to comply with specific critical legal
matters. There is no doubt that this kind of behavior is a violation of
civil and criminal law, and for too long no one seems to know how to
deal with it. An increase concern for corrupt practices was first received
with indifference, followed with increasing local political scandals and

growing evidence of public disgust with corrupt officials, prominent personalities, and institutions. It seemed that in our dealings there was only one rule: bribery and kickbacks, which have become a common belief, a kind of Italian "Credo," as it embraces foreign investment capital. Corruption has been the first enemy and obstacle against the projected campus development since its beginning. Time after time, a few decent people have supported and asked for action on this important matter. These decent individuals and personal confidants have been aware that, above all, corruption in the long and short runs have eroded resources from the project main objectives, increased the cost of running business activities, and has also distorted those fundamental agreements on which the Campus of International Character at Avezzano was legally defined and endorsed.

Besides the many wrongdoings evidenced from the city hall of Avezzano, a fundamental law, #43/1956, is known to guarantee foreign capital investment in Italy; the whole treaty between the United States and Italy does not offer more than perplexities and dilemmas regarding how to enforce it. Also, evidence has demonstrated more than once that the dilemma derived essentially from the fraudulent behavior and conflict of interest in the Campus land dealing within the city hall of Avezzano come mainly from political party friction. It is quite evident from inquiries that within the city hall of Avezzano, on this specific matter, officials have lied repeatedly, still continue to lie, and worse continue withholding very important information. In fact, I have become so enraged over these kinds of behaviors that writing and examining these public performances became a learning experience in itself.

Inquiry, personal notes, written reports to concerned parties, and material researched in specific files have contributed to call attention to this important matter. There is clear evidence of conspiracy and denigration against the Campus promotional activities, especially from obscure forces, which have vilified almost everybody supporting the endeavor. In testimony about the personal inquiry and work carried on during all these years, the title "Fight City Hall" is timely and appropriate, if for no other purpose than to at least to disclose facts and allegations to concerned citizens of the related community. Recommended litigation against the city hall of Avezzano has last more than two decades, and in spite of questionable interpretation from Italian courts, it must be conveyed whether the right to a judicial review of the verdicts' findings and award of damage is required to prevent an excessive burden to legal justice.

The litigation against the city hall of Avezzano has also presented a challenge to a judicial system that has issued verdicts in a certain frivolous aspect. In the legal dispute, attorneys and judges have somehow tried and failed to articulate a basic right of mentioned law #43/1956, which is a growing concern to the business aspect of the litigation. The verdict and related award are so frivolous as to violate the fundamental requirement of international law. This case offered a legal vehicle for a broader ruling on whether the local court procedure must guarantee limits in handling punitive damage awards, especially in reference to cited international investment law. Under the international law, only a competent judicial forum may review these verdicts to determine whether there is sufficient evidence to support the ruling. There are all the evidence and reasons to submit the case and related verdicts to an international court of justice, as part of a tradition in international law disputes of providing judicial review for the Italian court's decision.

There are no doubts that the plaintiff has suffered enormous damage because of the wrongdoings. Although Italian court judges have ruled in favor of the plaintiff, a small percentage of fault in damages has been found against the city hall of Avezzano. But time has altered the reasons and political skirmish that brought the local government regime to failure. The undertaken personal investigation has not only revealed a sort of political cataclysm and twistings bottom-line contractual arrangements in the legislated land boundary margin but an alarming problem of corruption and deception. Manipulation of public funds, racketeering with crooks, abuse of public office, and many other illicit actions from the city hall of Avezzano are just a few to be analyzed and examined in the inquiry. During the early phases of this inquiry, it was conveyed and made clear that the essence of law was above any politician's short-lived promises. Also, during the course of the inquiry, it was properly suggested that, being a law enforcement investigation, the entire undertaken activity must hold itself to the highest professional and ethical standards. This activity has been carried on mainly to prevent and avoid possible public corruption and violation of public and private trust. The many contacts and discussions held with professionals have certainly helped to assess and continue on a specific task.

Time and time again, personal contacts were also called on to share information, provide skills in the investigation, and analyze evidence before another Trip-Memo and Report had to be submitted for consideration. Without any question, these skilled professionals and contacts are the few decent individuals who supported and were inspired to follow the standard of their professions in a system built on law, not on false promise. It must be added that since the beginning of the inquiry, to get to the bottom of facts, personal efforts were stressed on cooperation in the law enforcement investigation. One of the principal objectives has been to determine whether wrongdoings and judicial prosecution must sustain specific allegations against the Avezzano city hall culprits. However, the investigation got to a critical point to make available such evidence, facts, and events as clearly and expeditiously as possible. It has been suggested to do so in the interest of justice and fairness to all concerned. All evidence, facts, and events are presented in a chronologic history focusing on specific matters.

Perhaps it is relevant to remind about something which in the re-zoned campus is not heard any longer these days: moral values, civic responsibility, and virtue. *"Immune come la moglie di Cesare"* (Immume like Caesar's wife): once used as analogy for the undertaken project Campus activities, it must sound fussy now in a changing environment made of micro-chips and a few potato-chips that challenge each other. Despite the changing community environment, differences, disagreements, and points of view, the campus analogy has been taken very seriously. Supporters for the Campus development were and are realistic about environment and human nature. It is not difficult to realize that certain local politicians had no vocation or talent to become saints, and that is why the law required that city hall deliberations must be published. Government structures by constitutional laws establish checks and balances to circumvent abuses of power by those politicians and bureaucrats who may not be called for sanctification. It is also very important to remember that a democratic government must demand above all a degree of civic responsibility and a sense of virtue. These are certainly demanded of elected officials as well as the citizens who elect them. If the people of the community have forgotten and lack these civic qualities for self-government, then nothing less than social, economic, and political disaster can restrain them from destroying each others.

The issue on civil responsibility has been one of the most fundamental aspects of the Campus of International Character since its conception. The philosophical concept has been straightforward, to protect and keep alive not only the Campus's interest in the deliberated community site, but to maintain the sense of civic responsibility within the proposed activities. It is meant that to pursue specific objectives and related interest, there is commitment to justice and, above all, to truthfulness. Today more than ever, to defend the Campus rights, to pursue justice, to have a sense of civic responsibility, and to tell the truth is to install a canopy over the community public meetings. The several papers submitted, especially in "A Short Story To Be Told," and in many other topics, for that matter, it is not difficult to understand why the canopy becomes very necessary when obscure forces, political twists and turns, as well as questionable strange human behavior, are the main ingredients for a community.

The "Rezoned Campus" land dispute is about several other related issues, also. Since their origin, these issues are based on a culture where lying, false statements, and fraud have become the general rule, which contributed to bring the city hall to the local tribunal. It is about lying and fraud, mainly to divert and secure the re-zoned campus to another group behind the obscure forces. It is, among other things, facts and evidence that show that using fraudulent and false information, local politicians and connected crooks are able to manipulate binding agreements and avoid the due process of the law. Above all, in a legal dispute to the land title, local politicians, bureaucrats, and crooks have engineered bribe efforts to usurp the approved AUA project's program and related activities. The bribe is just a simple and normal phenomena from having a special appetite for US dollars that should have been used in a lot of different directions. Some of this money should not have been used to pay for services received from a local newspaper to write an article against the project development activities, and more to further politicians' ambitious careers, while some went to line the crooks' pockets.

The undertaken inquiries, among other things, are about breach of contract and fraud, conspiracy and cover-up. It is indeed about very serious questions to be asked, not ignored: whether there is deception or corruption and what really went wrong with the re-zoned Campus land deliberations? In the end, from the inquiry and evidence from documentation, it is easy to learn that there is a very closed and insulated circle between government officials, politicians, and local crooks who don't have too much concern for law matters affecting contract negotiation, payment for the land, project development activities, and subsequent investigations into the contact circle.

The Italian courts' sentence against the notorious municipality as a frivolous political cover-up for a very serious international legal problem is not any longer a secret. Whether or not, aside from court decisions, the Foreign Capital Investment Into Italy, its related treaty between Italy and United States, is to be kept at present, and whether law #43/1956 must be enforced, it is time to take legal action. If there are any other feasible alternatives to continue any efforts within the framework of this law and to demonstrate the many discrepancies of the Italian courts decisions, and of course the inefficiency of law enforcement agencies in Italy and United States, then it is time to sandbag and liquidate not only the projected Campus of International Character Program but all collateral project activities as well.

It seems that given the present circumstances, in other more promising undertaken collateral activities, in the region (ZAR), the present political deviations are not different than the projected Campus's previous court case. Evidence demonstrates once again a pattern behavior to conduct business in the region (ZAR), where local government authorities enable or encourage breach of contracts in matters of civil and penal laws; domestically, nationally, and internationally. There is at least some relevant evidence of improper manipulation and transfer of project files, either within local government itself and/or with the collaboration of connected agencies offices. These are not just rumors or street-talk or political finger-pointing, but solid evidence of how to cause economic and financial obstacles and to damage each endorsed project's development activities. A personal inquiry can demonstrate with logic, facts, events, and valid evidence that capital investment applied to specific project activities in the region (ZAR) is fundamentally of American dollars; and in accordance with the Law #43/1956.

In many instances it's true, and this must be kept in mind, that politicians, bureaucrats, and regional personalities quite often find their memory has failed, directly and indirectly, to find their way out. But project files requested and submitted to specific government authority and other related agencies, especially that project's file, mysteriously appear and disappear. This same file, among other valuable information, contains the source and evidence of the US dollars, a foreign capital investment into Italy. It must be said, any other expedient is just to make this specific investment law a mockery, and this is serious enough to call for proper attention. Personal inquiry into this matter and the project file itself should also reveal important information concerning the Campus's land dealing and other detailed political-bureaucratic maneuvers that are related not only to the region's (ZAR) past but includes present and perhaps future project implications. Whatever these implications are regarding the undertaken project activities, a final decision on this matter must be addressed to the concerned authority in the United States and Italy. This concerned authority may or may not be concerned with the region (ZAR) political play-off. The odds are that at least a portion of the file's contents will be leaked and exploited politically, as usual, aiming to delay, delay, delay—detrimental for the projects' development program objectives in-situ, related to the tunnel WCBMextraction and (PPP) conversion in the Subequana/Peligna Valley of the Abruzzo Region, Italy.

Foreign Investment Regulations in Italy

Legislation Governing Foreign Investment

Foreign capital investments in Italy are at present regulated by the following legislation and administrative orders:

1. Law No. 43 of February 7, 1956, effective upon its publication in the *Gazzette Ufficiale* of February 21, 1956.
2. Legislative decree No. 476 of June 6, 1956, introducing new currency-control regulations and establishing a free market in foreign state and banknotes, as amended by law No. 786 of July 25, 1956.
3. Regulations for the implementation of law No. 43 approved by Presidential Decree No. 758 of July 6, 1956.
4. Ministerial decree of October 26, 1967, setting forth the foreign currencies acceptable by the Italian Exchange Office for the purposes of law No. 43.
5. Circular No. 280 of August 6, 1956, issued by the Finance Ministry's General Directorate of Direct Taxation, concerning tax obligations to be met before transferring abroad foreign capital or returns therefrom.
6. Circular No. 288 of February 21, 1957, issued by the Finance Ministry's General Directorate of Direct Taxation concerning the transfer abroad of dividends and other income on which the R.M. tax (income tax) has been retained at the source.

7. Circular No. 137 of August 17, 1956, issued by the Finance Ministry's General Directorate of Customs, concerning the importation of machinery for foreign capital investments.

These form a body of regulations which, without placing any restrictions whatever on the freedom of foreign nationals (individuals as well as corporations and firms) to make any capital investment in Italy, establish different possibilities for the transfer of profits, interest, dividends, or disinvested capital under certain criteria, and make such repatriation conditional upon the meeting of certain currency-control and tax obligations. Limits are also placed upon the contracting of debts and floating of bond issues in the local financial market.

Foreign capital investments are divided into (1) investments intended for the creation of new "productive" enterprises, or for the enlargement of existing "productive" enterprises, and (2) "other" investment."

The power of actually applying this definition to specific cases rests with the Italian Treasury. A foreign investor wishing to take advantage of the benefits accorded to "productive" enterprises must file, either directly or through a designated representative, with the Italian Ministry of the Treasury's General Directorate, Inspectorate General for Foreign Financial Relations, an application requesting a determination of whether his particular project qualifies as a "productive" investment. Such applications can be filed through any commercial bank. In his application, the investor should include all the technical and financial information that would be useful to the Ministry in making the determination.

Within a period of thirty days the Ministry must notify the investor of its decision on the application. If the decision is favorable, the investor may proceed to put his project into effect, making whatever changes may be required for the economic and operating efficiency of the enterprise. On completion of the project, the investor should request that the Ministry of the Treasury ascertain that the investment has actually resulted in the establishment or enlargement of a "productive" enterprise. The Ministry of the Treasury must make this determination within ninety days of receiving the investor's request.

Screening Procedure and Criteria

"Productive" Enterprises—For investments in "productive" enterprises, made after the effective date of Law No. 43, permission is granted, without any limitation of time or amount, to transfer freely abroad interest, dividends, and profits actually received, as well as amounts realized from capital dis-investment. "Productive" enterprises are defined as those "which engage in the production of goods and services" and which require, for their business, investments in capital goods and equipment (e.g., factories, yards) normally involving the use of capital for a period of time and not on a temporary and purely speculative basis. Examples are enterprises engaged in land reclamation and improvement power production and distribution, mining and transport activities, highway construction, and the construction of buildings, including hotels.

The broad scope of this definition, contained in Law No. 43, permits granting the benefits of free reexportability of capital and returns on capital to the great majority of investments.

If the Ministry of the Treasury's determination is not applied for, transfer of capital and returns on the foreign investments would receive the less favorable treatment discussed below for "other" investments. However, the application to the Ministry of the Treasury to have a foreign investment certified as a "productive" enterprise may be made at any time, even after completion of the project in question.

Other Investments—The treatment guaranteed by law for investments not intended to create or enlarge "productive" enterprises, as defined in the preceding section, is comparatively less favorable than that accorded "productive" investments. For these investments, interest, dividends, and profits may be freely transferred abroad in an amount not exceeding 8 percent of the capital invested, the repatriation of capital may not exceed the amount of the foreign currency originally imported, and any such repatriation may not take place until two years after the date of the investment.

When the law on foreign investments was enacted in 1956, Europe's economic and financial position, although improving, was still characterized by unfavorable balances of payments, which justified a prudent control on the flow of exchange. This explains why the 1956 law grants complete freedom of movement to foreign capital, which, because of its use, does not lend itself to a rapid exodus that could suddenly upset the country's economic situation. But, since 1956, the overall balance of payments to Italy has improved steadily, and the country was able to embrace a policy of large convertibility, especially after the creation, in 1958, of the so-called "capital accounts." Anyone residing outside of Italy, whether of foreign or

Italian nationality, may open these accounts with Italian banks without any need of a special authorization. The "capital accounts" may be credited with lire obtained from various sources, as, for instance, from the sale of real or personal property in Italy, from the earnings of foreign investments in Italy, and from transfers from "foreign accounts" in lire. The lire in the "capital accounts" may be used for any kind of investment in Italy. The important feature of these accounts is that their holders may, at any time, transfer the lire in them to "foreign accounts" and then convert said lire in foreign currencies, even currencies different from the original one, and transfer them abroad. Thus, the "capital accounts" allow foreign operator to make unlimited investments in Italy without difficulty. Moreover, through the "capital accounts," under article 2 of the Foreign Investment Law, an investor may transfer abroad, at the official rate of exchange, funds in excess of the limits established by said article.

Investment in the form of machinery—Foreign investments in any field may also be made in the form of machinery, subject, however, to the general regulations governing the importation of goods into Italy. The valuation of capital so invested is based on the value assigned to the machinery by the Italian customs, upon importation. This valuation is used by the Italian authorities in determining the allowable transfer of profits or capital repatriation.

The foreign investor must make an explicit statement in the customs declaration that the machinery is being imported under the Italian law on foreign capital investments. The amount of profits derived from machinery investments that may be transferred depends on whether the investment qualifies as "productive" under the procedure outlined above.

For the repatriation of capital represented by investments in machinery or equipment there is, however, the limitation in all cases that repatriation may take lace only after two years from the date of investment and in an amount not to exceed the sales price. The sales price may, however, exceed the value of the original investment.

Contracting debts and floating bonds issues by "productive" enterprises—A specific article in Law No. 43 covers the provisions under which foreign investors, wishing to avail themselves of the liberal treatment accorded to "productive" enterprises, may under certain limitations contract medium—and long-term debts and float bond issues in Italy.

Factors Affecting Investment:
Government Stimulates Investments

The Italian government has been engaged since 1950 in a vast program for the development of Southern Italy, an area characterized by a generally depressed agricultural economy and relatively low living standards. In its effort to promote the economic development of the area, the government has followed two basic lines of approach. Firstly, it has carried on a large program of *public work for the purpose of providing the necessary facilities and favorable conditions for the development of private enterprise.* Secondly, it has adopted incentives of various types that would make it *more attractive for private enterprises to invest in this area.*

In the first seven years of its activity, the Southern Italy Development Fund, known as the Cassa per il Mezzogiorno (an institution created in 1950 for the purpose of planning and administering the program on behalf of the government) has concentrated its attention mostly on the first phase. The second phase, instead, emphasizes much more the participation of private enterprise. Law No. 634 of July 29, 1957, which continued the life of the fund until June 30, 1965, provided at the same time for a long list of new incentives calculated to increase the flow of private capital, both foreign and domestic, in the South.

There are incentives of various kinds: there are fiscal benefits, industrial credits, capital grants, equity participation, and other miscellaneous ones.

All of these incentives apply in the case of modernization and improvement, extension, conversion, reconstruction, and operation in

Southern Italy of technically organized industrial establishments and of annexed constructions.

The most important of the applicable *fiscal incentives* are the following:

1) The industrial income produced by establishments described above is exempt from the payment of income taxes (Imposta Ricchezza Mobile) for a period of ten years.
2) There is an exemption from the payment of income tax on such portion of a firm's income (but not to exceed 50 percent of such income) that is invested in Southern Italy for the construction or enlargement of industrial facilities. Firms located anywhere in Italy may benefit from this exemption, which applies only to amounts not exceeding 50 percent of the costs of the projects.
3) A 50 percent reduction in the turnover tax for the purchase, in Italy or from abroad, of building materials and machinery required for the erection and installation, extension, conversion, reconstruction, and operation of industrial establishments and annexed constructions. These materials must be used for fixed installations.
4) Exemption from payment of customs duties on the above described items when they are imported.
5) Reduction to a flat nominal fee of registration and mortgage taxes involving deeds connected with investments in the South.

As far as **credit facilities** are concerned, industrialists in Southern Italy are eligible to receive special low-interest loans under a scheme operated by special credit institutes set up in conjunction with the Southern Italy Development Fund. The loans, with maturities up to fifteen years, are extended to industries that establish themselves in the South or expand existing industrial activities there. The rates of interest range from 4 percent to 5½ percent per annum according to the amount (4 percent on loans up to the equivalent of $806,500 and 5½ percent on loans in excess of $1,600,000).

As an additional **temporary incentive**, a new law in 1959 further reduced the rate of interest to 3 percent for loans granted to medium and small industries, up to the equivalent of $1,600,000 for new plants and up to $806,000 for improvement of existing plants. The loans may be granted up to a maximum of 70 percent of the cost of the projects.

In the field of **direct subsidies**, the Southern Italy Development Fund may grant up to 20 percent of the expenditure for industrial buildings and masonry work; for line-ups with roads and railways, acqueducts and other services, and 10 percent of expenditure for the purchase of machinery and equipment, provided they have not benefited from exemption from customs duties. The 10 percent contribution may increase to 20 percent when machinery and equipment is manufactured in Southern Italy. Small and medium-sized industries are defined as those having capital of not more than 3 billion lire ($4.8 million) and with not more than five hundred persons employed.

Other sundry benefits are available to firms investing in the South, like the possibility of obtaining, under certain circumstances, freight rate reductions for materials used in the investment, reduction of municipal taxes, et cetera.

The Rest of the Country

Some incentives for investment in small and medium-sized industries are available also in certain localities of Central and Northern Italy. These are provided for in Law No. 635 of July 20, 1957.

The law provides that in all municipalities of Northern and Central Italy having less than 10,000 inhabitants and which have been declared "depressed areas," new artisan enterprises and new small industries will be exempt from payment of all direct taxes on income for a period of ten years.

The definition of "small industrial enterprise" is that of an enterprise with not more than one hundred workers (office employees and apprentices not to be included in the count).

A special Committee of Ministers has been given the authority to list the municipalities to be considered "depressed areas." The first such list came out at the beginning of 1959, and since then another four lists have been made public, listing altogether some 1,380 localities as areas entitled to the tax incentives.

Small and medium-sized business firms in Northern and Central Italy may also avail themselves of special credit facilities provided for in Law No. 623 of July 30, 1959. Under this law, special funds have been made available to special credit institutions to allow them the granting of loans at the maximum rate of 5 percent and with "ten year" maturity for the construction of new plants or for the expansion and modernization of existing plants.

ADVANTAGES OF LOCATION

Italy's geographic position in the center of the Mediterranean area makes it a natural marketing and distribution base for southern Europe, northern Africa, and the Near East. Its long coastline and many good harbors make it easily accessible by sea, and well developed railways and highway networks facilitate internal transportation. Italy also has a large pool of available labor, much of it already acclimated to modern industrial organization, as well as skilled engineers and technicians.

taly has a long history of excellent craftsmanship and inventiveness, which have been reflect in major contributions to world techniques. It has a highly developed mechanical industry, particularly well organized for work on small orders and special jobs involving a highly skilled labor content. The relative flexibility imparted by this intense but small-scale development makes for a greater ease in filling orders for special parts, pilot models, new designs, et cetera.

Although relatively poor in most natural resources, Italy does possess potential reserves of hydrocarbons, which may present significant prospects for development. In recent years production of natural gas has expanded considerably, and successful explorations in Sicily have created much general interest in possibilities of developing an important petroleum industry.

Convention For Avoidance of Double Taxation

To avoid double taxation and prevent evasion of income taxes, the governments of the United States and Italy signed a convention in March 1955 that became effective as of January 1, 1956.

United States-Italy
Income Tax Convention

To avoid double taxation and prevent evasion of income taxes, the governments of the United States and Italy signed a convention in March 1955 that became effective as of January 1, 1956.

The convention concerns the United States Federal income tax and related surtaxes and Italian National government income taxes on land, buildings, personal property (*ricchezza mobile*), agricultural income, and the National progressive income surtax (*imposta complementare progressiva*). The convention also relates to partial exemption in the case of a tax based on property and income; although expressed in reciprocal terms, this provision actually has effect only as to Italian law, because the United States does not impose a tax on property.

Regarding the taxation of income derived from activities carried on by physical persons, corporations, or firms, the convention provides that the income of an enterprise operating in both Italy and the United States will generally be taxed by the country to which the enterprise belongs. Only when an enterprise of one of the countries carries on commercial or industrial activities in the other country through "a permanent establishment" may the latter country tax the income of the enterprise to the extent attributable to such establishment. The test for measuring the income of a United States corporation that is attributable to the permanent establishment in Italy is the amount of industrial or commercial profits such establishment might be expected to derive if it were an independent enterprise engaged in the same or similar activities under the same or similar conditions and were dealing with the United States corporation.

The Convention also provides that the taxes imposed in both countries on dividends that are transferred from one country to the other shall not exceed 15 percent of the amount involved. This rate is reduced to 5 percent, however, if the recipient of the dividends is a corporation controlling, directly or indirectly, at least 95 percent of the entire voting power in the corporation paying the dividend, and of not more than 25 percent of the gross income if derived from interest and dividends, other than interest and dividends received from its own subsidiary corporations. Such reduction of the rate of 5 percent shall not apply if it appears that the relationship has been arranged or is maintained primarily for the purpose of securing the reduced rate (Article 7).

Regarding personal incomes, the convention provides for the exemption from taxes in the United States or in Italy on salaries, wages, and pensions paid by one of the countries to citizens of the other who are not permanently residing therein. Incomes derived from real property and royalties received from the exploitation of mines, quarries, or other natural resources are to be taxed by the country in which such resources are situated.

Furthermore, the convention grants reciprocal exemption to incomes derived from the operation of ships or aircraft registered in Italy and the United States; this proviso suspended the arrangement between the United States and Italy that provided for relief from double income taxation on shipping profits, effected by exchange of notes in 1926.

2. Local Government Taxes

The local governments, i.e. the provinces and the municipalities, are authorized by law to collect a number of additional taxes, under the control of an interministerial committee referred to as the "Central Committee for Local Finance."

The following is a brief summary of the most important taxes collected by provinces and municipalities.

a. Consumption Taxes

Consumption taxes are levied on the local use or sale of certain goods, either produced or used locally, including gas, electricity, building materials, cheese and dairy products, candy, beverages, meat, poultry, game and fish, furniture, phonographs and records, furs and perfumes.

The tax is mandatory, though the rates vary from city to city. As to certain other items, including electrical and household appliances, paper wrappings, boxes and cellophane, sporting goods, shoes, flowers, watches, textiles and clothing goods, glass and crystal products, and material for furnishings, the tax is optional with each municipality.

b. Taxes on Business Licenses, Signs, Et cetera

Municipalities also tax through the issuance of licenses for certain businesses, such as hotels, boarding houses, restaurants, bars, dance halls, et cetera, for all public signs and displays for the use of public areas, for domestic servants, for the circulation of horse-drawn vehicles, and for improvements (paving, road construction, sewage systems, et cetera) resulting in an increase in the value of neighboring properties.

Exchange Regulations
in Italy

Firms and individuals of Italian nationality domiciled in Italy must surrender to Ufficio Italiano dei Cambi, through an authorized bank, within thirty days, such foreign currencies as they may acquire, including foreign bank notes (this rule does not apply to gold and silver coins, the market for which is free in Italy). However, Italian exporters and any beneficiaries of remittances and allowances from abroad may, within thirty days, open a Foreign Exchange Account (Conto Valutario) with an authorized bank in certain specified currencies, including United States dollars. The owner of the account may draw on it in order to settle abroad (provided, however, the regulations in force are observed) for imports of goods, services, and other financial transactions. The use of a Foreign Exchange Account is permitted only during the six months following the month in which credit was received. If the beneficiary of a Foreign Exchange Account is unable to utilize the foreign currency himself, he may surrender it to an authorized bank, which buys it on behalf of a third party who in turn is credited with it in a new Foreign Exchange Account to be utilized within the six months following the month in which credit was received. Subsequent transfer, however, to another buyer in Italy is not permitted. If the beneficiary of a Foreign Exchange Account does not avail himself of the sum to his credit within the above time limits, he must surrender the balance to the Ufficio Italiano dei Cambi within the second week-day following the day of expiry. The Ufficio Italiano dei Cambi will buy the currency at the lowest official rate of exchange quoted during the period from the day of crediting to the day of surrender. Transactions in Foreign Exchange Account currencies take place in United States and Canadian dollars, Swiss francs, pounds sterling, Belgian francs, French francs, West German marks, Danish kroner, Norwegian kroner, Swedish kronor, Dutch guilders, Austrian schillings, Spanish pesetas, and Portuguese escudos on the basis of market quotations on the Italian exchanges. The official rate is fixed daily by the Ufficio Italiano dei Cambi and corresponds to the average of the closing rates on the Milan and Rome exchanges on the same day. It is possible to effect forward purchases and sales in the most actively traded currencies if they clear bona fide export-import transactions.

Italian citizens who have emigrated to the United States are considered, under the exchange regulations, as foreigners. Balances belonging to persons in this category are credited to a Capital Account or transferred abroad, at the then current official rate of exchange, on production of documents certifying that the interested party has transferred his residence abroad.

Inheritances in favor of residents in the dollar area countries may be transferred abroad, without limit of amount, at the then current official rate of exchange.

Italian banks may freely transfer to dollar area countries without any limit of amount:

a) Royalties accrued from the utilization of foreign patents, licenses, and trade-marks
b) Sums due abroad as a result of technical assistance

Current Accounts

The main classifications of accounts in the name of non-residents are:
Capital Accounts
Special Accounts—Ministerial Decree n. 211 of March 2, 1948
Special Accounts—Law n. 43 of February 7, 1956
Foreign Accounts in Foreign Currencies
Foreign Accounts in Lire

Capital Accounts may be freely opened in the name of banks, corporations, firms, and individuals registered or having their residence abroad, regardless of the country.

Such accounts may be credited freely by Italian banks up to any amount without prior approval of the Ufficio Italiano dei Cambi with:

1) Transfers from Foreign Accounts in lire or from another Capital Account
2) Transfers from a Special Account: Law No. 43 of February 7, 1956, or from a Special Account: Ministerial Decree No. 211 of March 2, 1948, in the same account holder's name with implicit waiver of the benefits of Law No. 43
3) Sale proceeds of movable and real property, as for instance

    a) Sale of securities already lodged in a Capital Securities Account subject to presentation of a broker's or a bank's contract. In case of securities not listed on the stock

exchange, the bank has to make sure that an adequate price
has been applied

b) Sale of real estate registered in the name of a person residing
abroad

4) Remittances of Italian bank notes in denominations not exceeding
Lt. 10,000 by mail effected by banks established abroad for the
credit of their account

5) Interest accrued on the account

6) Transfer from Resident Account when the holder of this account
has transferred his residence abroad

The balances may be utilized freely and up to any amount for:

1) Investments in movable and real property other than those
provided by the Law of February 7, 1956, n. 43, i.e.,:

a) Purchase of, or subscription to, government securities, shares
and bonds of Italian companies, purchase of option rights,
provided these securities are lodged in a Capital Deposit;
in the case of securities not listed on the stock exchange,
the bank has to make sure that an adequate price has been
applied

b) Acquiring a capital partnership in commercial and industrial
concerns

c) Industrial plants owned by a person residing abroad (extension
and replacement of machinery, et cetera)

d) Purchase of real estate and construction of building (for civil,
commercial, industrial and agricultural use): if the purchase
is made by a foreign government, the prescribed Italian
Presidential permit authorizing the sale to be presented

2) Settlement of expenses pertaining to the administration of foreign
investments in Italy, as for instance: safe custody charges and
commission on security deposits; outlay for reconstruction,
alterations, repair, improvement, et cetera of real estate; outlay
for tilling of soil, land redemption, insurance premiums, taxes,
contributions, dues, cost of services, et cetera relating to the
investments, et cetera

3) Transfer to Resident Account when the holder of the Capital Account has transferred his residence in Italy
4) Transfer to another Capital Account or Foreign Account

Special Accounts—Law n. 43 of February7, 1956

These Accounts are established to record all transactions concerning investments, returns therefrom, and disinvestments under the provision of the Law n. 43 of February7, 1956. These accounts shall be opened with the Bank of Italy and its authorized banks in the name of foreign citizens residing anywhere and of Italian nationals residing abroad, who, having invested in Italy the sums in lire derived from the surrender of foreign currencies or drawn from Foreign Accounts in lire, wish to take advantage of the permission, granted by Articles 1 and 2 of Law n. 43, to transfer abroad the interest, dividends, and profits actually received and the capital deriving from subsequent disinvestments.

The basic purpose of these accounts is to make it easy for the holders, when applying for transfer of incomes or disinvested capital, to prove that the conditions required for such transfers do exist. For each investment operation there shall be opened a Special Account, bearing a progressive number, in which shall be entered all transactions (crediting and debiting) concerning the investment.

These accounts may be freely credited with:

1) Lire arising from the sale of the following currencies: US dollars, Canadian dollars, pounds sterling, West German marks, French francs, Belgian francs, Swiss francs, Dutch florins, Danish kroner, Norwegian kroner, Swedish kronor, Austrian schillings, Portuguese escudos, Spanish pesetas, remitted to Italy for investment purposes under Law n. 43
2) Transfers from Foreign Accounts in lire opened in the name of banks, companies, and individuals residing abroad
3) Lire arising from disinvestments under Law n. 43
4) Income from investments under Law n. 43
5) Transfers from Special Accounts: Ministerial Decree n. 211 of March 2, 1948, for the quotas of income (8 per cent) that have

become available for transfer abroad on investments effected under M. D. n. 211

6) Transfers from Special Accounts: Ministerial Decree n. 211 of March 2, 1948, for the quotas of capital that have become available for transfer abroad with the prior clearance of the required documents by Ufficio Italiano dei Cambi for the utilization of this account

7) Value of machinery imported in accordance with Article 5 of Law n. 43

8) Transfers from another Special Account: Law n. 43 of February 7, 1956 with the prior clearance of the required document by the Ufficio Italiano dei Cambi for the utilization of this account

The balances may be utilized

1) freely for:

a) Investments in Italy.

In the case of purchase of securities, the securities must be deposited in a Special Securities Account—Law n. 43 of February 7, 1956

b) Transfer abroad of income from investments in the same currency originally surrendered, as follows: with no limitations for income originating from capital invested in productive concerns (namely, those so recognized and authorized by the Italian Treasury upon demand of investor); up to 8 percent per annum for income originating from investment for which the said authorization has not been requested and/or obtained. Income exceeding 8 percent per annum may be credited on behalf of the beneficiary to a Capital Account. The purchase of the foreign currency to be transferred abroad as stated above takes place at the official rate

c) Transfer of income that has become transferable to a Foreign Account in lire

d) Transfer to Capital Account with implicit waiver of the benefits of Law n. 43

2) With the prior clearance of the required documents by Ufficio Italiano dei Cambi for:

a) Transfer abroad of capital disinvested (to the holder of the account) in the same currency originally surrendered, as follows: without any limit of amount and at any time, provided the investment has been recognized as made in productive concerns; up to the amount originally surrendered and not before two years from the investment, if the capital is not recognized as invested in productive concerns. The eventual surplus of capital in respect of the amount originally invested must e credited on behalf of the investor to a Capital Account. The purchase of the foreign currency to be transferred abroad as stated above takes place at the official rate.

b) Transfer of the quota of capital that has become transferable under the provisions of the law to a Foreign Account in lire

c) Transfer to another Special Account—Law n. 43 of February 7, 1956

A one and a half per mille exchange commission is charged in accordance with the regulations of the Ufficio Italiano dei Cambi on:

1) All credits in Special Account—Law n. 43 derived from the sale of foreign currencies or transfers from Foreign Accounts in lire

2) All debits in Special Account—Law n. 43 for the purchase of foreign currencies or fro transfers to Foreign Accounts or Capital Accounts in lire

All other entries in Special Accounts—Law n. 43 including credits and debits arising from sales and reinvestments are free of commission.

Special Accounts: Ministerial Decree n 211 of March 2, 1948— These accounts were opened in conformity with M.D. n. 211 for foreign banks, companies, and/or individuals wherever residing, or for Italian citizens residing abroad who made investments in Italy before Law n. 43 of February 1956 came into force, of lire amounts arising from the sale of free currencies, and who wish to avail themselves of the right granted them by Article 2 or Law n. 43 to transfer abroad the income from investments effected under M.D. n. 211 and the proceeds of subsequent disinvestments.

The Ufficio Italiano dei Cambi has prescribed the progressive elimination of this category of accounts directing that the proceeds from the sale or disposal of Ministerial Decree n. 211 investments (if not transferred abroad) be reinvested into Law n. 43 of February 7, 1956 accounts.

The accounts may be freely credited with:
1) Lire arising from disinvestments under J.D. n. 211
2) Income on investments under the said Decree

The balances may be utilized
1) Freely for:
    a) Transfer of income abroad, in the same currency originally surrendered, up to 8 per cent per annum.

    Income exceeding 8 per cent per annum may be credited on behalf of the beneficiary to a Capital Account. The purchase of foreign currency to be transferred abroad as stated above takes place at the official rate.

    b) Transfer of the quotas of income that have become transferable to a Foreign Account in lire

    c) Transfer to a Capital Account with implicit waiver of the benefits of Law n. 43 of February 7, 1956

    d) Transfer of the quotas of income that have become transferable to a Special Account—Law n. 43 of February 7, 1956, for subsequent reinvestment

2) With the prior clearance of the required documents by the Ufficio Italiano dei Cambi for:
    a) Transfer abroad of capital disinvested not before two years from its investment and for the same amount of foreign currency originally surrendered; the eventual surplus of capital in respect of the amount originally invested must be credited on behalf of the investor to a Capital Account. The purchase of the foreign currency to be transferred abroad as stated above takes place at the official rate.

    b) Transfer of that quota of capital which has become available for transfer to a Foreign Account in lire

    c) Transfer of that quota of capital which has become available for transfer to a Special Account—Law n. 43 of February 7, 1956, for subsequent reinvestment

A one and a half per mille exchange commission is charged in accordance with the regulations of the Ufficio Italiano dei Cambi on debits in Special Accounts—M.D. n. 211 for the purchase of foreign currencies and for transfer to Foreign Accounts in lire. All other entries in Special Accounts—M.D. n. 211 are free of commission.

Foreign Accounts in Foreign Currencies (US dollars, Canadian dollars, Swiss francs, pounds sterling, Belgian francs, French francs, West German marks, Danish kroner, Norwegian kroner, Swedish kronor, Dutch guilders, Austrian schillings, Portuguese escudos, Spanish pesetas) may be freely opened in the name of banks, companies, firms, and individuals registered or having their residence abroad regardless of the country.

These accounts may be freely credited with:

1) Remittances from abroad of the following foreign currencies: US dollars, Canadian dollars, Swiss francs, Pounds sterling, Belgian francs, French francs, West German marks, Danish kroner, Norwegian kroner, Swedish kronor, Dutch guilders, Austrian schillings, Portuguese escudos, Spanish pesetas;
2) Payments of goods imported into Italy and other current payments permitted to be settled in one of the foreign currencies mentioned in 1) above
3) Transfers from another Foreign Account in foreign currencies
4) foreign currencies purchased with funds of Foreign Accounts in lire
5) foreign currencies purchased with another foreign currency
6) interest accrued on the account
7) amounts pertaining to Italian capital investments abroad

The balances may be freely used for:

1) Payments of goods exported from Italy and other current payments
2) Remittances abroad
3) Purchase of lire at "official" rate of exchange for the credit in Foreign Accounts or in Special Accounts Law n. 43
4) Transfers to another Foreign Account in foreign currencies

5) Conversions into another foreign currency

6) Amounts from repatriation of Italian capital investments abroad

7) Withdrawals in cash by the owner

Foreign Accounts in lire may be freely opened in the name of banks, corporations, firms, and individuals registered or having their residence abroad, regardless of the country.

These Accounts may be freely credited with:

1) Lire arising from the sale of the following foreign currencies: US dollars, Canadian dollars, Swiss francs, pounds sterling, Belgian francs, French francs, West German marks, Danish kroner, Norwegian kroner, Swedish kronor, Dutch guilders, Austrian schillings, Portuguese escudos, Spanish pesetas, remitted from abroad or transferred from Foreign Accounts in Foreign currencies

2) Payments of goods imported into Italy and other current payments permitted to be settled in one of the foreign currencies mentioned in 1) above

3) Transfers from Special Accounts—Ministerial Decree n. 211 of March 2, 1948, or from Special Accounts—Law n. 43 of February7, 1956, for the amounts transferable under the said laws in foreign currency

4) Transfers from another Foreign Account in lire and from Capital Accounts

5) Interests accrued on the account

6) Repayments of loans and financing of any kind done with funds of Foreign Accounts

7) Amounts pertaining to Italian capital investments abroad

8) Dividends and interests on securities in custody in "deposito capitale" accounts

9) Income on dividends of securities circulating abroad and sent for collection with the required affidavit

10) Granting of loans of any kind abroad

11) Inheritances and gifts

12) Other invisible transactions

The balance may be freely used for:

1) Payments of goods exported from Italy and other current payments
2) Conversion into one of the following foreign currencies: US dollars, Canadian dollars, Swiss francs, pounds sterling, Belgian francs, French francs, West German marks, Danish kroner, Norwegiankroner, Swedish kronor, Dutch guilders, Austrian schillings, Portuguese escudos, Spanish pesetas, to be remitted abroad or credited in Foreign Accounts in foreign currencies
3) Withdrawals in cash by the owner or other authorized person
4) Transfer to another Foreign Account in lire or to a Capital Account
5) Transfer to Special Accounts—Law n. 43 of February 7, 1956
6) Loans and advances in any form provided the resident borrower has obtained the necessary license from the Italian Treasury
7) Amounts pertaining to the sale of Italian capital invested abroad
8) Repayment of loans granted abroad
9) Other invisible transactions (see the Bundle in USA)

Securities Accounts—The main classification of securities accounts in the names of residents abroad are the following:

Capital Securities Account
Special Securities Accounts: Law n. 43 of February 7, 1956
Special Securities Accounts: M.D. n. 211 of March 2, 1948
Foreign Securities Accounts

Capital Securities Accounts—These may be freely opened in the name of banks, corporations, firms, and individuals registered or having their residence abroad regardless of the country. The following Italian securities may be deposited freely in these accounts:

1) Securities purchased or subscribed to with funds transferred from Capital Accounts
2) Bonus shares granted on those existing in the same Capital Securities Account
3) Securities transferred from a Special Securities Account—law n. 43 of February 7, 1956, a Special Securities Account—Ministerial

Decree n. 211 of March 2, 1948, or from another Capital Securities Account

4) Securities circulating abroad, dispatched from abroad only to an authorized Italian bank and accompanied by the prescribed affidavit providing that the securities belong to a person residing abroad. These securities must bear the following stamp: *"circolante all'estero—ex deposito capitale"*

5) Securities received as a result of inheritances and gifts

Securities may be withdrawn freely for:

1) The administration of securities (grouping, division, substitution, renewal, or coupon sheets) and in general for transactions requiring the actual presentation of the securities or for the constitution of temporary deposits with the issuing company or with banks as directors' bonds, or in order to take part in shareholders' meetings

2) Sale in Italy with payment of proceeds into a Capital Account

3) Transfer to another Capital Securities Account

4) Exportation abroad of shares, bonds and State funds in accordance with the prescribed procedure. The securities must be stamped "for circulation abroad" by an authorized Italian bank

5) Inheritances and gifts

Special Securities Accounts—Law n. 43 of February 7, 1956

The following securities may be freely deposited in these accounts:

1) Italian securities purchased with funds from the depositor's Special Account—Law n. 43

2) Shares gratuitously granted on securities existing in the account

3) Securities transferred from another Special Securities Account— Law n. 43 registered to another name from a Special Securities Account—M.D. n. 211 registered in the same name

4) Securities circulating abroad, dispatched from abroad only to an authorized Italian bank and accompanied by the prescribed affidavit proving that the securities belong to a person residing abroad. These securities must bear the following stamp: *"circolante all'estero—investimento No . . . ."*

5) Securities received as a result of capital increases on investments made under Law No. 43 of February 7, 1956

Securities held in these accounts may be withdrawn by:

1) Continuing to enjoy the benefits of Law n. 43 of February 7, 1956
  a) Sale, with payments of the proceeds into the depositor's special account b) Transfer of another Special Securities Account—Law n. 43 registered to another name
  c) Any operation required for the administration of the securities
  d) Exportation of shares, bonds and State funds in accordance with the prescribed procedure. The securities must be stamped "for circulation abroad" by an authorized Italian bank. To this effect the securities are stamped as follows: "circolante all'estero—investimento No . . . ."
  e) Inheritances and gifts.

2) Specifically renouncing the facilities stated in Law n. 43
  a) Transfer to a Capital Securities Account

Special Securities Accounts—Ministerial Decree n. 211 of March 2, 1948

These accounts still exist with the authorized Italian banks for the custody and administration of securities purchased under M.D. n. 211. They enjoy, however, the facilities granted by Article 2 of Law n. 43 of February 7, 1956 (namely transfer of income abroad up to 8 percent per annum and re-export of capital arising from the sale of securities after two years from the original investment and for the same amount of foreign currency originally surrendered).

The Ufficio Italiano dei Cambi has recently prescribed the progressive elimination of this category of accounts that the proceeds from the sale or disposal of Ministerial Decree n. 211 investments (it not transferred abroad) be reinvested into Law n. 43 of February7, 1956 accounts.

The following securities may be freely deposited in these accounts:
  1) Shares gratuitously granted on securities existing in the account

2) Securities circulating abroad, dispatched from abroad only to an authorized Italian bank and accompanied by the prescribed affidavit proving that the securities belong to a person residing abroad. These securities must bear the following stamp: *"circolante all'estero—ex D.L. 2. 3. 1948, n. 211"*

3) Securities received as a result of capital increases on investments made under D.L. March 2, 1948, No. 211 limited to the value of the option rights pertaining to old securities deposited in "dossier ex D.L. No. 211"

The securities held in these accounts may be withdrawn by:

1) Continuing to enjoy the benefits of M.D. n. 211 and Law n. 43 for:
    a) Sale, the proceeds thereof being credited to a Special Account—M.D. n 211 belonging to the owner of the securities account
    b) Transfer to a Special Securities Account—Law n. 43 of February 7, 1956 registered in the same name
    c) Any operation required for the administration of the securities
    d) Exportation abroad of shares, bonds and State funds in accordance with the prescribed procedure. The securities must be stamped "for circulation abroad" by an authorized Italian bank. To this effect the securities are stamped as follows: "circolante all'estero ex D.L. 2. 3. 1948, n. 211"
    e) Inheritances and gifts

2) By specifically renouncing the benefits stated in M.D. n. 211 and law n. 32
    a) Transfer to a Capital Securities Account

Foreign Securities (in Foreign Currency) Accounts

The name applies to accounts opened for the safe-custody and administration of securities whether of Italian or foreign origin, issued in any foreign currency whatever, belonging to, and owned by, aliens.

Credits and utilizations of these securities accounts are free from any restriction on transactions abroad and in Italy.

Translation by Author
Italian Republic

Summing up for the Plaintiff: "Please the Tribunal, reject any contrary instance, to accept the plaintiff's claim as proposed in the summons with the whole consequences for expenses and fees."

Summing up for the Defendant: "Please the Tribunal, inattentive to any adverse request and defend, to reject claims proposed by AUA author and promoter, on his own and on behalf of the American University of Avezzano, because groundless in fact and in right, inadmissible and without legal proceeding, with expenses and fees victory."

Trial Development

By summons notified on June 6, 1976, the author and promoter, on his own and on behalf of the foundation "American University of Avezzano" in Cleveland (Ohio), United States of America exposes:

> On his behalf, in 1969 he was scouting for a feasible location to develop facilities and buildings of a higher learning institution for foreign students. At this time, contacts were made with the Avezzano city hall authorities to determine where he could establish this project. At that time, the undertaking was supported and carried on also with the Department of Physical Education of Case Western Reserve University, which would have

provided academic know-how and development expertise. Avezzano's city hall authorities immediately demonstrated interest in this project to such a degree that by means of deliberation, dated October 31, 1969, the city council approved a variation to the building code zone in order to provide the destination of an area in the location "Tre Conche" to establish the International University of Physical Education.

Soon afterwards it was agreed upon that the area to be assigned to establish the University would have had an extension of about 250,000 square meters. In particular, it was established that such an extension, the main part owned by the city hall itself, should have been sold directly, and the remaining, owned by third parties, to be set aside as a park and for following enlargement and development. It should have been acquired at farming land price.

In such an option, the city hall pledged to let the project's promoters obtain the property and also, eventually, sustaining it in the competent offices case to issue a public utility decree of the project to be built. Considered such favorable premises, the project's supporters instituted, by means of a special legal foundation, the "American University of Avezzano," giving successive impetus to the whole propaedeutical and promotional activities for the project realization.

The organs of the American University of Avezzano made out a financial plan, especially in reference to the necessary procurement of available funds, for the construction of various facilities and to provide for operational needs of the University. Such a financial plan was submitted to the city hall authorities along with the documentation concerning the objectives of the American foundation and the powers of attorney to its appointee. Then, the prefect Commissioner adopted a deliberation for which the real estate outline of city hall's property, consisting of about 73,000 sq.mt. and held suitable for the objective referred to previously, should have sold to the foundation by a private transaction prior tutelary authorization (which supervened on May 11, 1971). At this point, contacts were intensified between the American foundation representatives and the city hall, particularly with the mayors, as they followed up as time went by. In spite of combined efforts from all of the American foundation representatives, the foundation was unable to achieve the anticipated objective.

Inexplicably, city hall representatives, with a wearing and dilatory attitude, made sure that the project's objective and, in particular, the stipulation of the sale contract deeds that would have permitted the foundation to acquire the land and start the works, never came to completion. Notwithstanding the continued written and verbal assurances and the accomplishment of some deeds, such as the final draft of Public Sale Contract and the payment of the agreed upon price by the foundation, it was not possible, as mentioned, to arrive to the stipulation. In consequence of such a behavior from the organs of the city hall, the summons explicitly invited the mayor of the city hall of Avezzano, with registered mail dated February 10, 1975, to execute the project commissioner's deliberation #219 of September 1, 1979, already mentioned, and to stipulate the land sale contract by public deed to the American University of Avezzano. The target time established, once again, was not complied with. Further attempts carried out in extremes were all futile.

Whereas the judgement in front of this Tribunal hearing to condemn the city hall of Avezzano, prior declaratory of its responsibility as of Article 1337 Civil Code, to restitution of the perceived sums and indemnity for damages sustained by the plaintiff.

It appears before the court, that the city hall of Avezzano assumes that the plaintiff has exposed in the summons facts which are related only to his defensive thesis stopping on in the year of 1970. He makes any hints to successive facts (letters, proposals, et cetera) which made the city hall administrators maintain that it was not, and is not, on the side of an effective interest to cultivate the creation of the proposed institute, and that there was not the necessary economic and material strength to make it. Therefore, the defendant concludes to reject the claims. Determined the conclusions, the case was referred to the College, which reserves a decision in the public hearing on November 14, 1984.

Reason of Decision

Two preliminary exceptions were raised by Avezzano city hall: the lack of active legitimation of the author and promoter to have the same act on his own, besides representing the foundation "American University of Avezzano" of Cleveland (Ohio), USA. In spite of any substantial legal interest, and as a second exception, the lack of representation in the trial of same mentioned foundation, such exceptions are groundless.

As far as the first exemption is concerned, there is no doubt that, at the moment in which the interest to act must exist, is maintained to be that of judgment and not necessarily that of claim.

But included in the summons content among the actual damage items explicitly discussed are among other things, travel expenses, and these obviously could not refer but to the person.

Now the rejection of the above preliminary exception, not without underlining once again the subsistence of interest to act, does not require any investigation upon the truth of the claim, which instead concerns the merit of the claim, and it is determined, therefore, independently from the dispute's outcome.

Also without merit is the other exception concerning lack of representation in the trial of the foundation "American University of Avezzano," in the sense that the author and promoter would not have power of attorney in the trial to represent the foundation. The Tribunal points out that in the documentation results that the mentioned nominative is in possession of the power of attorney to negotiate, as well as the trial power of attorney. Thus, it is helpful to rememeber that with the joint decree of this Tribunal deposited on this date, June 4, 1982, the case was deferred before the investigating judge to allow the plaintiff to obtain the delivery of authorization or to produce it in February, 1969. N. 300 in Giust. Civ. 1. page 947. As a matter of fact, from the documentation submitted emerges the grant of power of attorney to negotiate and to sue.

In respect to this last, from the affidavit signed and dated February 24, 1976, with the signature authenticated by a notary and legitimized by the competent Italian Consulate of Cleveland, Ohio (USA), it is clear that the author and promoter has the authority to act on his own and on behalf of the American University of Avezzano, as well as to choose and to entrust an attorney to conduct negotiations and to promote the trial. It is in combination with such an appointment to the attorneys who represent him in the present trial.

In fact, from the existing documentation from the hearings and especially from the deeds completed in Italy by means of the various city council deliberations and from the notary's Land Sale Contract, as well as from numerous letters of correspondence between the two parties in the case, indicate in a clear manner that the American University of Avezzano is a foundation legally registered in the state of Ohio (USA) and has had the power of attorney to act legally against the city hall of Avezzano in the name and on behalf of the above mentioned foundation. It seems at least strange that the city hall of Avezzano, during the long process of negotiations generated to arrive at the realization of the facilities and building of the educational institute at the international level with the offering, also, of land and other items, never expressed objections and doubts about the seriousness and legal existence of the foundation, as well as the representative powers,. Turning to the merit of the case, the following considerations are worthwhile.

The plaintiff relied on the application of Art. 1337 C.C., according to which the parties, during the negotiation proceedings of that contract, must behave in good faith.

It is clear that the city hall of Avezzano must compensate the plaintiff for the expenditures that he incurred and that he would have not confronted if he had not trusted in the contract stipulation.

As justification for his requests, the plaintiff has submitted a signed financial statement. The president of the American University of Avezzano sent a check of $300.00 at the request of Avezzano city hall as the price amount anticipated for the expenses pertinent to the acquisition of the city's lands(see letter of Avezzano mayor dated March 2, 1972).

As for Art. 1278 C.C., the defendant must return to the plaintiff the correspondent value in Italian currency equal to the exchange rate of $300.00 at the day of effective payment. As far as the financial-economic statement is concerned. But such juridical possibility could not be invoked because the board of trustee president could not be considered a third party in the present dispute but interested party. For Art. 27 of provision of the law in general (see Provisional Law of Civil Code), the competency and the formality of the trial are regulated by the law of the place where the trial is developed.

At this point, given the nature of the affairs handled, as well as of preparatory documentation, the travel expenses for negotiations developed over a long time, and for probable cost of the work and advice requested of technical people and for projects, this Tribunal maintains it is proper and equitable to liquidate, as breach of contract, the sum of Lit. 35,000,000.00. (This documentation shows that this number is US dollars and not in Italian lire) The payment of such a sum and that corresponding to the value of $300.00 dollars will be condemned the city hall of Avezzano, which must also pay legal interest upon such sums since the day of the claim until the actual payment in full. The city hall must repay to the plaintiff the trial expenses, which are liquidated in Lit. 70,000.00, for disbursement. in Lit. 514,000.00 for rights to public attorneys and Lit. 1,600,000.00 for the lawyers fees.

P.Q.M. (for this reason)

Definitively pronouncing the civil lawsuit promoted with summons notified on the date of June 10, 1976, on his own and on behalf of the foundation of the "American University of Avezzano" of Cleveland, Ohio (USA), against the city hall of Avezzano, in the person of its pro-tempore mayor, thus is provided:

> Reject the preliminary exception of lack of active legitimation and lack of power of attorney to represent in the trial the foundation of the "American University of Avezzano" raised by the city hall of Avezzano; condemn the city hall of Avezzano, in the person of his pro-tempore mayor, to return to the plaintiff the corresponding value

in Italian currency equalized to the value of $300 from the day of actual payment and to apply to the same plaintiff, for breach of contract, the sum of Lit. 35,000,000.00 (thirty-five million) with obligation to correspond this sum and on that corresponding to the value in Italian currency, plus interest on $300 from the day of the claim to the actual payment, in full. Condemn the defendant to reimburse to the plaintiff the trial expenses liquidated in total Lit. 2,184,800 (two million one hundred eighty-four thousand eight hundred) and subdistinguished as in the reasoning part over IVA and CPA (taxes and court duty) as per law. Thus decided April 3, 1985.

The President Writer

Update Event and Points

—Re-appealed the verdict to reevaluate the sums, plus to make correction to interest as explained in the reasoning.

—It seems to me this line (35,000,000.00 lire) was maliciously made mainly to eliminate interest on the capital investment calculation.

—I have mentioned this peculiar error to my attorney, who will present it to the court of appeal of L'Aquilla.

—Awaiting Court of Appeal's decision at the end of this month of October, 1987, to take further legal actions.

The Only Alternative and Final Decision To Resolve Project AUA And Its Collateral Business Activities

Whether or not the verdict against the city hall of Avezzano, Italy, has been a frivolous court decision, and because the Project AUA activities connected with the Campus Program must be liquidated, it is overdue. If there are any other feasible alternatives to put aside and save them from the many evidenced wrongdoings in the long litigation of the Italian courts, then it is time to differentiate them openly and squarely. It seems that given the present circumstance and problematic situations, it could be said in few words: Put up or Shut up. But, is it fair just to shut up?

Everybody knows and it is very well evidenced that the city hall of Avezzano has incurred a breach of contract and related wrongdoings in a matter of civil and penal laws: domestically, nationally, and internationally.

There was and still is at least an improper transfer of the Project AUA file, Confidential/Restricted matters, either within the city hall office itself and/or other connected entities. Of course, there have been rumors, and although rumors are not evidence, an undertaken personal inquiry can demonstrate with logical relevancy, facts, events, and validity of evidence many times ascertained that the investment of foreign capital for the Project AUA plans, Within a Campus of International Character, is defined in dollars (USA); the whole according to Law #43-1956, treaty between Italy and the United States of America. Collateral business project activities, such as construction of parking garages, bridges, WCBM tunnel, recovery of $Co2$, ultra-lightweight materials, and AMICA information file and data as endowment have been also submitted accordingly.

True, in many instances, memories often have conveniently failed for some of those connected directly and indirectly with the longest litigation in the Italian court's history. But these particular files submitted to the city hall of Avezzano and other government agencies for the Campus site deliberation, information which should have been subpoenaed by the courts, mysteriously disappeared, and as just mysteriously reappeared. These files show reported detail of involvement in a fraudulent land deal (See Campus Reports). Whatever final decision on this matter should eventually be made, there have been suggestions that a summons should be addressed to a US Federal Court; it may or may not be concerned with political pay-off. Odds are, however, that at least a portion of this content would be leaked and exploited politically. Foes in many ways would have tried again and again to use the Campus land deal to politically damage whomever might have taken a different position from the original deliberation, voted unanimously.

The controversies in which the city hall of Avezzano has found itself and some Obscure Forces are now very much politically involved and are legitimate fodder for opposition and non-opposition of this local political dilemma. In fact, it is possible that the city hall of Avezzano, in spite of evidence, may once again seek to use excuses to deny and cover up wrongdoings. On the other hand, it could be proved that a personal investigation has emerged from relentless efforts to get to the bottom of this matter. It must be underlined that this investigation by the end might lead to a courtroom, inevitably to US Federal Court, mainly related to the International Law (Rico Statute), and not to the Court of Public Opinion. This is a practical legal instrument that is allowed to recover the invested USA dollars for all the undertaken project activities, and these are not rumors. This avenue will legitimate the invested capital as per Law #43-56. Thanks for your attention. GDG.

"To Re-Appeal a Judgment"
(Project AUA vs. Avezzano's City Hall)

In reference, and following information derived from my last phone conversation on December, 1985, I should underline a few points of main concern to the decision to re-appeal the case against the city hall of Avezzano. Before anything else, I must state once again that as of this moment, I have received no copy of the verdict issued by the Avezzano Tribunal, in spite of the attorney's assurance he mailed it. Nevertheless, it must be stated very clearly that the basic strategy ought to be a tough battle in the appellate courthouse of Aquila and eventually tough negotiating at the bargaining table. From a legal point of view, the strategy is pretty clear, which is to push ahead with every step of the legal battle, starting with a motion including the many wrongdoings and related criminal activities previously presented (see Trip Memo, 1978).

In some of the verdict findings there are errors in the Avezzano tribunal judge's decision and in the framing of the comment submitted by the tribunal's president, as well as the adequacy of the evidence from the legal documentation to support the conclusion, particularly the reexamination of properly defined damage amounts. That's the main issue to be pushed ahead. The attempt will be made to present all the related substantiated legal questions with the aim of to going eventually into the Supreme Court. It might even be possible to try for a ruling that the tribunal of Avezzano's judgment *violated due process of law because the amount of damages is grossly misrepresented.*

It also should raise wrongdoings and criminal or penal issues (Delitti Contro La Pubblica Amministrazione). In effect, the Lit. judgment (the amount defined for damages) is another kind of takeover by the same "interest group" for the land ownership. As a matter of fact, it should be argued that the proper right of ownership to the land negotiated and defined for the campus of the projected AUA interferes with the "land use" established in the city of Avezzano's deliberation and "Piano Regolatore" approved by Ministero Dei LL. PP, and other deliberations are, therefore, invalid because state law has supremacy.

The major approach and concern now ought to be to keep the legal fight a going concern, which means a lot of talking within the community and with citizens, supporters, and concerned persons to inform them that they have joint venture deals with the projects' activity and to make sure they will continue to support the Campus of International Character's efforts. As in the past, at some point there may be such a lack of confidence that some people may back away and that can destroy planned activities very quickly. One of the ways to keep all those persons interested in the legal matter is to pursue the fighting and bargaining strategies vigorously.

Proclaiming the evidenced wrongdoings in the Appellate Court must be making certain people and government officials very, very nervous. One of the main approaches that should be taken is to tone up the PR activities. The position should be taken that all legal remedies are being pursued, but it is also business as usual, and one way or another they're going to work those problems out, so let's not panic and run for the exit for quick solutions!

Another reason the PR should be toned up is that it may boomerang in L'Aquila Court in spite of hurting some local politicians' credibility. It is conceivable that continuing to shout about some "illegal activities performed" will, to a certain extent, hurt the city hall of Avezzano's position in the appeal. It seemed that the Court of Appeals of L'Aquila does not like to feel outside pressure.

The other thing to contemplate is filing the financial statement for $100,000,000 (including punitive damages), thus trying to obtain the previous recorded judgment and start to consider liens on the city hall of Avezzano's assets. It is not expected to see any rush into bankruptcy at this particular stage, but some political and bureaucratic alternatives are anticipated that are made available for the city hall local government. Hence, the city government would get a lot of leverage in negotiations with the projected AUA's principal; on the other hand, litigants must threaten to treat the city of Avezzano's government as unsecured and unstable, fronting a political bankruptcy reorganization since the day that the City Council unanimously voted for the projected campus land use.

It also seems to be possible to notice a kind of cautious at this stage because of the many "unstable mayors" and their broken promises. This and the political bankruptcy results should permit setting aside considerations of liens that have been obtained on the "piano verde" city political decision (see entire documentation, since project's representation included this in the philosophical material). There is certainly room and motivation to make some concessions to the local government in order to keep it out of political and bureaucratic bankruptcy.

If this present approach is rejected, then it should be followed by the legal appeal and procedures and trying to assume the property ownership rights give to the projected AUA principal's fundamental defense. It would produce long delays and legal complications, neither of which the city of Avezzano nor any project's supporters could afford. The main problem of the Campus of International Character at this stage is that business uncertainty and the passing of valuable time without the resolution of this conflict can further affect other parallel projects' development for endowment. Even if a full reversal of the previous judgment is won a year from now, any investors in that parcel of land would suffer considerable financial damage from the higher interest rates. In addition, it would have to pay on the "commercial paper" and the uncertainty of the status within its community and among concerned citizens, friends, and remaining supporters of the Campus of International Character. It must be concluded that the city hall of Avezzano's defense lawyer continues to be the plaintiff's best dream coming true.

I must thank you very much for your attention and support for this and other efforts.

Determination of Capital Originally Invested for Project

AUA'S Activities

The cost reevaluation and determination of the capital invested for the American University of Avezzano (AUA) Project, within a Campus of International Character, must be based on the price level or ISTAT index, as stated in the sentence N= 336/86 from the Court of Appeal of L'Aquila, Italy. This appears to be a problem of statistics only and can easily be resolved. In spite of the legal logic connected to the "just and fairness" reevaluation of the invested capital, it is possible in a certain sense to make some hints when determining the statistical index. All this is proceeding according to notes and discussions held with concerned parties. In fact, as is very clearly explained and suggested, it is necessary to determine which index to make reference to for which group of economic goods or work activities performed. These factors are to be used to calculate the value of the work performed and other money related to the invested capital for the specific projected Campus activities development; to take into consideration either the original money invested in US dollars or that of exchange, such as Italian lire, the overall employed and tightened to the law #43, February 7, 1956, in substitution of the "Letter of Intent," which provided the most solid guarantee for foreign investment into Italy as recommended letters and specific law.

Another problem to take into consideration before determining the statistical index of price to be used for reevaluation is to define exactly the territorial dimension on which the Project AUA activities are referred to. If these activities are of international character or less, then the problem is whether to hold in account only those sums spent for travel purpose, ignoring the rest without a plausible reason, or whether to keep in consideration those other maintained expenses, and whether to include in the reevaluation calculation of the price index the whole amount of the sums used for specific Project AUA activities. For instance, why are the attorney's fees together with other court expenses listed in the verdict and not those that have been employed directly and indirectly for other connected activities of Project AUA? These expenditures are very important for the purpose of Project AUA activities and strictly tied to fluctuation of prices, their reevaluation carried on by an independent and impartial arbitration, which is what the verdict was established to achieve. In any event, it is important at this point to put in evidence that this problem of cost reevaluation for each activity in phases of development was already tackled by the concerned parties before arriving at the legal dispute introduced to the local Court of Avezzano. Mutual agreements were made between concerned parties, and a specific request was made to attach to the legal documentation the capital originally invested for the Project AUA and the following cost reevaluation in US dollars in reference to the time and place (See: Cost Reevaluation and Financial statements).

Even if it is considered only one aspect of the reevaluation based on the Italian statistical index ISTAT as stated from L'Aquila Court of Appeal verdict, at this point it is obvious that the Italian national price index may represent only an average for an arbitrary interpretation, mainly due to the elements gathered from the version presented during the meetings held with the Avezzano city hall officials on May 28th and 30th of 1995. During these meetings inconsistent positions were taken by the city hall of Avezzano authorities, which presents the serious merit of the knowledge of facts and evidence to be used for this problem's resolution. Not all the information received during and after these meetings was relevant, and it was worthless for the purpose of reevaluation. Some of these versions lacked logical validity, and they seemed to be a result of ambiguity in the absence of the documentation originally submitted to the city hall of Avezzano for the Campus program. It must be said that these city hall officials' behavior and dealings were very strange, especially when a request was made more than once to claim property rights to the Project AUA documentation. The same denial by city hall authority to have open access to the documented evidence is corroborated by an alarming "confiscatory" policy practice, now told as another expedient.

Because of such dubious behavior on the part of city hall officials, it is necessary to ask the following questions: After all the documentation was provided to the competent authority, and the denials of evidence supported only with missing information on the part of the official's version, how can a reevaluation from ISTAT criteria proceed? Is the medium price fluctuation that each single "price of goods" have encourred in the Campus zone from one period to another generalized or only representative? Assuming the relative validity of the version given for the land price value for the Campus and that at present time, which is the necessary determination of the year to be assumed as point of reference to get to the index of reevaluation to technical instruments and legal implications? On the whole, how is the ISTAT reevaluation to be approached, and from which arbitration authority and/or legal institution? From these few questions, it is clear how important it is to relate the entire reevaluation process to the original documentation and how much the transparent evidence of the capital originally invested for Project AUA activities is needed. (See: deliberations for the Campus' location from the city hall of Avezzano and Provincial government decree.)

Reevaluation of sums according to index and ISTAT techniques: It is necessary to keep in mind that in the determination of the ISTAT index, the research of information consists in the selection, collection, analysis, and evaluation of all factors that have contributed to the disclosure of the undertaken activities related to Project AUA. This intelligent, continuous, and systematic flow of information aimed to rationalize the Project AUA activities must be based on facts and not on intuition and casual attempts. Therefore, the concrete application of economic and financial techniques of specific activities must be considered and be oriented to the reevaluation that is also required to have direct references to general and specific data that has been provided. If these data have been misrepresented or are incorrect, incomplete, and/or diverted, then the whole direction of the reevaluation calculation must lead to a wrong determination of the results, of course with incalculable consequences.

Given the fundamental importance that the ISTAT reevaluation has in this legal matter, it is absolutely necessary that where it is possible, professional specialists must be called to perform such a technical calculation. For the whole matter, which refers to data already submitted to the competent authorities, the ISTAT must have the possibilities together with its authority to give access to the entire legal documentation in order to exactly follow the formation of the capital invested since the beginning of the activities connected with Project AUA and the Campus of International Character's development. As matter of fact, the ISTAT's most important inquiry aspect must be concerned with disclosure from the submitted documentation, in which a major or minor accuracy might affect the followingreevaluation development. The formation of the capital originally invested for Project AUA in US dollars and Italian lire, employed for specific activities, must be taken as the most fundamental aspect to allow more precise understanding of the amounts allocated for the whole Project AUA's program.

The numerical value stated in the verdict from Italian Court: The number stated in the verdict has a very meaningful value. (The number is correct, but the assigned value in lire is wrong.) The assigned value of the amount must be changed and stated in US dollars, and this is evidenced by the legal documentation submitted to the competent authorities in the United States and Italy. To have stated the verdict value in Italian lire is a pernicious, deceitful, coercive, and wrongful attempt to disguise the real value of the capital invested for Project AUA activities—particularly the costs related to Campus facilities development in Avezzano. Even at the present, a certain meaning is maintained to be subjected to a careful reevaluation (ISTAT or not), based mainly on price variation, which are supported already by the Project plan materials from the Campus program to be determined for the rezoned acreage defined within the municipality of Avezzano. In fact, it is the technical-legal aspect of the rezoned area defined as the campus that must be taken as one of the first approaches to evidence for the reevaluation—the first step to determining the amount of dollars and the work performed for the feasibility study and location research, the presentation of the Campus program, and rezoning of the area (See: city hall of Avezzano deliberations). Moreover, it is logical to maintain that when a reevaluation of all cost factors related to Project AUA activities are worked out through the statistical method, that amount must be taken into consideration other than certain values by approximation. It is obvious that this method may limit itself to avoid those factors that are interconnected with the property rights of Project AUA material; to claim a confiscatory policy and conflict of interest, not only for calculation purposes but for the legal obligations and inquiry as well. Hence it is possible to realize that the entire matter is more than a mere financial mathematical calculation; the main issue rests with an area that involved the criminal law, called obstruction of justice. In deducting, the result is very clear, arriving at the conclusion about why the amount of the capital stated in the verdict had to be written in Italian lire and not in US dollars, as originally reported through the proper channels. (See: Draft and Final

Contract of the "Campus land" sale and agreement documentation from concerned parties.)

In order to reevaluate the original capital invested for specific activities one needs to recall a basic financial-math formula, where (M) is the quantity of money invested in a determined period of time (at least thirty years), (V) is the velocity of money circulation, (P) is the median of price considered or the price of land defined for the Campus from 1.00 lire/sq. m to 100 thousand lire /sq. m taken in reference), and (Q) is the total quantity of each unity of price or cost account. Therefore, the following equation is determined: MV=PQ and P=MV/Q, which is the general price level.

The investment, therefore, is far more interested in the return that must be received than local government's speculations. The first technical term that one would come in contact with while considering the capital investment on behalf of Project AUA's activities is that of "yield," or "basis." In finding the present worth of the capital invested, it is first necessary to consider the formula for computing compound interest (according to ISTAT). This is derived as follows:

> Let u = number of interest periods
> Let N = rate per period

Then the valuation of $1.00 at compound interest for u periods at N rate is (1 + N)^u.

Thus, let us assume that $1.00 is invested at compound interest, computed semiannually, for ten years at 6 percent. Substituting this in our formula, we have:

$$(1 + N)^u = (1.00 + .03)^{20} = (1.03)^{20}$$

The computations in this case are facilitated by the use of logarithms.

> The log of 1.03 = 0.012837
> Log (1.03)^20 = .25674 = log of 1.8061
> 1.8061 is the desired amount

(The present worth of a sum discounted at a given rate of interest is the reciprocal of the sum at compound interest. That is, compound discount is the reciprocal of compound interest. The present worth of $1.00 at compound discount for u periods at N rate thus becomes $1/(1 + N)^u$.

A comparative method for Project AUA Costs Reevaluation: In real business practices and in legal rulings, the interpreting business practice has given virtually no consideration to the problem of changes in the value of money, although it is obvious that money(in the value invested for the Project AUA). However, facts do not always coincide with the political cost from the city hall of Avezzano, particularly the changing point of view by politicians, with or without conflict of interest.

For example, an individual buys seventeen acres of land between 1969 and 1970 in Avezzano, Italy, for $300 and sells the same in 1995 (legally or illegally) for lire 100mila/sq. m; the whole business seems to be justified and reasonable only for the arguments of politicians. Ignoring all kinds of claims and carrying legal charges, this individual has ostensibly made a lot of dollars or lire in profit. If, however, the purchasing power of the dollar or lire in 1995 through 1997 or any other year is only half of what it was in 1969 and 1970, the profit actually will be only 50 percent in terms of 1969 and 1970 monetary value; the seller made a 50 percent in 1969 and 1970 dollars, or greater than 100 percent in 1995 and 1997 dollars or lire.

In reevaluating Project AUA costs as per verdict for the periodic project activities since the beginning of the acute price fluctuation situation have taken place in a specific location. (See: A Short Story to be told for reference.) Nevertheless, it is true that conventional costs of investment in a period of sharply rising or falling prices often fails to represent actual money value terms or purchasing power, and over a period of years the surplus land price amount may come to express merely the application of a new measuring unit (in this case the value of land for calculation comparison is used) to resources that have not been expanded from the standpoint of a productive capacity. The reevaluation may well further examine the possibility of applying some commonplace methodology to the accounting figures, particularly in connection with the preparation of comparative reevaluation techniques used (for instance, for present land price appraisal) for the purpose of showing tangible results as they would appear with changes in the general price level of the specific location.

Another reasoning for the reevaluation purpose and calculation simplicity, or to take a more extreme case into consideration, suppose that the same individual at the same time invested the same value of $40,000 or lire 35 million between 1969 and 1970 in security (SOHIO shares, as proposed in the financial plan) and sold the same in 1997 or any other year of the activities. According to conventional views, the seller would have made a lot of dollars and also lire; the legal taxable income on the transaction (assuming no intervening transaction affecting principal, or other complexities) would be very profitable. If, however, money has fallen in value through the change in the price level so that the purchasing power of money in 1997 is 50 percent of that in 1969 and 1970 money, the proceeds in 1997 money amount only to three-quarters of the value. This figure compared with the investment already made between 1966 and 1970 shows what kind of loss and why a reevaluation of the sum invested must be done before any other aspect of the entire matter.

Similarly, if between 1970 and 1975 the investment is made in SOHIO shares at their nominal values and sold in 1997, whereas the value of money has increased 25 percent due to a general decline in price levels in Ohio, that same sum invested will go as far as a hundred times the value, including the splits and dividends. The maintenance of the integrity of money as capital invested, the dissipation of real capital spent, is a serious situation in the economic and legal senses. In the case of an appraisal involving an increase in dollar-value in excess of the increase in the general price level, there would be some point to a method of recording the appraisal by which that part of the nominal enhancement corresponding to the change in the value of money were set up separately. Take into consideration the land "zona campus," which cost of $1 to $2 sq. m. at original value is appraised at lire 100 thousand/sq. m., and that between the date of purchase and date of appraisal the value of money had fallen 50 percent. In this case the effect of the appraisal might be recorded as indicated by the following:

Land-appreciation . . . . lire 100/sq. m.
Capital adjustment-land valuation . . . . lire 100
Surplus adjustment-land valuation . . . . lire 100

On the other hand, in cases where the increase is no more than sufficient, or is less than sufficient, to recoup or maintain capital in the sense of purchasing power, there would be no occasion for the use of two accounts to absorb the credit. It is not intended to imply by this reasoning (and suggestion) that the part of the nominal element of appreciation in excess of the amount that merely reflects the change in the general price level as suggested in the verdict should be viewed as realized capital recovery. However, it is true that there is a distinction between an increase in the proprietary equity, which represents, in effect, merely the application of a new measuring unit to the situation, and an increase advantage in recognizing this distinction in the financial statement submitted to concerned parties (See: Reevaluation of Costs).

Similarly, in the case of a reevaluation involving a decrease in monetary value, it would not be unreasonable to attempt to separate the element of change in relative economic resources from the purely nominal adjustment. Thus, if the land in question, which cost lire 1 sq. m. (as legally documented), is appraised as lire 100 thousand/sq. m., and in the meantime the value of money has been reduced to 100 percent (for the lire), the effect of the appraisal might be recorded for Project AUA material to have allowed the change from rural to a rezoned campus (See: /deliberation and submitted Project to Avezzano city hall and Provincial Prefect). Again, if the decline in nominal value is but 1000 percent, as for the Italian lire, other conditions should be taken into consideration (*danni emergenti e lucro cessante*). There would be no other excuse for the city hall but to accept the adjustments as already submitted previously, on the grounds that the reduction in capital has been more drastic than the change in the value of money. The difficulty of readily and accurately measuring the change in the value of money as it applies to the particular situation already enhanced is a practical obstacle in the way of making analyses of the type indicated. Uncritical use of general index numbers in terms of statistics cited in the verdict is certainly to be avoided.

Interest on investment-affirmative argument: The cases for inclusion of interest on investment of sums used for Project AUA development, especially as operating expenses, are stated in details as submitted reevaluation costs. The arguments offered follow the lines indicated by the following verdict from the Court of Appeal (L'Aquila):

"The inclusion of interest in operating expense (*rivalutazione dei prezzi in $ or lire?*), results in a more rational and significant expense figure, as interest is a true cost of production."

The inclusion of interest in detailed operating costs is essential to the process of making comparisons and formulating the whole project costs reevaluation. It must be pointed out that virtually all experts contacted on this matter agree that pure interest, the reward for those furnishing capital as such, is a price-influencing cost of production and/or service. It is also pointed out that to treat interest on borrowed money as an expense without the inclusion of any allowance for interest on proprietary investment, as is often done by accountants, is illogical, as one element of interest is no more a price-influencing cost than the other.

It illustrates the point that to the hired manager or consultants, whose point of view is becoming increasingly important, there is no distinction between capital derived from proprietary sources and capital otherwise acquired. To capitalize interest during project development activities and to refuse to recognize interest during the course of these activities as expense is more or less illogical. In conclusion, it must be stated that from certain Project AUA activities a strenuous hostile campaign has been waged for a number of years, designed to foster "particular personal interest" other than of recognizing imputed economic-financial costs to specific Project activities. However, it is held that true business profit is not the legal income the ownership invisions or a corporation, but the amount realized after proper allowance has been made for interest on investment, personal services, and all other contributions made to the enhancement of specific activities other than that of ultimate responsibility and risk-taking.

-trip memo—Italy
(May-June 1995)

Direct Foreign Capital Investment into Italy (Relationship with European community and United States)

Given the circumstances and events concerning Project American University of Avezzano (AUA) within a Campus of International Character, there is still a natural and also an inevitable tension between concerned parties and the city hall of Avezzano-related governments. The purpose of this work is to examine this escalating tension and the historical background of the problem and to make some preliminary suggestions, especially about the verdict of the Court of Appeal of L'Aquila (ISTAT reevaluation) and how it might be resolved. It would be agreeable to think that a definitive solution can be put forward, but that seems to be awaiting more information about ISTAT procedures, principles, and definitions and the techniques involved for calculation. One of the main questions appears to be are we at the stage of gathering information and trying to interpret the significances, or should we just proceed with the end solution of the problem? If this work can help to solve the problem, it must be said to have succeeded in its objectives.

The undertaken work is divided into specific topics, which can be considered either separately or in sequence, such as the historical background from the verdicts and the problem concerning law #43. Feb. 7, 1956: Foreign Investment in Italy, a treaty between Italy and the United States, to the present situation, by providing supporting documentation for ISTAT reevaluation and the capital originally invested for connected activities. The city hall of Avezzano's deliberations and law #43-1956 (Prof. N. Irti) are taken as primary supports to invest in Project AUA's activities, and the most frequent source of dispute and conflicts have been, and still are, the enormous amount of money and work done on behalf of the entire Project activities since its early days. The investment is a great amount of capital and human energy, about which for at least three decades an enormous giant wave of tension has been building up from one country to another, along with considerable additional amounts of personal frustration. The scale and course of this tension are also influenced by government agencies, acting alone and in concert, but often finding themselves beyond their power of control to help resolve the problem of how to enforce law #43-1956.

It must be said that the movement of invested capital on behalf of Project AUA, based on the mentioned law and following the same government policy, can in a certain sense threaten and sometimes destroy personal finance resources and/or national policies with regard to currency exchange rates, balances of payments, and the availability of credit. All this must be taken into consideration by the ISTAT reevaluation. Project AUA's activities over the course of years have not deliberately set out to challenge the city hall of Avezzano or other connected government agencies. Nor is it in the undertaken activities about the manner in which the invested capital has been transferred or generated. The activities implied were to conduct normal business operations: providing a program for other investments, repatriating profits as per the mentioned law, and controlling the program's objectives. Among the ways law #43-1956 defines and supports foreign investment into Italy include the movement of money, profit dividends, royalties, and interest payments; loans, and other capital investments; and payments for goods, services, and "know-how" wherever and whenever Project AUA's activities take place.

At the present time, through the General Agreement on Tariffs and Trade (GATT), NAFTA, and market globalization, Italy, the United States, and other countries have also accepted a common set of principles to govern their international trade, instead of negotiating mutually exclusive trading agreements with each other. Despite frequent backsliding they have been consistently dedicated to removing tariff and other non-tariff barriers to trade and, of course, investments. These two factors especially have opened the way to the establishment of inter-related programs and has been considerably helped by the formation of the European economic community and the European free trade area, within which financial investment can be operated on a continental scale, which formerly was possible only in the United States. It is not only boosting opportunities for international direct investment that have improved since World War II, but most "solid guarantee" and support given by law #43-1956.

The attitude of local government toward foreign capital investments has also changed, and it is easily realized by the related deliberations and documentation evidences. It is not a secret any longer to find out that central government and local authorities have been obsessed with the need to achieve a high level of foreign investment to reduce a high level of unemployment. Ever since 1945, governments have been competing with each other in their efforts to persuade international investment to help them. From the outset, US capital investment have been better placed than others to take advantage of the post-war changes. In the early years, most of US investment rivals were either completely or partially destroyed, and this is true of financial-economic resources in Avezzano (Italy). There, community voices were asking loud and clear for the Campus program, dependent on the financial-economic plan submitted to the city hall authorities. It is true also that since foreign investment has become much easier, most governments have continued to restrain capital outflows for reasons of balance of payments. This is true to some extent even within the Common Market, although the treaty of Rome laid down that there should be free capital movements between members. US companies project activities, such as the undertaken activities in Avezzano, Italy, were not only free to invest abroad when others were not, these groups were positively encouraged to do so. The policy of the US government in general has hoped that a flow of independent-private capital investment abroad, and in Italy in particular, would have helped to reduce the level of official loans and grants needed to launch the country's economic recovery. It encouraged generating project programs overseas and took practical steps to help them by negotiating agreements with a large number of governments and by guaranteeing their investments against restrains on the repatriation of projects.

Not only Italy, but most of the European governments for their part, have welcomed the US investor as an invaluable helper in the task of rebuilding their war-shattered economies first, and obsolete technologies and know-how after. Some have established offices in the United States in order to attract American companies and projects to their countries, and most of them offered financial inducements and tax incentives of various sorts. Avezzano's land dealing for the Campus program is a case in point; deliberations speak for themselves. The formation of the European Economic Community, or Common Market, in 1957 and the treaty between Italy and United States law #43, Feb. 7, 1956, had a decisive impact on the attitude to pursue Project AUA activities, in spite of litigation and following the city hall political chaos. Project principals saw that if the hopes of the signatories to the treaty of Rome were fulfilled, other Continental opportunities similar in scope to the United States would be also created. The formation of the Community also convinced investors that Europe would eventually combine political stability with economic expansion, R/D activities, education, and technological innovation, recreation, tourism, and community concern for health and environmental issues.

But other considerations must also be taken into account the relationship between oligopolistic market structures in the United States and the foreign investment activities of US companies. In an oligopolistic market, it becomes increasingly difficult for the leading companies to capture a larger share of the total sales. Each additional percentage point in a company's share of the market becomes more expensive to secure than the one before. The easiest way to grow is through the acquisition of rival concerns. But if the rivals are all about the same size, this is frequently impossible. Even when it is practical, it is very expensive. Moreover, the Department of Justice since the war has become progressively more reluctant to allow mergers or takeovers by large companies that would have reduced competition. Consequently, foreign expansion has offered companies in oligopolistic industries the best prospects for further growth. The Department of Justice has also done much to encourage competition in foreign markets (See "Direct foreign investment and international oligopoly," by Stephen Hymer, June 1965, mimeographed). For a further discussion of this point see "American Direct Investments in the Common Market" by Bela Balassa, (*Banco Nazionale Del Lavoro Quarterly Review,* June 1966).

It is important to also recognize that in the last few decades a special breed of vast business organizations have been developed—based in one country and with subsidiaries throughout the world; i.e., Texas Instrument; Bailey System; BP; other multinational companies). These organizations are able to transfer vast sums of money between their branches and also to resolve and/or precipitate financial crises, despite all attempts to regulate them by the political governments under which they operate. As governments are asked to assume greater responsibility for the economical and social stability of all their citizens, it is most important to get facts for ISTAT at this point.

Service Transactions

Many varieties of international commercial transactions, other than those which involve the movement of capital merchandise or material goods, affect the supply of and demand for foreign currency. Among these are the so-called *service transactions*. The payment of miscellaneous charges, fees, and commissions affects the supply of foreign currency in the same way that it is affected by payment by the American credit/debt account. If Project AUA, for instance, pays the expenses in dollars, the balances of foreign banks in the United States are increased; if it is paid in foreign currency, then the foreign balance of American banks are reduced. Similarly, for the trips made to Italy for Project AUA's activities or any other places for the same reasons, expenditures for lodging at hotels, eating at local restaurants, and using services and local transportation are ordinarily made payment in dollars (by credit card or by exchange into local currencies). If before leaving the United States, the dollars are converted into Italian lire, the bank account in the United States is reduced and affects the formation of capital investment overseas. The demand for Italian currencies are also affected by all kinds of international capital transactions.

It must be underlined that considering all problems and risks involved, the flow of private investment to the Avezzano campus in Italy has been also severely limited since the beginning of litigation at the local courts, and most potential investors have shown little enthusiasm for external loans (except for investment in T.I. because of Italian government grants—See newspaper and magazine articles). These generous grants and other loans of the Italian government have temporarily made up for the dearth in private lending, but it is generally believed that this kind of government generosity should rather quickly give way to businesslike investment transactions. The problem is then to eliminate those special risks that would have been incurred by the Project AUA principal investor to go ahead with the financial-economic plan submitted to the city hall of Avezzano and concerned parties. Although a private capitalist may be quite willing to accept the ordinary risks of business failure, he must shy away from the added danger of having interest and related funds (ISTAT reevaluation) immobilized because of local politics and encountering all kinds of difficulties in withdrawing the principal of the Project AUA's total investment, and of having the foreign account holdings, whether earnings or principal, converted to domestic money at a much lower rate on account of devaluations that prevailed at the time investments were made.

The solution that appears to be most favored at the present time is the working out of a system of guaranties whereby the city hall of Avezzano, or its representatives, inviting further private investments, will give full assurance of immediate conversion of investment earnings "at a prescribed rate of exchange," as well as further assurances of conversion of the principal in US dollars. The International Bank for Reconstruction and Development and other financial institutions have the capacity from the government of Italy where the investment is made to obtain a guarantee (Law #43-1956), but little or nothing has been accomplished thus far in the use of such guarantees. The whole matter of promoting further private investments for Project AUA activities awaits further developments, from not only the Security Exchange Commission (SEC), but above all the European Court of Justice.

Foreign Operations and International Cooperation Administrations: A further step toward the unification of all foreign-assistance programs within the jurisdiction of a single agency was taken as of August 1, 1953, when the Mutual Security Agency was replaced by the Foreign Operations Administration, according to the terms of a presidential reorganization plan. The new agency was given the authority to direct several programs that had never been included within the purview of the Mutual Security Agency, such as those of the Technical Cooperation Administration and the Institute of Inter-American Affairs, both of which had been in the State Department. But the State Department in turn assumed the commanding position with respect to the Foreign-Assistance Programs when, as of July 1, 1955, its newly formed agency, the International Cooperation Administration, absorbed the functions and powers of the Foreign Operations Administration.

Although military-aid operations continue to outrank by far all other kinds of assistance accorded to foreign countries at the present time, and although such operations are chiefly the concern of the Department of Defense, the International Cooperation Administration, like its predecessors, has the general responsibility for coordinating the military and non-military programs, as well as the specific responsibility for supervising and directing the latter. The work of the International Cooperation Administration may be said to fall into seven major categories: mutual/ defense assistance; direct forces support; mutual defense support; technical cooperation; development assistance; relief; rehabilitation, and other multilateral programs; and emergency programs. (On many occasions, at least at the beginning of Project AUA's activities, it was mentioned and suggested to me directly to approach the Defense Intelligence Agency (DIA), which would have helped the first-phase program of the Campus to get off the ground with

Eximbank, Washington, DC (Financial Institutions.)

Authorized to carry on a general banking business to promote the foreign trade of the United States, the bank grants both short-term and longer-term loans to American importers and exporters, to foreign governments, and to nationals of foreign countries, who (as a rule) can obtain the support of their governments. Congress directs it to grant loans, as far as may be possible, only for specific projects and only upon reasonable assurance of repayment; moreover, the bank has instructions to supplement and encourage, rather than to compete with, private lending for international purposes. In the latter regard the bank prefers to receive loan applications of American importers and exporters through the commercial banks rather than directly from the prospective borrowers, and it welcomes commercial bank participation in the loans it approves.

Nevertheless, investment of capitals (home or abroad) are subject to a variety of regulations imposed by the state governments (Italian and United States mainly), but the most significant body of regulations with which the Project AUA activities must conform are those described by the law #43-1956, recommended by Attorney as was indicated in the law and related correspondence; this law especially offers the most solid guarantee for the investment. In addition, other provisions of this law are designed to prevent abuses in the development process, such as fraud and other wrongdoings. According to the Court of Appeal of L'Aquila (Italy) verdict, particularly all the financial-economic statement aspects submitted to the city hall of Avezzano are satisfactory as far as the Campus program development. There are reasonable prospects that the Project AUA concern would have taken the investment capital, the originating budget, and cash flow for operations and been prepared to work out the final investment details according to the development phases of the project.

Law Enforcement in Capital Investment: Long before the specific law #43-1956 was adopted to protect capital investment into Italy, it was possible to prosecute dishonesties under contractual law; that is, the law found in the decisions of judges from the earliest times in the countries involved. Thus, fraud has always been subject to punishment under Italian and United States law. And fraud is not too difficult to prove in this specific case. In fact, to convict the city hall of Avezzano of fraud on the Campus land deal, it must be clearly stated once again that a misrepresentation of facts is made by the city of Avezzano's officials, that this misrepresentation was made knowingly in the past as well as at present, and that the law enforcement agencies (SEC and Italian counterpart) should act upon the misrepresentation and that the Project AUA and its main principal suffered large damages as a result of not acting upon it.

For many years the United States criminal code has made unlawful not only security deals (but others, of course) to use the mails in promoting "any scheme or artifice to defraud" (United States Code Title 78, Par. 338.) (See letters from city hall to request money for payment.) Under other legislation the Postmaster General is authorized to stop the delivery of mail and the payment of money orders to anyone who attempts to obtain money or other property "by means of false or fraudulent pretenses, representations or promises" (US Code, Title 39, Par. 259 and Par. 732). The state legislators took steps (with Kansas in 1911) to protect investors by the adoption of "blue-sky laws" and fraud laws. The "blue-sky laws" generally require the registration of security dealers, or the presentation of a financial-economic plan (or prospectus), which are to be implemented within a state or abroad. The fraud laws obligate investment banking houses to publish notices and authorize government officials to institute criminal proceedings because of fraudulent character.

Theoretically, capital is entitled to a return that is devoid of all risks and which is in no way associated and/or evidenced with the management of Project AUA's activities, for the return allocated to the entrepreneur or business manager is known as "profits in economic theory." But if it completely overlooks the practical aspects of the situation, then the entire matter should end at this point. It is, in fact, compelled to recognize both the practical, as well as the theoretical aspects, of the capital invested. Practically, therefore, as well as theoretically, the return on such investment should appear as a participation in profits, in that it is a residual, not fixed, claim in the financial-economic plan and specific financial-statements. Yet, the return on investment (ROI), which represents the ownership equity in the Project AUA in part, at least, must be considered as a return on capital similar to interest paid on the bank-loan, even though some economists make distinction between profits and interest. Hence, it seems apparent that in the "remainder" shown in the financial-economic prospectus submitted to concerned parties, it will be unable to adhere strictly to the economic distinction between profits, interest, and the return for risk.

As is expected, the task presented by the ISTAT reevaluation verdict seems to be somewhat more complicated than easy, dealing only with pure interest rate calculation. At the time of the litigation dispute over the Campus property, legal action was dealing with a definite phenomenon, which has long been discussed and studied and for which there is a mass of related and consistent information. In considering the return on various investment activities on behalf of Project AUA at this point, where interest, profits, and a return for risk are all present in varying degree, and if that is the case in question, then it must be contended with less satisfactory, less well-defined, and less supportive evidence. The question of procedures in developing these evidences from documentation also presents some difficulties with this situation; however, it is important first to proceed to an analysis of the total capital invested for the entire Project AUA's activities (including those for endowment purposes, such as a mobile laboratory; parking garages; Labortec and Albpetrol joint-venture; Silva Co.; and Lab. Int.). Thereafter it is possible to take up in more detail the return on each capital investment activity. In a study based on personal inquiries within these activities, one of the common characteristic found among concerned parties (public and/or private) are repetitive behaviors of unreliabilities in the ratio of earnings to investment endorsed presumably by the "obscure force" to obstruct related development plans. This contains, however, an excellent lesson to be learned for further investment prospects. Countries, as well as their public and private corporations, failing to consistently balance their budgets and avoiding legally binding commitments should be taken very seriously for purposes of investment. Such poor performances are manifested with the city hall of Avezzano and remained unfavorable for a long time; when the internal currency of Italy is depreciated and destabilized—these two phenomena are frequently associated—it must be stated that the payment of financial obligations is also made increasingly difficult and very alarming.

The relation of the financial obligation of a foreign country (city hall of Avezzano) to its position as a debtor is highly important. As matter of fact, the external obligations of a country, as well as those of its subjects, require payments in foreign currency and, therefore, involve the whole problem of international balance of payments. The "Trip-memo" report regarding travel to Italy in 1982 has been already considered among the various aspects of undertaken activities.

It is important that credits exceed debts in the form of exports over imports, or in the form of an excess of services rendered to beyond those performed by foreigners if a community in question is ultimately to pay interest or principal on its debt. It should be rememebered that the capacity of a nation to meet the service on its foreign debt, therefore, is closely related to its total international trade balances, including both visible and invisible items. It is also true that many aspects of the "instruments" under which foreign investment is made are similar to those found in the corporate deed of trust or the mortgage under which domestic loans are floated, or in the contract made between the civil unit and the lender, in the case of domestic civil loans. For reasons already stated, particular attention should be paid to the purpose for which the investment was undertaken on behalf of Project AUA's activities, especially in the case of Campus land acquisition and project development. Investment for purely productive purposes, such as campus program facilities, rehabilitation of devastated regions (Albania's activities), and for currency stabilization, where properly supervised, are perfectly proper and legitimate. Investment for military expenses and for the purpose of balancing budget deficits instead, indicate poor financing and should be avoided. A quotation from an address by President Coolidge, Nov. 19, 1925 (*Commercial and Financial Chronicle*, Nov. 21, 1925, p. 2482) stated: "If rightly directed they (American loans) ought to be of benefit to both lender and borrower. If used to establish industry and support commerce abroad, through adding to the wealth and productive capacity of those countries, they create their own security and increase consuming power to the probable advantage of our trade. But when used in ways that are not productive, like the maintenance of great military establishments, or to meet municipal expenditures which should be either be eliminated by government economy or supplied by taxation, they do not serve any useful purpose and should be discouraged."

In view of the ISTAT reevaluation, then, a close relationship between business conditions and total capital invested ($35 million US dollars— See related documentation), the investment is required to keep in the closest touch with changes in the economic and business situation within the city hall of Avezzano. This can be done only by an intimate study of a substantial body of the statistical data, which have been available for sometime. Such a study is required and is still needed, not only regarding the ability to properly interpret the available material, but knowledge as to its sources as well. Unquestionably the professional specialist who has had statistical training is in a better position to deal with the various events and evidence that are commonly used to measure business conditions than is a person who lacks such training. It is not the purpose here to go into an elaborate discussion of the techniques that should be used by the ISTAT in preparing and analyzing special documentation. It is, however, necessary to call attention briefly to any relevant interpretation of the already submitted data and related statements.

Most of the data used in measuring business and economic-financial activities are described in the related submitted documentation known as "Financial-Economic Statement." It may be defined as consecutive events and data representing, for specific stated periods (trip memos and other reports) the Project AUA development changes that took place in respect to a definite factor of the Financial-Economic Plan as an investment into a foreign country: Italy. Thus, the amount of capital defined in the cost reevaluation (as requested by the Italian court) over a specific period also constitutes very important evidence. These important data of the time may be put in the form of a computerized schedule, or the entire evidence may be represented in graphic form by means of a curve for the ISTAT analysis and interpretation. Regardless of any particular form for the data presentation, the so-called "first-hand information" and original capital investment statements are still essential and frequently required by statistical treatment before the entire financial matter assumes practical significance.

Trip Memo to Italy—July, 1985

First, from several phone calls made directly and indirectly, it was possible to learn the status of the lawsuit introduced some years ago to the Avezzano Tribunal. In summary, this information is what transpired from the phone conversations: "The verdict has finally been decided by the president of the Avezzano Tribunal. It is in your favor; the city hall of Avezzano is found liable for damages as inserted into the summons . . ." At that point, to find out more about the verdict's content, a trip to Italy seemed inevitable. As a matter of fact, persons in contact were informed in advance to schedule meetings with me personally in Italy during the month of July.

The first person contacted was the judge at his tribunal office, while waiting for the attorney. meeting. The verdict's file was no longer deposited in the bailiff's office; it was already sent to the registrar's office for the legal procedure of registration and fees payment. The judge curiously informed me that, indeed, the verdict was in my favor. However, he was not in a position to define, in details, the findings nor to elaborate much more on the finance matter involved related to the amount of damages in US dollars. It must be pointed out that he recognized the enormous amount of work performed on behalf of the entire project's endeavor and the money spent. He admitted and almost suggested that, perhaps, a higher court (like la Corte di Appello dell' Aquila) would have addressed an accurate and realistic definition on the specific financial matter much better. Whether or not to reappeal the case should be discussed with the lawyer. The judge briefly conveyed his thoughts and the reasoning of arguments that led him to the verdict's findings. There were no questions nor doubt about the inquiries and the undertaken investigations, especially those carried on his part to determine the course of the case and its related decision.

And, as the judge openly admitted, this case's final decision was based more on "moral values and principles" than on the matter of "peculiar" financing. In a few words, I had not too much to add to my understanding on this subject, given the time and the proper place, but was very much in agreement with the judge's philosophical reasoning. Related material would have been sent to him to validate the logic of the discussion undertaken and the validity of a kind of work performed in line with the development of a Campus of International Character. (See related material: Morality as Philosophical Concept within the Projected AUA.)

The lawyer was met at Avezzano's tribunal, where he was working on other kinds of professional businesses. While awaiting this meeting, a former mayor of Avezzano, made clear that the case was in my favor and that I won it because of a good cause and that the local political system in town was and still is corrupt and that's all. He had to leave; somebody called him out. It must be stated that the mayor was and still is a friend and supporter of the Campus of International Character in Avezzano. In the meantime, the lawyer finally took a few minutes to get to the registrar's office where the verdict's file was held. Walking from the tribunal to the registrar's office, I mentioned to him the discussions with the judge and my disagreement with the amount of Italian lire defined by the court. I had to read the contents of the verdict before the lawyer could have elaborated and answered. I was allowed to read the findings and the conclusion of the verdict. But copies of this verdict were not allowed until it was registered according with the law, after a fee equal to 1,500,000.00 (almost $800.00) was paid in full. This fee was not paid at that time because I was not informed to provide the needed money before I left Cleveland. I promised to send the money to pay this fee.

In following meetings held with the lawyer focus was given to what kind of action to take against the city of Avezzano once the verdict was registered. Suggestions were given and taken to approach the newly elected city administration with different alternatives and to submit some specific financial proposals before asking for the verdict enforcement and/or to reappeal the case for a larger amount in damages not properly defined on this one. In any event, the political instability of the new elected city's government (the same mayor in charge) was learned of and of the related personal and impersonal problems in connection with the specific land purchased for the campus. It was explained in detail how to get the amount of damages, and how it is funneled through the various governmental channels. Many times I made the lawyer aware of my doubts and all kinds of pressure on me, mainly from the delay in the lawsuit's procedures. He reassured me I'd have back the sums spent on behalf of this project and be compensated for related damages.

During discussions held during these meetings, references were made to other previous understandings and agreements. Specific materials and references were convalidated by the written and legal documents made available from sources and files. At this point in time, it was decided to perhaps wait a little bit longer before making and taking the proper legal actions. On the other side, a target time was mutually agreed to: not later than the coming fall.

Other meetings and times were focused on collateral business activities, especially in relation to material submitted to introduce Petrolio Roccioso in specific locations of Italy. Some suggestions on how to approach the specific areas of concern were offered. Me and the lawyer personally went to visit some of these areas to make sure the geophysical aspect was well understood. The validity of this work was recognized, and the lawyer promised to file for the patent application previously submitted to him.

Phone contacts were kept with two generals to arrange a meeting and to be introduced personally to the new ANFI's elected president. This meeting could not be scheduled due to time conflicts. Therefore, a meeting with one of the generals at Cuneo turned to be a feasible and valid alternative. In fact, a variety of issues, topics, and discussions relevant to material previously submitted to the general and ANFI's office in Rome were acknowledged and given the proper attention. Emphasis was given, also, to material submitted and related to collateral business activities, particularly "white coal" patent applications in Italy. Also explored were possibilities for developing lines of import/export between Italy and the United States, with approaches for potential products and firms to be identified. Some of the proposals would also be addressed to key people, given the nature of the unique type of work and the technical know-how required. The general promised to assist in identifying key persons in Italy in order to expedite the endeavors. He advised to meet personally with another general, the newly elected ANFI president. Attempts were made to arrange this meeting as a top priority in the working agenda, but because of time and schedule conflicts it did not take place. Another date was considered. This was also suggested and supported by Gen. another general during my short visit to his ANFI's office in Rome. Material concerning "A Short Story to be Told" was given to him to be enclosed in the ANFI's file related to Project AUA. One general would be informed directly by one of the other two generals of further information pertinent to the status and the project's progress in connection with working activities in Italy.

It must be mentioned that a few days during the course of this trip were spent with members of my family, relatives, and close friends living in different locations of Italy. Time spent among them could be considered as sort of a physical relaxation on one hand, but for up-to-date events a kind of mental refreshment, above all. Trips and short visits were made to Torvaianica, Percara, Sulmona, Ascoli-Piceno, and other nearby towns and villages.

A special trip was also made to Caramanico, where an appointment to take physical therapy under my doctor's recommendation was made possible. Upon the Therme doctor's suggestions, a physical examination was required, and the therapy for the mud bath applications was postponed to a later date, perhaps during the coming fall, when weather should be cooler. A courtesy visit was made to a former Abruzzi senator, in Sulmona, a supporter of the projected campus's activities in the early days of the promotional stages. He was still enthused about the several programs with which he was acquainted. After receiving the usual congratulations for my endurance in pursuit of a "great cause" for a "great initiative," recognizing the validity of my work performed, he had the obligation to inform me that a similar project equal to the Campus of International Character was under construction in the Sulmona area. The president of the State of Venezuela sponsored this "specific" project in this "specific" location. Some newspaper clips were very much informative, after all! (See related material.)

An excursion was also made to survey a specific location where ALF's samples were collected from my previous trips there. Most of the time spent on this specific site was dedicated to understanding more deeply the topography of the area. A variety of information would have been needed to follow up on those works and studies already undertaken, including a more accurate analysis of the specific area's geophysics and the sources of the white coal rock's formation, as well as other chemical components; all those needed more supportive information. (See: Study and analysis related to Grotta Dei Saraceni and its H_2O underground work.)

At this specific location, an attempt was made to meet with key people such asa mayor and a doctor. A summary of my work and study of "P.R." and "W.C." was informally introduced to both these gentlemen. Although the presentation and discussions were limited to cover a few aspects of the entire endeavor, they had a pretty good understanding of the potentials involved and certainly of the various positive results that could be achieved; they both offered their support and cooperation. Different sources for planning and community concern were suggested in advance. A common suggestion was that a formal presentation of the undertaken activities should be presented officially to a consortium of this location's community representatives. This was a quite appealing suggestion, to be considered further.

At the conclusion of this trip, only by a coincidence, I happened to meet, inside a bar near the Avezzano Tribunal, the past and present mayor in charge of legal government affairs. The mayor identified himself as a self-proclaimed "champion" of those evergreen trees, to be protected in connection with the project campus, during contractual negotiations, and other stories written and not written in reference. Often I invited him to visit Cleveland, Ohio, USA, to better understand the position of the projected AUA, Within a Campus of International Character in Avezzano, Italy. Maybe to avoid an embarrassing situation or other reasons, he seemed almost disturbed. He had no other word to give but: *"Mai verró in America"* (I will never come to America), and he left immediately. His behavior is understood and not a surprise at all. After all, he is not the only one in a certain coincidental encounter.

Trip Memo to Italy
July, 1985

Morality: A Philosophical Concept To Develop a Campus of International Character

(This philosophical concept was very much in agreement with the judge's reasoning and thoughts—July, 1986)

Not too many people these days believe that morality is important in the development of young people, as well as in endeavors such as the projected American University of Avezzano (AUA). But certain prominent people and institutions of various entities hid their support to the cause of this project and ignored how effective it is to provide an essential climate that is conducive to moral development as a corollary to the philosophical concept of the Campus of International Character.

In spite of concern from "prominents" about lack of moral values, there were methods and tactics to divert this endeavor's efforts, the facts are often too elusive and not too difficult to isolate them from the development of this project. Quick "solutions" have been offered by such political interest groups about morality, although political parties or interest groups and movements seldom work toward developing individual moral maturity for either people or for projects.

As a number of people who supported the projected AUA development became more vocal in their concern over their community affairs vis-a-vis moral values, independent promotional activity turned to be more than absolute. By virtue of this insistence on being in a strong position, indeed, the promoter had an obligation to make a commitment to moral issues within the main project's effort and to develop activities and programs that will develop moral awareness among the projected AUA's supporters. While responding to the concerns of these loyal supporters, the independent approach for project development, at long range, should provide leadership in developing the Campus of International Character's structures and facilities, and above all developing programs for moral awareness, which could be appropriate to the benefit of this institution and other supporting organizations.

As a matter of fact, the "moral issue" must be stated and accepted as a goal of the Campus of International Character, along with its activities and curricular concerns. The promoter or governing body of this Campus of International Character must be articulate in communicating and delivering the elements of this goal. The commitment to integrity must be visible, and it must never be, or seem to be, compromised. People connected with the campus's activity must be given ample opportunity to discuss the state of moral issues on its campus and how to improve it. Ideally and practically, the philosophical concept of the Campus of International Character should be well articulated with the principals and supporters or any concerned citizen encouraging a common interpretation of its goals. Each member of this projected campus needs to think how his or her own value system relates to the values espoused by the projected AUA within a Campus of International Character's philosophy.

Because it is rarely possible to find special time for these kinds of "exercises," the campus's activities should offer a program or hold a retreat to initiate the process and continue to hold retreats as the person or persons in charge learn to deal with increasingly complex and difficult issues. As one immediate goal, the projected AUA must have a person who is directed toward human relations as well as academic concerns. Writing and approving this person's position is not enough. Understanding and learning to live with this position is a developmental process. Expectations appropriate to people of varying ages must develop to reach agreement on how these people will communicate these standards and maintain them with their surrounding community. Principals of the projected AUA need time to discuss and evaluate campus activities to be sure that it is taking full advantage of opportunities to deal with ethical and moral issues. Literature, history, sports, politics, and social studies have long been viewed as fertile disciplines for introducing such discussions. People in charge of these disciplines need to be skilled leaders in the discussion of moral dilemmas and value systems.

But people and students can learn to solve problems and recognize open-ended issues through all disciplines and campus activities. In the sciences, skills of accurate observation must be developed. Mathematics should inherently promote recognition of patterns and respect for laws of nature. Sports discussions and political analysis relate to corruption exposures. Relating problems of another culture and other people to current problems can become part of the study of history. Introducing "new thought" into the campus through visiting speakers is particularly valuable when the university community has been struggling on its own to deal with ethical issues. People both inside and outside the campus activities need the insight and prospective that can come from the outside, as well as the recognition that many issues are universal.

People in charge of campus activities must recognize that group relations within the various activities are basic to achieving a climate of moral awareness. They must be willing to spend time originally planned for programs and activities to work through problems that are adversely affecting the morale of the group. People committed to campus activities need help in developing skills for guiding young people with logic and compassion in dealing with their own problems. These people must be involved in developing the regulations that govern the campus's activities, the related community, and programs in enforcing them. The Campus of International Character must be a democratic society in microcosm; people connected with it need to learn the responsibility that is imposed on each individual in a democratic society. People connected and involved in the campus's activities need guidance from the governing body of the institution to identify the kind of community they want, the rules needed to govern it, and ways of carrying out those rules.

Morality is intricately involved with the total development of a human being. No one can become mature without a well-developed value system and without having worked through difficult ethical issues. Morality is intricately involved with total development of a human being. When people connected with the campus's activities are given extended opportunities to grapple with ethical issues together, it becomes clear that "grown-ups" do not always have the answers, and the line between certain people becomes less distinct.

The End of a Case

The judge's final decision could end the long legal fight over the multi-million-dollar damages caused to the project American University of Avezzano, which began between 1974 and 1975 in the Avezzano's local tribunal. This case is thought to be one of the biggest scandals in recent Avezzano political and judicial history. Many prominent political figures, as well as other noble and not too noble personalities, have stumbled over this specific project. The promoter of the project brought suit against the city hall of Avezzano upon valid suggestions and related recommendations. He is seeking to recover damages totaling near ten million dollars, plus other damages from the city hall of Avezzano. There were council deliberations and agreements between the city of Avezzano administration and the promoter of the project campus. Based on written documents and other negotiations, the promoter and author of the project understood precisely that the city of Avezzano would secure a deed to the property recommended, selected, and defined with the city hall of Avezzano's and other government approvals for the campus's structure and facilities. Consequently, power of attorney was made to recommend lawyers in Italy sign contractual documents and accept delivery of land title. The agreement was drafted by a local public notary. A final draft of the contract was already signed by one of the parties. Several mayors of the Avezzano city hall maliciously delayed to avoid signing the contract and delivering the title to the land. This title was needed for the project's development and to procure funds to start building the facilities and to implement operational programs in line with the submitted Project AUA plans.

Story Center Place. This is the story of what can happen to an Italian city that rolls out the red carpet for a high-risk land development and sees its dreams of rich promises end in frustration and controversy.

In the fall of 1969, the city of Avezzano, Italy, set out to attract a new and exciting educational-recreation project in the area of the local "Piano Regolatore," zoned for urban renewal. City prominents and connected private and public personalities envisioned a day when new jobs would be created and thousands and thousands of dollars would fly from one end of the town to the other.

In pursuit of this goal, lavish, and some said questionable, offerings of city land were made. Some critics claimed that Avezzano came very close to being plunged into a real estate sale, almost equal to the amount of flow determined and experimented in the same area since the drainage of "Lago Di Fucinoi."

This story centers on a of land-purchase deal, known locally as "Zona Tre Conche." A multi-million dollar project was forecast for scores of first-phase building structures and an education-recreation-tourism program (see attached project presentation). The first phase project and programs were to be build and implemented within the 73, 000 square meters of land (as part of other options, a total of 250,000 square meters of land) defined by the city hall government. The offering and the content of the city of Avezzano deliberations and other agreements related to this location where the international campus was defined, have now all but vanished. Also vanished were Avezzano's dreams of quick prosperity. As one local city official summed it up: "What really happened, and in total confidentiality: The city council and the administrations in charge—these are the people who run the city—just went crazy over this specific project, the Campus of International Character. Every politician, bureaucrat, and businessman in this city thought they were going to get rich overnight. It became an issue like talking about a project second in magnitude only to the drainage of "Lago Di Fucino," or Santa Claus, or the gifts from the public Christmas trees. Recommendations at that time were clear; you did not dare say that you were against any part of this package-gift which the city of Avezzano was offering."

In the almost fifteen years after the Project AUA Campus of International Character was introduced to the city's local government, provincial, and other public and private agencies, Avezzano has:

—For all practical purposes, offered for sale to the projected "campus" 250,000 square meters of land defined in the city urban renewal, "Piano Verde," *to develop them as proposed from "land-use" according to specific conditions lined out directly with the city hall*

—Promised to build the infrastructure to connect, *to bridge*, and to provide access to the campus's site location

—Offered to cooperate, through a *"Decree of Public Utility,"* a public domain-type of acquisition for adjacent lands within the option agreement and to help procure other parcels of nearby land in the site already defined and approved by provincial government

—Directly and indirectly spent more than thousands and thousands of dollars financing a similar project-venture, which now appears will never be built

—Launched on a nearby site location the construction of a sports facility and hospital complex at the cost of highest estimation.

—Offered to participate and support in an endowment and other business ventures, such as in parking garages, tourism, and other capital investment activities, such as tax-exempt revenue bonds, in order to provide Project AUA with fixed income.

The Background. Project AUA seemed to vanish in the midst of the "Pianura del Fucino," the name of this location. In so much as it stands, one of the remaining principal supporters has been forced to delay all the possible approaches, at least for the time being. The question to be asked is: What happened to the campus, to the Avezzano dream? To answer and to somehow understand these questions, it is necessary to go back to the beginning of this project, almost fifteen years ago.

In 1969, the promoter for AUA was scouting for a suitable place to locate a program in recreation-education. The project was called "A Campus of International Character." More than a dozen sites and regional areas were surveyed to determine where to establish this project. At that time, this was a supported undertaking with the Department of Physical Education of Case Western Reserve University Cleveland, Ohio, USA, and other potential persons and institutions which would have provided academic know-how and development expertise.

Promising Location. This supporting venture settled on Avezzano because this city offered an excellent site for the building facilities and was showing what one of the many council deliberations describe as: "A wonderfully cooperative attitude." (See related material and deliberations.)

Project AUA principals and sponsors accepted the site in Avezzano, confident that once the campus facilities were built, it would draw at least one thousand people a year (a conservative estimate) and employed between fifty and a hundred people. It would have generated a cash flow of at least one million dollars yearly, according to the proforma of that time.

Proponents and supporters of the project also calculated that the proceeds from AUA activities and its employees would have added nearly one million dollars in tax revenues a year to the city and national governments. They also envisioned a multi-million-dollar capital investment for endowment that would largely benefit the area of Avezzano. It must be said that civic leaders went all out to smooth the way for the project, as described by one local attorney: "As a matter of fact, when another project similar to the campus was introduced to the same community, the same concerned persons just jumped into the local and national government decision-making process. They did everything they could have done (joined the right clubs, rubbed shoulders with the right local politicians), and after a few meetings of wheelings and dealings, the city of Avezzano could have been theirs in a matter of a few days and for one dollar, more or less."

Unfortunately, a site was also needed for this "new project" where the collections of "Don Orione" could have assembled the world's first "opere pie," personalities and famous donors of certain facilities for displacement, as one local newspaper quoted: "The Avezzano absolute power instantaneously recommended that the already promised land defined for structure of Project AUA should be revoked and cashed-in for land sale. At first, members of the local political establishment, formally and informally, offered the site defined for the project to "Fox and Company." This name is altered because of the pending litigation in Avezzano court. The price of other developmental land in the nearby area was already running up from one thousand to ten thousand lire per square meter. As a matter of fact, in Via Tiburtina Valeria, some advertisement signs with the related name mentioned for land acquisition and other ventures were posted stating: "Willing to buy real estate and other property for transactions."

No Lost Promises. Written into the agreement drafted and signed for Project AUA was this money-back guarantee: (1) If Project AUA within a year was unable to start a building and complete these within five years, it promised to refund the purchased land, plus other expenses for the transferring of the deed. (This is in reference to the draft made by the notary) In addition, if Project AUA could have found another developer for the real estate suitable for the city, it would be allowed to recoup out-of-pocket expenses, including site improvement, salaries, subcontract costs, advertising, and promotion.

To date, Project AUA has expended an enormous amount of dollars, lires, and work hours. The majority of this amount has been paid and anticipated by its principal promoter. The closing date for the land deal should have been five years after the signing of the contract for the title to the land. Instead, after a few years, the city council, without any notification to the concerned party, decided to revoke, unilaterally, deliberations and past agreements. There have been postponements in the agreements, and the final contract was never signed by the city of Avezzano's mayor, although a check was cashed for the land sale.

Because of this delay, Project AUA was unable to follow-up on promotion and phases implementation. Project AUA was also forced to delay a fundraising campaign and missed the target for promotion obligations. These damages range from five million to ten million dollars, depending on what version of the estimation is accepted, either the city hall of Avezzano's officials or Project AUA's executives.

In coming to face Avezzano's attitudes, the Project AUA principals and executives knew they had a number of major problems to overcome.

For example, if the campus's main programs and other related activities were going to employ one hundred people, there was a very concerned question about where these employees should have come from and how they should have been trained. The answer suggested it was to aim at a new low-cost approach to train key personnel or emphasize voluntary work. This approach was going up near the nucleus of few members of the board of trustees to work out and carry on the decision making process. Impetus for the project advancement was solicited time and time again, and suggestions were provided by the concerned offices and individuals. Public and private personal recommendations and the very need for such an approach became almost obsolete for the promotion of these project's activities.

Some of the Difficulties. Another of the obstacles to overcome was whether the principals of Project AUA Within a Campus of International Character would have enough capital available to promote such a project and to carry on the related programs. But these "thoughts" and other planned excuses appeared after a few years, after a check was already cashed by the city hall of Avezzano for the sale of the first parcel of land (73,000 square meters) and the drafted contract was finalized for the signatures. In fact, to make sure there was no shortage of cash to promote the project, the principals of this project solicited the board of trustees to start a venture capital investment as part of an endowment for the educational-recreational aspect of the campus. Suggestions were also introduced to sell municipal tax-exempt, revenue-type bonds for Project AUA business activities. Such a proposal would have saved Project AUA millions of dollars in interest by getting a loan in municipal bonds rather than at commercial rates (see financial economic statement material).

The local authority assured principals that the construction of a tunnel or a bridge to cross the nearby railroad tracks for access to the campus's site was anticipated. As a solution to a problem that would have eased the "traffic jam," as the crowded "Passaggio a Livello" was often referred to, an engineering study was made public. These facilities would have crossed the existing railroad tracks and thus provided easy access to the campus site. These facilities would have connected a residential area on one side of the city railroad with another particular area defined as "Il Concentramento." Politicians and local business leaders, however, had put in a more attractive concession: to develop "*Il Concentramento.*" This slum area, once very well renowned in the "Fucino," would have *transformed* the scarcely populated north of the city *into a booming district for land development.*

The cost of the bridge, or the tunnel, as well as the hospital and sports facilities were estimated at multi-million dollars, financed from the renowned "Cassa del Mezzo Giorno." To re-pay these millions of dollars, other kinds of planning for this kind of work were made. In the midst of construction, the city professionals could have raised costs as usual on all the building activities. This specific area had the highest construction costs, including the bridge, and did not matter if it had the lowest return on one dollar capital investment. Obviously, it was, and still is, another blunt related to the zone "The conche." Some local critics have charged that these costs nearly put the city's political system into bankruptcy. On the other hand, proper suggestions were given: If the campus was going to be a success, it would have needed a different kind of development approach.

Opposition to the Project. The drive to push the purchase of the land through without delay was intense and touched off the first real planned opposition to the support of Project AUA.

One side of the issue was represented by a local newspaper, which stated: "If the city of Avezzano can find some way to sell the land to another group, local government ought to do it even if the cost is much higher, because those 'clear' dollars would be coming back to the community." (See related material and paper clips.)

Another point of view: "The city of Avezzano should not subsidize any 'crooks' just because an ambassador (Fox and Company) is just coming to the city of Avezzano. It is rather logical to take the money from the city taxpayers and distribute it to the already famous personality or the concerned group."

As debate and opinions heated up in the summer of 1973, a city official described the scene: "The newspaper *Il Tempo (Pagina Marsicana)* carried major stories almost every day related to Project AUA and told how this project would have taken profitable land from the community. It was just an amazing time; the newspaper, *Il Tempo*, was wholly owned and under full control of the opposition to Project AUA and the landlords who wanted access at any costs to the land defined for the campus. This group claimed to gain considerably from these specific local real estate holdings, if the related tactics were proven to be successful. That's why the local political machinery has supported the attempt to pass the deal to a more favorable group (Fox and Company). And so the newspaper *Il Tempo* had to carry on the 'slanders' in banner headlines and other editorials, day after day, in the local Pagina Marsicana."

A Local Landlord. A councilman, or vice-mayor, or businessman, or landlord, or a "crook," as some of the local people defined him, took away and exploited a vast parcel of land, buildings, and a variety of properties and real estate in the city. This prominent "crook," as some sources often referred to him, also holds some kind of peculiar business and other exploited financial activities. Above everything else, he has taken to promoting other "illegal political activities" within the municipally owned properties, real estate, and several other tracts of land, especially within the area defined for the campus.

The city's always-changing new political administrations during the years between 1973 and 1975 entered the controversy. At first, the proposed contract, ready to be signed for the delivery of the land title, was reaffirmed for reconsideration. Then, supported tacitly by the newspaper "propaganda" to discredit. Project AUA's efforts, city hall's "professionals" and others started to put forward wrong information and slanders to discredit promotional activities. All this was a kind of effort to win public opinion, based on sharp criticism against the agreements, although there was no reference made to negotiations undertaken and works already accomplished.

A final decision was made in all secrecy within the local landlords' circles and delivered to their related political "cronies" that reasonable and prudent public officials' decisions, even if legal in their procedures, were not going to follow-up, in spite of previously approved deliberations, or any other government law that would have authorized the execution of the contract already drafted. The tone of the language made sure that it would have been an "arbitrary" and capricious action in the part of the city hall of

Avezzano and, quote: "openly contrary to public interest to deliver the title to Project AUA." (Also see article printed by *Il Tempo*, 1973.)

A public authority in Avezzano later said that it would have been just a matter of years before the new group, supported by the local newspaper, and interest for the campus's land, the "Fox and Company," the entire "enterprise" would have gone bankrupt by trying to make payments in the illegal activities already locally undertaken. It is not a secret any longer that the local landlords, plus "Fox and Company," could have ended up owning all "Fucino," using only bribe money and political manipulation.

This respected public authority said also that, in reference, there was a serious question in the minds of the majority of concerned citizens: How and whether the famous and powerful "Fox and Company" could have successfully floated the millions of dollars to Avezzano's very well renowned "crook." However, this was not the prevailing view at the time, and it was evidenced from personal inquiry held within the specific community.

A Cool Council Meeting. After the land dealings and other questionable attempts from "Fox and Company" and the day-by-day slanders from *Il Tempo, Pagina Marsicana*, legal criticism, and several stormy sessions from the city government council, finally it was made clear that the letter of intent already given to Project AUA and related previous deliberations were revoked in the spring of 1975. This decision was enforced without notifying the concerned principal of Project AUA. Prior to this decision, however, the principal of Project AUA requested that the Ethical Commission of L'Aquila check for several cases of possible conflict of interest from some public officials. The request was presented to the specific commission, which should have ruled on the contents of the deliberations and informed the city government of damages derived from a clear breach of contract. The Ethic Commission avoided ruling on this specific request, unless the city hall officials who were themselves involved in the possible conflict of interest requested a judgment directly from the Provincial Government Commission. As a matter of fact, none of the Avezzano public officials in charge of this matter had made a file for such a public ruling.

Prior to withdrawing from the approved agreements deliberation, the city hall of Avezzano secretly had made approaches to contract the new group,

"Fox and Company" (See *Il Tempo's* article), for a more "practical" delivery of land title. "Fox and Company" did not give any down payment to the city hall for the land, just bribe money to an anonymous journalist and some politicians who were responsible to support and to put together the majority of the council's votes to revoke past deliberations related to the site recommended and selected by the same city hall of Avezzano. It now appears likely that all bribe payments were lost, unless the powerful "new group" could take or contract another area, perhaps in the nearby location of Sulmona (see *Il Tempo's* articles).

Promotional Activities Canceled. In the midst of all the city of Avezzano's problems, the promotional activity of Project AUA was having its own. At one time, it had the letter of intent, the deliberations, to proceed with the fundraising and other project development activities, especially the reassurance of the city's mayors and suggestions from a lawyer and other government officials. The future looked bright and promising, especially with dedicated sponsors to implement these activities.

Then, during the summer and fall of 1973 and 1974, the recession was deepening and the response from Avezzano made clear what had already happened. The promotional aspect was hit along with other Project AUA activities. The lawyer's letter of intent definition and city hall deliberations lapsed in the spring of 1975. This was only revealed a few months later after Mr. Palli was sent to Avezzano (see the letters' explanation and report).

After the city of Avezzano's decision was made clear, some of the supporters of the projected campus also pulled out. The board of trustees submitted a file to the United States IRS that it was going to delay the activities until a legal matter was decided by the Avezzano local court (see related court materials).

Some prospects were submitted as proposals for development of projected parallel activities, and without the reassurance of the related letter of intent, as well as the delivery of land title, works completed remained on standby.

Work Achieved and Development Activities Reconsidered. Some persons committed to the various activities cut their support and their involvement with the project's development. The welcome received at Avezzano in 1970 was no longer warm for the promotion of the project, but in every aspect very hostile. Those concerned citizens and some specific persons who offered their support, for one reason or another, withdrew based on good and bad assumptions and hence their disconnection with the project development activities. The local political machinery, the "bosses," were committed to support another similar initiative, and their "turning around" and "questionable" maneuvers, as well as their personal attitudes, were and are fully clear. The city hall of Avezzano, the "secret circle" of prominent personalities close to "Fox and Company," still wait for the land defined for the campus. The promoter and principal of Project AUA is continuing the search to find an answer from lawyers and from Avezzano's tribunal.

Meanwhile, someone locally described the situation as: "At the beginning (in Avezzano), there was nothing dishonest in the city's dealing with the promoter of Project AUA. It became more a situation of a lot of exploitation by local and international politics, business, and "crooks," and these are who control the city of Avezzano inside and outside, thinking they had found the pot full of gold at the end of the rainbow.

"If the principal promoter and his supporters of Project AUA had not already advanced money, paid for work done and results and services clearly accomplished today and yesterday, nobody would be questioning at all how it was done to help the campus's effort in Avezzano. As it turned out, there was more money spent and work done than many people thought. Maybe some prominent politicians in town have learned a lesson, but there are doubts also. A lot of people in Avezzano, in the Abruzzi region, as well as all over Italy, in Cleveland, and everywhere else Project AUA had exposure, and some other concerned people still believe that the Campus of International Character should be built on the selected site, defined previously, at Avezzano (L'Aquila), Italy."

Abruzzo Region, Italy: Is This Also a Zone At Risk (ZAR)?
(Foreign Capital Investment, its Treaty and its Law)

The Italian Courts' verdict against the notorious municipality was to be just a frivolous political cover-up for a very serious international legal problem; this is not any longer a secret. Whether or not, aside from the court decisions, foreign capital investment in Italy and the related treaty between Italy and United States to be mintained, law #43-1956 must be enforced. It is overdue, and it is time to take legal action. If there are no other feasible alternatives to continuing efforts within the framework of this law and to revealing the many discrepancies in the Italian courts' decisions, and of course the inefficiency of the law enforcement agencies in Italy and United States, then it is time to sandbag it and liquidate not only the Campus of International Character program but all the collateral project activities undertaken as well.

It seems that given the present circumstance, regarding other more promising collateral activities undertaken in the region, a zone at risk (ZAR), the present political deviations are no different from the Campus project's previous court cases. Evidence once again demonstrates a pattern of behavior to conducting business in the ZAR region, where local government authorities enable and encourage breaches of contract in matters of civil and penal laws, domestically, nationally, and internationally. There is some relevant evidence of improper manipulation and transfer of project files, either within the local government itself and/or with the collaboration of connected agencies. These are not just rumors or street-talk or political finger-pointing but solid evidence of how to cause economic and financial obstacles and to furthermore damage each endorsed project's development activities. A personal inquiry can demonstrate with logic, facts, events, and valid evidence that the capital investment made for specific project activities undertaken in the ZAR region is in US dollars, and in accordance with law #43-1956.

In many instances, and this must be kept in mind, politicians, bureaucrats, and ZAR personalities quite often assert that their memory has failed, directly and indirectly. But undertaken project files requested by and submitted to specific government authorities and other related agencies have mysteriously disappeared; in this same file, among other valuable information, is the source and evidence of the US dollars, a foreign capital investment in Italy. It must be said, any other expedient is just to make this specific investment law a mockery, and this is serious enough to call the proper attention. Personal inquiry into this matter and the project file itself should also reveal important information concerning the Campus's land dealing and other detailed political-bureaucratic maneuvers that are related not only to the ZAR region in the past, but to the present and perhaps future projects. Whatever these implications are to the undertaken project activities, a final decision on this matter must be addressed to the concerned authorities in the United States and Italy. This authority may or may not be concerned with the ZAR region's political play-off. The odds are that at least a portion of the file's content will be leaked and exploited politically, as usual, aimed to delay, delay, delay the project's development program objectives in-situ: the related tunnel WCBMextraction and (PPP) conversion in the Subequana/Peligna Valley of the Abruzzo region, Italy.

Notes and Thoughts from Meeting Discussions (Concerned Key Persons)

Records from local court litigation in Avezzano clearly show file manipulations of all kinds and political pressure to keep the city hall of Avezzano officials' secrets, which led to being overwhelmed by requests for information about the Campus land sale deal. Unable to manage the voluminous paper file translations (Italian-English and English-Italian) and unprepared by the complexity of related council deliberations, city officials chose secrecy during a review of the contractual Campus land sale deal process that dragged on for several years before it was decided to summons the local tribunal of Avezzano as per the lawyer's recommendation (See Letter and Summons). During all these years of litigation and court appearances and final meetings to review documentation, the city hall of Avezzano has refused repeatedly to open its own Campus files related information relevant to Project AUA, including materials about the program, structure designs, and correspondence used for past and present land zoning modifications. There is no doubt that decisions by the city hall of Avezzano officials to keep these records secret broke not only Italian law but international laws under the RICO Act as well.

Expert and informed persons contacted forthe campus land sale deal have been convinced for sometime that an open process of the entire matter might have shortened the review by competent government authorities and, as a result, would have prevented the financial-economic difficulties for Project AUA's activities which have occured during these years. The Campus land sale deal would have been settled long ago and probably new proposals from another "concerned party" would have been made aware that its dirty laundry would have been disclosed from the beginning. Instead, the fact of the matter is that this "concerned party" interested in the Campus land might have felt more confident about slipping this dirty deal through. Perhaps, it was ignored or forgotten that public records laws require the local, regional, and state governments to open their business books to their citizens. It is a common notion that the law must protect the public by guaranteeing that it remains safe and sound.

In addition, the city hall of Avezzano has for years refused to return Project AUA's material and abused the discretion of property rights by keeping nearly all the records concerning the Campus land sale secret. Concerned citizens are aware that Avezzano city hall officials let them down by keeping this information about one of the biggest and most contested wrongdoings in community secret. Even at present, citizens concerned with the Campus program development and protecting community interests are again at center stage, with new Campus land modifications that were made to keep them in the dark about this crucial problem. There is a kind of secretiveness about the whole new Campus modifications that, to say the least, is very disturbing. It would be very interesting to find out who really has sponsored these "new modifications." For years, city hall of Avezzano officials have given conflicting signals about the fate of the rezoned Campus land for the proposed program activities, fostering all kinds of speculation about the reason for the delay. It must be said that Project AUA's financial condition, because of delay, has deteriorated and concerned land speculators rifts widened, while the public has remained much more in the dark about the Campus land sale deal.

In spite of so many meetings and discussions, it is still unclear why the city hall of Avezzano (Ufficio Tecnico) has taken so long to admit a dubious decision to rename "Zone Campus" to "Park of Sports and Recreation" in the Contrada Barbazzano. Although there are many versions, one of them is that city officials traditionally are used to making these kinds of decisions behind closed doors, which is historically how many mayors and administrators have dealt during all these years. This is the kind of closed-door process, as in reference to deliberation transcript N. 255/1975, that the local politic in the city hall of Avezzano quite often flourishes in. It is admitted very openly, however, that the new change in Campus modifications, had the city hall of Avezzano promise more than once the realization of Project AUA's program, averting a lot of political turmoil.

In the Campus land deal, there were subterfuges arranged by urban affairs specialists on behalf the city hall of Avezzano, including, of course, the falsification and omission of documents, and professional specialists have made sure to include the construction of a hotel and other services in the new approved modifications. The problem from these modifications to be resolved by an interest to pursue the Campus program is enormous, although it made public the alliance among the "new land ownership," local politicians and government and the bureaucracy. Perhaps new talents for corruption, bribery, and other kind of wrongdoings won't end with the Campus land deal, even though efforts to curb them are a main concern. Persistence and pervasiveness are not reasons to acquiesce, totally or partially, to the corruption and to the unscrupulous enrichment of the community's crooked few at the expense of those who have invested toward Project AUA's activities. Without any doubt, law #43-1956 must be reviewed regarding relevance in its connection with RICO Act, as recommended. It means focusing on the city hall of Avezzano's relationship with the new "campus modifications" sponsor to work in partnership to manipulate the land use.

Concerned citizens are outraged over this land-use manipulation; it never looked carefully into the kind of local government interest in partnership for the Project AUA's campus activities. Citizens were not given the proper consideration in this matter because the city hall of Avezzano seemed not to care. But an investigation and a study of the city hall of Avezzano concerns for the Campus program since its early beginning might show the danger of the other side. Corruption is endemic, and a bailout to pay for it would have forced the city hall of Avezzano to wait additional decades to get its economic and financial resources in order. There should have also been an investigation committee appointed to review the endemic corruption in the Avezzano community. Now, citizens are crying to be bailed out and promise to follow the investigation with related trials, but it must be awaiting in fine variety. The whole might be explained to the distinct disadvantage of Project AUA's plans for ground-breaking, such as the price asked for the land and if the costs of reevaluating the entire program are exorbitantly higher. This is one of the main reasons why government authority under the RICO Act must take the proper steps on this specific matter. In fact, from discussions with concerned parties, critics point out that agreement on RICO law enforcement leaves the definition of infractions and delineation of penalties to each signing nation. The prohibitions omit altogether bribes to political parties, their officials and candidates; bribes to state-owned but unsubsidized firms, which is rather a contradiction in terms; and bribes that the city hall of Avezzano in this case permitted.

Some thoughts concerning the meeting and rezoned Campus—property rights and conflict of interests: The rezoned Campus property rights in Avezzano (L'Aquila), Italy, appear that the local laws have no significance at all. It is true that an individual's property rights in land and project materials might not be remembered often, even if they are not entirely forgotten, because if there is a conflict of interest as stated and validated from different sources, then there is a good reason to accept the notion that the only outcome would infringe on the rights of another. Rather, the definition of Project Campus property rights in the rezoned land (See: Variants al Piano Regolatore) must be recognized as a balance between the conflict of interest on one end and as vested interested and other concerns in the other. For example, assuming that those vested interests and their conflicts of interest, as already stated, decide that they intend to construct a farm for weaning pigs; under the local rezoning law is not that "vested interest" absolutely right to do so, despite the noise, traffic congestion, environmental health problems, and other illegal changes that are likely to result?

It is believed that the local zoning law and other types of limited property regulation (such as the designation of a Campus zone) are essential to protecting one's own right to freely enjoy property, knowing that its character and value cannot be arbitrarily stripped away or to be viciously confiscated under false pretenses. Is a confiscatory law between Italy and USA? A petition to the International Court of Justice and/or related local magistrates should make sure to raise a valid point concerning both the value of the real estate and the updated reevaluation of the project's cost development for the rezoned Campus without diminishing both the program and the historic character of the entire undertaking. The city hall of Avezzano failed to note that the once rezoned Campus designation can be challenged by the project's Campus ownership and removed after no more than a few days; therefore, the property rights are not confiscatory under international law. It is a common impression that in ignoring the property rights claims to the project materials (not yet acknowledged as requested) that was passed by the vote of the whole Council and signed by the mayor, new members of Avezzano City Council were responding in a certain sense to the constituents' concerns for specific conflicts of interest and connected cover-ups.

Ultimately, the designation process for the rezoned Campus must protect everyone's property interest based on valid evaluation of evidences and work democratically without any conflict of interest to ensure that a reasonable balance of a fair reevaluation of the entire matter is achieved among concerned parties. Since time is very important and since any confiscatory policy approaches and/or blocking efforts will have no credibility without the participation of all concerned parties, responsible citizens of the local community should suggest or demand that their council get ready to openly divulge the content of Project Campus file materials, which have been hidden for the last twenty-five years. The council should pass such a disclosure resolution at once, or councillors will have no one to blame but themselves when the floodgates are opened and traffic and pollution overwhelm the local environment in that once tranquil area of the rezoned Campus.

More than once, directly and indirectly, in the interest of concerned parties for determination and claim to property rights connected to the projected American University of Avezzano (AUA) Within a Campus of International Character, material was previously submitted to the competent authority of Avezzano city hall. A copy of the same file was also submitted to the Prefect of L'Aquila Provinces as public domain for this specific project activity. The entire matter was properly discussed and requested during meeting discussions on May 28th and 30th, 1995, at the same city hall.

The possession and findings of this material, the claim to property rights, and having access to the original documentation files are necessary to determine a fulfillment of obligations and, above all, to facilitate the cost reevaluation of specific project activities. In the event of another futile and inconsistent version given by the city hall, for the purposes of ostracism and to alter the objectives and property rights of such a project, then it must be stated with much regret that legal action as another recourse becomes imperative. Thank you for your attention.

A Campus of International Character in the Center of Italy

(Feasibility Study and R/D Activities of Location)

The presentation of the documentary related to snake charming (I Serpari Di Cocullo) is the precursor and the corollary to the Campus of International Character program development. Research and feasibility studies of the Abruzzo Region, Italy, especially in the "Marsica e Peligna" valley, are the fundamental historical-cultural background for the Campus program definition and related project activities. The location to establish the Campus facilities and program objectives implementation is where once the Great Lake of Cliternum, now Celano, at present shows vast cultivatable fields. From the heights of Celano, or from the hillsides above Avezzano (at the San Pietro Church Hill), on the slopes of Monte Velino, that it can be recognized with horror, or satisfaction, according to the interest that predominates, environment changes in landscape, agriculture, industry, and housing. A few decades, or a century—the implied time is not enough to make a thing of beauty of a dried lake, of course; but a hundred more years, or thousands, would be insufficient to obliterate the chosen plan, that of geometrical precise design over an area of endless parallelograms edged with spiky poplars, the whole like a fancy chessboard. Even its glorious fields of sugar beets, potatoes, and waving corn lose their beauty by the neat measurement to which the "rezoned area is subjected.

But the last few decades have defined more dramatic changes in the environment where plans existed to establish a Campus of International Character. The spokes of these changes come from different sources, mainly the expansion of commercial-industrial, residential, and other kinds of urban development that take place, above all, in the importance of community land preservation. Although Campus Project development should logically be reevaluated, it is certainly valid to recognize that the new urban area modifications are essentially the force used as an external threat to enhance the undertaken activities closer to the archaelogical site of Alba Fucens. It must be stated that the destruction of health and environment, and especially the neglect of archaelogical remains, by economic and urban development is not only the problem of this specific location—it is a prevalent world-wide problem. Like other archaelogical sites, Alba Fucens offers a beneficial effect, in that it has an enormous potential for new discoveries from the prehistoric era of the Pelasgian civilization to the contemporary cultural-social society.

The contribution of a Campus of International Character program closer to the archaelogical site of Alba Fucens can help to support further research and development about previous ideas of the wealth of Pelasgian archaelogical material potentially available. It is both possible and feasible to carry on field-work on a larger scale than ever before, and this means a major contribution in the way research and development activities at the Pelasgian site are organized. Students and faculty and staff members of Project AUA are directly and indirectly involved in these activities. Direct participation in archaelogical and related activities as a model project can especially support efficient changes and meld practical method with theory, in order to deal with the problems of the location.

A feasibility study of the specific location, together with a research design, is proposed for investigating the structure and functioning of extinct and present cultural systems and how these relate to one another regarding the processes of change and evolution. An essential aspect of this design is the fact that it is a multi-project activity. It is recognized that the most satisfactory framework for field research is the one that begins by examining, in a preliminary way, the archaelogy and cultural past of the Abruzzo Region as a whole and then focuses on increasingly limited sections of it with increasing intensity. Work and R/D activities, such as On the Slope of Monte Velino, a Campus of International Character; Mobile Laboratory/white coal; the Pescara River Bank and its Upstream Tributaries; and others as a whole, is an indispensable initial phase of the undertaken project. The acquisition of reliable and representative information about specific locations, past and present human activities, including the relationship with environmental variables and with one another, are very much relevant regarding the Campus program determination.

Information from the potential Palesgian archaelogical site may require a three-dimensional imagination, as much to grasp not only the ancient cultures in time and space but to understand and to visualize buried site modifications nearby. Maps and timecharts remain the evidence of the plans and historical process that guide the patterns that underlie and make sense of the complexity of the real world. Although there are divergent points of view and wide disparity in the knowledge of Project AUA's activities, it is especially important to appreciate the alternatives that are presented and the process as a whole, including the interrelationships within it. However, to understand the reconstruction of the prehistoric past and contemporary events requires some acquaintance with the methods and techniques provided to get relevant information. Recent modifications and other changes in innovations of the specific location fundamentally affect not only the view of the past but that of present. The whole might give an better, accurate perspective of the Pelasgian archaelogical site and the potential for Campus Program development.

Project AUA's activities and interests in the Pelasgian age include a rediscovery of the history of Western civilization, which will give a fresh impetus to a new scale of construction and excavation that can bring to light many of the remains of early man and his work. High technology and new science in geology will provide a time-scale beyond the scope of earlier imagination, while interpretations of early life are broadened by the frequent encounter with less developed peoples in many parts of the world. It is certain that contributions to the enhancement of the Pelasgian archaelogical site exploration of early civilization also will give a new dimension to historical records through the discovery and evidence of the cyclopean fortress stone wall foundation. In front, on the neighbouring hill, stands the San Pietro Church, superbly located under the twin peaks of Monte Velino, which change, depending on the weather and time of day, from blue to dove color and opal. Set high and steep, it commands all the surrounding country and the plain that once was the Fucino Lake, whose waters of old came up nearly to its rocks. Probably a natural earthwork, this location has a magnificent outlook, or a place for meditation on the ruin of things. Project AUA intentions are also to deal not only with the ancient artifacts and monuments but above all with the whole landscape of the surrounding area, as this can be reconstructed by increasingly sophisticated methods and investigating analysis.

Suggestions and criticisms are welcomed.

Submitted by:

Author and Promoter
(Project AUA)

NEAR THE "CAMPUS" PROJECT A.U.A.   CELANO

BEFORE THE 1915 EARTHQUAKE   THE CASTLE (ORSINI)   **AVEZZANO**

MORE THAN A CENTURY AGO   THE MARKET-PLACE   SOLMONA

NEAR THE "CAMPUS" PROJECT A.U.A.   SCANNO

An international camp with an Outdoor Education in the Midst of Abruzzi's Mountains

An international camp with an outdoor education in the midst of Abruzzi's mountains is nature's laboratory. It is a setting that will offer excellent opportunities to learn much knowledge and skill and to develop wholesome attitudes. That which can best be learned inside any classroom can also be learned at this international camp. Outdoors, more will be learned through direct experience and dealing with native materials and life situations in the midst of Abruzzi's mountains.

International camp and outdoor education are not synonymous here. Outdoor education will include camping. The international camp will provide will provide a laboratory by which many facets of the outdoors can be studied first-hand. The international camp experience will help to develop qualities especially important to preparing young people for the lives they will live.

The value of this international camp and the outdoor education related and connected to some school programs will also be well established. Teachers from elementary through college levels will also benefit from studying the objectives, contributions, programs, administration, and other aspects of these important fields of camping and outdoor education. As a matter of fact, there is a greater need today than ever before for camping and outdoor education, which are emphasized more and more in schools and colleges and in conservation, recreation, and other agency programs.

Some important objectives outlined for this international camp with outdoor education precisely match the nature of Abruzzi's mountain location. Here, campers, visitors, and students will learn to live democratically with other children and adults. It is a place to learn more about the physical environment and the importance of a wealth of natural resources. An appreciation for the out-of-doors and the contributions it can make to enriched living will be certainly developed. Those qualities that make for good citizenship, such as responsibility, leadership, teamwork, and honesty, will be also developed. While camping, students will be stimulated to learn about native materials and to see their relationship to the learning that takes place in the classroom. Worthwhile recreational skills, such as map reading and other benefits, will be derived from wholesome work experiences. Moreover, campers will learn some of the basic rules of safety and to depend on personal resources in practicing the rules of healthful living.

These objectives are worthy goals and tie in closely with the social, intellectual, and health aims of general education intrinsic to this international camp and outdoor education. Students will develop socially by learning to live democratically. Responsibilities for maintaining the camp will be assumed by all. Each student, regardless of national origin, color, or other difference, will be respected as an individual who can contribute to the group enterprise. He also will develop intellectually as he satisfied his lust for adventure. He will see the wonders of nature first hand and learn about conservation, soil, water, and animal and bird life. Certainly the international camp's character-building experience will also promote good health, and the outdoors, together with healthful activity, interesting projects, and congenial classmates, will improve the general fitness of the student, who will leave this international camp site with a rugged glow to his cheeks, sparkling eyes that reflect the new things he has seen and learned, and an extra notch in his belt. If some education is "preparation for life," then surely this international camp with outdoor education experiences is an essential and worthwhile part of it.

As a result of the many surveys and studies that have been conducted throughout this location, the feasibility and value of this international camp with outdoor education in the most primitive and still sublime Abruzzi Mountains are very much in evidence. For the purpose of feasibility, in fact, it might be deduced that the intrinsic values of such camping experiences and studies will be three-fold. First, they meet the social needs of the student; second, they meet the intellectual needs of the student; and third, the meet the health needs of the student.

The international camp and outdoor education experience will be an essential part of a child's school experience because it helps to develop the child socially. In this international camp setting, children will learn to live democratically. They will mix with children of various creeds, national origins, races, economic statuses, and abilities. They will assist in planning the program that will be followed during their camp stay. They will assume part of the responsibility for the upkeep of this international camp, such as making their own beds, helping in the kitchen, sweeping their cabins, and maintaining the tennis courts; and they will experience cooperative living. The children will get away from home and from their parents. They will lose their feeling of dependency upon others and learn to do things for themselves. This is especially necessary in modern society, where divorce, separation, and the desire of mothers to seek careers of their own are so prevalent. The child will learn to rely on his own resources. The international camp with outdoor education experience will also provide an enjoyable experience for the child. He will be naturally active and seek adventure. This experience will provide the opportunity to release some of this adventure and satisfy the "wonderlust" urge.

The international camp and outdoor education experience will be an essential part of a child's school experience because it will help to develop the child intellectually. While living in this camping and outdoor education setting, the child will learn about such things as soil, forests, water, and animal and bird life. He will learn about the value of the nation's natural resources and how they should be conserved. He will learn by doing rather than through the medium of textbooks. Instead of looking at the picture of a bird in a book, he actually sees the bird chirping on the branch of a tree. Instead of reading about soil erosion in a textbook, he will see how it really occurs. Instead of being told about the seven basic groups of food, he will have the opportunity to live on a diet that meets the right standards. Instead of reading about the values of democratic living, he will actually experience it. The child will experience many new things that he cannot possibly experience at home or within the four walls of a school building. This style of camping will also be of special value to children who do not learn easily from books. In many cases, the knowledge accumulated through actual experience will be much more enlightening and beneficial.

The international camp and outdoor education experience will be an essential part of a child's school experience because it will help to meet the health needs of the child. This international camp will be located away from the turmoil, confusion, and noise of urban life. Children will experience having their meals at regular times, obtaining sufficient sleep, and participating in wholesome activities in the out-of-doors. They will wear clothing that they are not afraid to get dirty, that does not restrict movement and permits the absorption of healthful sun rays. The food will be good. They will do things that are natural for them to do. It will be an outlet for their dynamic personalities. It will be much more healthful, both physically and mentally, than living a "push-button" existence, with its lack of recreation, relaxation, and opportunity for enjoyable experiences. It will be like living in another world; the children will come away from such an experience refreshed.

Outdoor education at the international camp in the midst of Abruzzi's mountains will cut across areas of studies and subject matter lines. It will apply equally to art, science, physical education, or home economics. Opportunities for outdoor education will be unlimited in this international camp's environment. In addition to the fields, woods, and potential facilities and equipment, many private or public sanctuaries, museums, parks, camps, farms, and other local resources can be used for such purposes.

Outlined here are some common avenues for the outdoor education at this international camp:

1. *Classroom-Related Experiences.* The trip into the outdoors becomes a "lab" period related to planned activities in the curriculum. They may be short trips to the camp site or extended experiences in connection with a special field, such as science, physical education, conservation, or recreation.
2. *School Ranch, Farm, Forest, and Garden Programs.* This international camp will have its own facilities and access to lands that will serve as laboratories. Private farms near the location can offer general

instructional opportunities, as well as a place for agricultural practices. In specific areas, these programs will include a suitable ranch where children have the opportunities to live together, observe and care for farm animals, participate in gardening, and roam over the wooded "back forty." Gardening may be one of the most practical activities in this outdoor education because of its recreational value.

3. *Extended Educational Programs.* One of the newest and most sensational developments in this international camp will be the use of outdoor education for an extended educational program, whereby democratic social living will be combined with learning about the natural environment and adventures in outdoor living. In this Extended Educational Program, children and teachers, together, will have direct learning experiences related to many areas of the curriculum.

4. *Day Activities and Club Activities.* Such activities will usually be considered part of curricular offerings and will be provided for organized special-interest groups. While usually conducted on an informal basis, such activities may be related to areas including physical education and recreation, science, and others. Activities will often include camping, hiking, and other student interests, such as archery, arts and crafts, and bird study. Day activities in this international camp will be used by affiliated schools, colleges, recreation agencies, and youth-serving groups. Special classes and different organized groups will also have opportunities for field study combined with the outdoor recreational skills.

5. *Winter Sports and Others.* Skating, skiing, toboganning, showshoeing, and other winter sport activities will be included. These activities are gaining in popularity in this location, and programs of this international camp may offer appropriate training for participation in such activities. Other sports will be related to specific interests, such as hunting and traveling, and will be related to safety, conservation, and outdoor skills.

6. *Adult Outdoor Education and Recreation.* A wide variety of activities will be offered in keeping pace with the public's great surge of interest in many outdoor activities for adults. Some of these adults may focus on their hobbies, such as making outdoor equipment and training for advanced skills in outdoor sports.

The international camp with outdoor education will be set up and run primarily for young people, a place in which they live more or less in a world of their own, working, playing, worshipping, and carrying on the various activities of living under the watchful eye of a qualified staff of adult counselors and other responsible staff personnel. This international camp will be located in a spot of rustic beauty in a remote and somewhat isolated area.

The type of this international camp will be known as a resident camp, where campers will spend their sleeping as well as waking hours for a period of several nights, weeks, or months. It will have its own personality and, consequently, not exactly like any other camp in existence. Nevertheless, most of its programs will have certain points of similarity. It will be a large and elaborately equipped camp, where there will be acres of trees, paths through trees, and some sort of water. There will be rustic cabins, tepees, Adirondack shacks, and tents on wooden platforms for the campers to live in, as well as a common dining room, a lodge or recreation building, a handicraft shop or workshop, sanitary facilities including showers, a well-equipped kitchen, a camp office, tool houses, and sheds for caretakers. Various other buildings would be scattered about to provide shelter for the health center, trading post, counselors' retreat, nature museum, and library and to house supplies and equipment for trips out of camp.

In the open, there will be a large riding ring, a stable for horses, ranges for archery and rifle, an outdoor swimming pool, an outdoor chapel, an amphitheater, a council ring, and several outpost campsites where campers could go to sleep and cook out. There will also be fields and courts for such organized sports as tennis, archery, badmitton, horseshoes, golf, baseball, and football.

This international camp will be quite a thriving community. A modern, fairly large camp will represent an investment of hundreds of thousands of dollars. Yet, as with most other great institutions, this international camp will be on a very modest scale, and it will be interesting to follow its development through the years.

Aspr Surd

A Bridge with Three Double Lanes of Traffic in Abruzzi

A cooperative endeavor to efficiently meet the regional environmental problems: Project American University of Avezzano (Cleveland, Ohio); Instituto Studi Abruzzesi (Pescara, Italy); Abruzzi Regional Governments (National-Local)

It was already stated that the projected works and studies inherent to the proposed campus at Avezzano were conceived as a philosophical-educational bridge between the country in which the author was born and the country in which the same author and promoter received his college education. This bridge, so defined, was envisioned as essentially providing a new and unique university, its curriculum well-balanced in health and physical education and their training programs, in the liberal arts and sciences, as well as cultural-tourism exchange programs, located in Italy.

In crossing and traveling this bridge, some of the project's analysis took place, work-implementation was made, and a comparative study for the purpose of project-research was undertaken. The analogy is related closely to the problem of actual projected traffic on one side of the bridge and avoiding confusion and delay. Thus, with all the respect to the bridge analogy, the problem exists. It is connected directly to the project's endeavor, and is relevant, valid, and feasible. It must be said that, regretfully, this problem was interpreted and related to other smaller and bigger regional problems, detrimental and discouraging for any progress.

It is quite known that traffic and congestion represent the character of a city and, more appropriately, a portrait of its society. Traffic is where the people are, and the majority of them now live in urban areas that cover a small percentage of its land area. Still more travel to the central city each day to work. Studying this traffic problem that parallels the course of this bridge shows that the amount of traffic within a few-mile radius of a regional major city center is four to seven times as great is it is outside these areas. Here are the constituent elements of day and evening traffic jams and worker psychosis when all of them want to go home at the same time. Here, also, are the elements of the city's parking problems: the capacity of already insufficient traffic lanes further reduced by parked cars. Here, also, is the political engineer's excuse for those Autostrade on vast embankments of fill that are now splitting apart so many long-established communities. These are "desire lanes," directed by a single purpose—automobile traffic speed—with no thought given to the possible social, economic, and esthetic side effects. Nor, indeed, to the problem of where to park all the cars that the new Autostrade will bring to the city center.

Motorists cannot be shoppers, workers, or cinema-goers until the car is parked at the right place and they can basically can afford to do so. The new road construction has been, to a large extent, the great arterial highways (often toll roads), which speed traffic only between one area and another, but evidently also increase traffic congestion within the central city area by dumping an increased traffic load on the unimproved street system. At the same time, the improved highway and Autostrade seems to encourage more of some of the region's natives to leave quickly for harder and often unknown destinations. More sophisticated motorists still drive their cars downtown rather than take some other form of transportation. This increases still further the congestion within the city and emphasizes the disparity in size between approach roads, on the one hand, and parking facilities and city streets on the other. It is as though some drunken planner had zoned the roads in reverse.

Still, the great percentage of travelers, particularly the inhabitants of this area, for obvious reasons will continue on the same old roads. City or town streets carry almost the total vehicle-miles. These local streets, as is expected, will continue to attempt the hopeless compromise of carrying the project traffic efficiently while at the same time serving as a parking garage, a pedestrian walk-way, a political forum, a retail shopping area, a play space for children, a track for local buses and other buses and trucks, an interant hiring hall for taxis, and often as a processional way where businessmen, politicians, churchmen, lazy-men, and others burst out in their costumes.

Obviously the need here is for specialization. Nevertheless, it must be pointed out that there's a need to attack this and other problems in a cooperative and constructive effort. Hence, the projected international campus at Avezzano is not concerned only with the pursuit of knowledge and the training of its students. As a matter of fact, in recent years, such preoccupation has perforce been widened under economic pressures of a concerned society and government for the increased involvement of the university in the affairs and problems of the times, including adequate numbers of efficient specialists. Even in its unique role and with its limitations, this projected university shall have an essential part to play in local and regional development, providing training through higher education and other services. Higher education is central to economic growth, not only through this projected American University of Avezzano but also within an inter-related pattern of all types of technological, academic, commercial, or social science-based institutions.

In a direct sense, inadequate higher education provisions in a region impoverishes the supply of a trained elite and, furthermore, detracts somewhat from the general quality of the cultural or living environment. Through the multiplier effect on the general services, the presence of a very well-equipped institution, such as the projected University of Avezzano, shall also indirectly make a distinct contribution to the economic growth of the Abruzzi region. In this sense, this institution will have a dual significance in any strategy for growth and development. It will be very much more than a status symbol of international educational respectability. There will be indeed, based on several studies and considerations, a strong case for incorporating phased investment for this higher education provision within the ground-plan of any international or regional development program.

The pressures are of course considerable, and they are not absent in the Abruzzi region, for the local universities to produce the numbers and kinds of specialists in the areas of studies required to meet the needs of the local and nationwide communities in the immediate future. Because the approach of this projected university of international character would be an ever more costly process, the expenditure will largely be borne by the Promoting Committee supporting the project; such direction, some critics would say distortion, of the purposes of this university will be increasingly difficult to resist, either in principle or in practice. Indeed, this "projected philosophical bridge" should tend to relate most efficiently to the regional development process. There may, in addition, also have to be some exchange service for the needs of regional cultural tourism, industry, and commerce. Even without some bending or enlargement of the main purposes of the projected University of Avezzano to include some service to regional and maybe national needs, there will be likely be continuing benefit from the general research of individual scholars, even if not carried out with an applied purpose in mind.

Fundamental research will always be based on the possibility of practical application, but clearly there will be also a break point where fundamental research will be guided or harnessed precisely in order to further practical outcomes. There, of course, will be a continuous spectrum between the cumulative benefits derived from random, unplanned scholarly contributions and, at the other extreme, carefully planned, phased, and integrated programs in which particular scholars, disciplines, or departments of this institution will be assigned a role and financed from appropriate funds, either by outside agencies or industry or government grants.

It may be useful to look at and examine briefly the stages of this certainly progressive and innovative implication of the projected university. For instance, individual consultancy is the most straightforward and traditional form in which scholars in pure and applied sciences or other disciplines would be cited for the solving of particular problems on a personal contract basis. Here, these problems will involve close and continuing contact between the projected university's faculty and the regional community. It will be, without any doubt, an advantage to the specialists within and connected with this university campus, who are going to generate some relationship to the characteristics and needs of the regional resources in terms of tourism, commerce, and industry.

It is a prerogative of this project, however, to explore and accordingly concentrate in all its fields of application a team or group, which shall be the most effective way of organizing to solve real-life problems. Allied with this will be the need to promote interdisciplinary thinking and work within the intellectual climate of the campus and its affiliate institutions. Such interdisciplinary groups must ideally have both an academic and a practical purpose and be concerned with intellectual exchange between the disciplines to their mutual advantage, but primarily focused on contributions to common problem-solving. Such involvement shall be clearly advantageous to both the giving and receiving institutions and connected communities, particularly when such problem-solving relates to real-life situations with intellectual feedback.

The problem of research integration presented here is an analogy to a "bridge with three double lanes of traffic," involving the projected University's Campus of Avezzano in one lane and regional institutions or organizations (like the Abruzzi Studies Institute) and regional-national government on other lanes. Following this pattern, very much remains to be done if the greatest benefits will be accrued at least cost and with maximum satisfaction to all three parties. Particular types of relationships at this point merit some consideration:

> *1st Lane*—The projected American University of Avezzano, national and regional governments, regional institutions (Abruzzi Studies Institute)

> *2nd Lane*—The projected American university's developments; national-regional tourism, trade, development agencies; governments.

> *3rd Lane*—The projected American University's centers, local governments, scientific-technological organizations, and industries.

There are now many embryonic organizations developing on the same basis in various limited forms and often for specific short-term objectives; there are many other possible interinstitutional approaches and alternatives.

At the base of all should be some kind of interdisciplinary committee within the projected American University of Avezzano's framework, perhaps resulting from a combination of university representatives and all relevant higher educational-cultural-developmental institutions within the region and state and from other countries. Adequate financing is required for continuity; if such a project is to flourish, there also should be integration within the teaching life of the same projected Campus of International Character and a continuity of research involvement with outside problems, probably on a contract basis, which almost certainly will require a corpus of full-time research workers from this university. The rapport between the research workers and the academic staff would be a two-way advantages and enable the American University of Abezzano's contribution to be most effectively made.

A second, more promising "lane flow" on the projected "bridge" could also be an American University of Avezzano, state and regional government, industry-trading complex. Basic to this notion is that technological innovation in science-based growth industries will be likely to originate, at least in part, within the project's fundamental research approach. The development of such a project within an industrial or commercial framework must require, furthermore, close collaboration between the American University of Avezzano, the research innovator, and those agencies and industries concerned with technological development. Such development itself would often offer further opportunities for innovation and continuing research commitments. Hence, the concept of the projected American University of Avezzano's campus and a close partnership with industry in developing inventions or new ideas, among which there might be some confusion and delay, poor incentive and cooperation, and most of all a high commercial-industrial mortality rate and financial instability to the regional community problem.

Developing this concept further, it may be quite feasible to involve the cooperation of other universities or institutions and other industrial concerns in order to develop a more sophisticated research-technological center. Central to this endeavor must be the common use of an up-to-date technology complex, allied with the intellectual powerhouse of the connected universities and their research laboratories; the whole, of course, must be located near the campus of the projected American University of Avezzano. State and regional legislation is already provided, mainly to act as a magnet to attract and develop science-based industries, and it is interesting to note efforts and establishment of industrial complexes in some regional area (i.e.; Nuclei Industriali), although it winds-up for the expectation. Some of these regional level developmental projects are very well known for their economic-social status, their difficult problems with unemployment, and the lack of available skilled labor, as well as the need to redeploy men from the declining staple industries to the growth industries already introduced or also being brought with the support and endorsement of government policies. Consequently, part of the regional planning strategy should be concerned with maximum support for promoting the projected American University of Avezzano, which will become a center of a new environment to replace the wornout fabric of its stagnant socio-economic problems.

A cooperative effort so conceived and anticipated must attract additional science-oriented and—based industries and thus directly aid in the process of regional problem-solving. Additionally, there will certainly be a multiplier effect from attracting the research laboratories and production facilities of lead firms in leader industries. This effect will include contributions to and from the regional cultural and living environment experiences made by those presently inadequately represented immigrant executives, teachers, students, visitors, and tourists.

These are but some of the various possibilities available through the "three double lanes of traffic" across the philosophical bridge: the university campus and government and institutions (Istituto Studi Abruzzesi and other feasible associations) to cooperate in problem-solving, plus industry to develop the socio-economic-education process. Policies from such cooperation will, no doubt, vary according to place, time, and organization, but a positive approach to the necessary liaison and wide circulation of the achievements and setbacks involved in such collaboration are highly desirable.

Particular attention to the following is indicated:

1. Define and build up balanced disciplines within the American University of Avezzano, which will directly or indirectly contribute to the regional development process in education, cultural-tourism, industry, commerce, and technology. Work out interdisciplinary arrangements for intellectual and practical collaboration by these disciplines within the university's campus and other affiliated institutions. Create a balanced team from these disciplines, capable of functioning as the directorate of a research group for

collaboration with government and/or industry on applied research projects.

2. Elaborate the liaison arrangements for interchange in the research field among the project American University of Avezzano, government, institutions, and industry. These should cover the research group's proposals, coverage for financing in short—and long-term projects, and mutual agreement on major research objectives.

3. Maximize support for the promotion of science-humanity-technology, the AUA Center. Clearly this must involve concentrated effort and be unique nationally, even though there would be strong arguments for locating such developments apart from government promotion policies or regional policy balance in supporting development areas.

In conclusion, such a multiple purpose "bridge" will be likely to generate "traffic lanes" of growth and a healthy economy, and it is quite optimistic to affirm that their direct and indirect contributions to immediate regional problems will be also potentially outstanding. To be successful, the collaboration should include positive and reliable commitment by all the concerned parties. Finally, there is a little to fear and much to gain from such involvement for every organization or institution, each individual or community, especially if governments (local and national) and related communities accept, as they must, their increasing, indeed inevitable, responsibilities to the life of the project and any long-term problems.

One week was spent in the north of Italy (Milan, Domodossola, Macugnaga) where by phone and correspondence the colonel provided to attend the ceremony of the Corpo Guardia di Finanza, held in Milan, with me and my son. The ceremony itself and being back among members of "Fiamme Gialle," and especially the feelings from that "esprit de corps," certainly made it worthwhile and a little difficult to describe in a few words. An excursion was planned to Domodossola on the route to Macugnaga (Monte Rosa, Alps). A visit was made to the frontier post at the Domodossola railroad station where old memories and exchange of information about old comrades were shared with Finanzieri in service at time. The reception was warm, cordial, and illuminating in many different aspects of learning about new and common old experiences of work and achievement.

Once at Macugnaga, at the foot of Monte Rosa's glacier, in Valle Anzasca near the Swiss border, a few thoughts were put together before starting to climb to the glacier. A survey of the location was made and a few pictures taken. An analysis of rock samples collected from specific points of the location helped to reinforce my thesis for a feasibility study of Petrolio Roccioso in Italy (See related material: Description of the Monte Rosa's Glacier as an Introduction of Petrolio Roccioso in Specific Areas of Italy).

After few days spent at my family reunion and visiting friends and relatives, a meeting was scheduled with my lawyer in Avezzano to discuss the litigation pending at the local tribunal regarding the projected AUA vs. the city hall of Avezzano and the newspaper *Il Tempo, Pagina Marsicana.* This meeting was conducted informally, and only few written notes were taken to list specific documentation requested by the lawyer. Those documents must be submitted to the court in order for the judge in charge of the litigation to be able to make the case's final decision. According with my lawyer's explanation, some documents were missing from the tribunal's file, or they were not submitted when the summons was introduced. Reassurance that those document were submitted to the court had to be proven by comparing the file from the judge's desk with my personal copy. The missing documentation included: Projected AUA's financial statement and cost analysis of the first phases of the campus buildings, facilities, and operation. Evidently these important documents were missing from the Avezzano's tribunal without any plausible and convincing reasoning. At this point, a decision was made to check and verify all documents deposited with the Court in another meeting scheduled for one week later in our native hometown; Cocullo. That meeting was held at my lawyer's family home; attending were just the lawyer and myself, and the tone of discussion became very friendly and informal. Fragmentary notes of these discussions were taken and most of the questions and answers were given and taken orally; no transcript or recording device was used. Once again, page by page the documents from the Avezzano tribunal were checked and verified with my personal file. The only documents missing were those submitted at previous meeting. Therefore, my lawyer requested that those documents be sent to him as soon as possible (**). To the specific question asked, once again reassurance came from my lawyer there was a 100 percent chance of winning the case. But when asked about the possibility to have a solution for the delivery of the land's title from the city hall of Avezzano or by means of other legal instrument from the tribune, he stated that the delivery of the land contract was over; nothing could be done within the spirit and nature of related council deliberations. As a matter of fact, he pointed out that building residential villas was in process on the site proposed and defined for the Campus of International Character. With this information, no more questions were asked concerning Avezzano's promised land. I would have to send just the documents requested for now, as far as the litigation pending in Avezzano's tribunale was concerned.

The remaining time at the meeting and other discussions was focused on the possibilities of using the specific studies, proposals, and project work completed in the areas defined as colleteral business activities and/ or endowment projects submitted to the lawyer on previous occasions. Suggestions were given to implement some aspects of these activities in Cocullo, my own town. My lawyer is personally aware of the importance of my work performed and the potential of results that could be attached to this specific location. He anticipates no major block to develop activities related to livestock, especially for sheep, swine, and cattle (See: Studies and Proposals of Projected Sirente Ranch.) There should be no legal problem to implement some phases of these studies and projects insomuch as the material is authored and promoted by myself. It will not interfere with the case pending at Avezzano's tribunal. Although suggestions received offered a positive outlook, it was also agreed to make a more accurate analysis of this location before the final plan is presented to private and government organizations. At this time, another invitation was offered to my lawyer to visit the state of Ohio in order to be able to better understand some aspects of my work performed in connection with these specific projects in Italy. He accepted the invitation, but he will take the trip only when the case at Avezzano's tribunal is over. For the lawyer it is just "a matter of principle," as was personally stated few times.

---

*   They are sent and phone confirmations followed as soon as my lawyer received them.

A meeting was also scheduled with Generals of ANFI, in Rome, to inform them of Project AUA's status, the impasse of the litigation, as well as future plans of ANFI activities in the United States. Unfortunately, this meeting had to be postponed because my briefcase, where material and documentations of projects in Italy were kept, was stolen. (See claim to Police Department in Rome). This briefcase was found after few days at the Gregorian University of Rome. My lawyer was notified by a university official to inform me that I could claim the briefcase from the receptionist at the university. Only a book and my eye glasses were missing; the rest of material and documentation were not damaged, just disorganized. It took a while to put all the pieces together. Only one thing was found to be a little bit strange; on the top of the first file was a label that said: "Inspected by a Number One".

A few phone calls were made to the colonel in Milan, to thank him for his kind assistance in North Italy and to also inform him of my impressions traveling around the peninsula (See: Analysis from the Extreme North to Extreme South of Italy, June-July '82).

Finally, a visit to the generals of ANFI, who learned of past and future programs for the Association, my personal feelings and attachments, and my respect for a noble institution, which its motto describes: "*Nec Recisa Recedit.*"

Thank you very much for the attention and consideration.

Around Italy

Trip to Italy, June-July 1982

I thought for awhile before taking another excursion around Italy, but those thoughts were challenged by an old man (one of my old but still very young friends) with whom I used to talk and walk under those familiar trees, sometime discussing matters under one of those big umbrellas with blue and white stripes. He was still alive and staying there in his homeland. We had exchanged a few words and salutations early in our previous meeting. He had offered something to drink, and after I had ordered my cappupccino freddo, we sat side by side and talked in our familiar language, without concentrating on the proper accent, grammar, syntax, and other formalities. He was and still is the typical old man of my country, such as one sees in every location in Italy, with a strong face and sturdy frame. "These youngsters today are looking pretty happy," I remarked, as a group of them marched by with their Italian soccer flag. He shrugged his shoulders and drank some of his coffee. "It is all wrong," he answered. "It is just another great parade." My old friend was loud and careless about being overheard. "The whole system is wrong," he continued. "They are marching steadily toward disaster." Personally I found that hard to believe, by the new look of that familiar location, and especially the surrounding communities, where everything looked prosperous. Thewaiter in his impeccable suit looked like the owner of a private yacht. A luxurious car arrived, depositing an elegant young man in search of a drink, plus two lovely ladies in filmy transparent garments; I recalled when to greet them was just a matter of an eye expression. "The government," said my friend, careless of being overheard, "builds roads to create work. It distributes money for food to political cronies and the professionally unemployed. It gives the people with political luck expensive trips to resort areas and back. All very nice for them, of course. But who buys Italian produce or Italian goods? Who helps the Italian manufacturers and businessman, who have been ruined—who are already ruined, like me?"

"As bad as that?" I asked.

"Worse than that," he said, looking across those mountain peaks as though staring at a scene of ruin and calamity, instead of having before his eyes a vision of dreamlike beauty. "Property in Italy," he said, "is without any real common sense value. How can a nation carryon when that happens? It is ridiculous to be a business-oriented man of prosperity in Italy because one is the victim of the government, corrupt politicians, bureaucracy, and all kinds of political parties that take away everything and then ask for more. One is robbed while the political cronies may have expensive trips to selective resort locations, inside and outside Italy, and, look at the new way of living, made as an experience and of course as a memorial to their "Godfather" 's politicians. One is robbed also for public works that are unproductive. One is robbed to maintain an army of servants for corrupt politicians, bureaucrats, and an army of petulant professional crooks. One is robbed until all one's profits have disappeared and until one declares oneself bankrupt. All that is mockery under another name. The corporations of which you hear and see so much are the same kind of people under another name. Everything now being done in Italy is a step towards another new government formula. The men of positive initiatives are disposed. Business profits are nonexistent. Only the politicians and bureaucrats have priviledges, and those will not last much longer because the nation itself is bankrupt."

From the interior of the good-looking foreign-made luxury car, into which the elegant young man and the two lovely ladies had now returned, came the blare of the radio's sport report. It was shouting out the results of the victorious national soccer team in the World Cup, the major summer sport event in Italy and around the world. "Who," asked my old friend, "will buy a business that is overwhelmed with debts?" I had no answer for that question. "As you are aware, I own a business," he told me. "A business that was worth millions of lire before the arrival of the last few government regimes. Now, if you like, I will let you have it for a few dollars. But I do not advise you to accept this offer. There are no profits; there are many debts; the government sends the officials to me with a demand for a new taxation. I say, 'Take over my business for a year; what profit it makes you shall have in payment of taxes.' They made a grimace and would not accept. They knew too much." Another group of young soccer fans passed nearby in a parade of cars, signing and shouting that Italy won another soccer game. My friend accepted another drink. It was the least I could offer to a businessman whose heart was bankrupt. "It is, of course, an advantage to be bankrupt these days," he said with sudden cheerfulness. "Formerly it was a great disgrace. Now it is almost a virtue. It is even the way to advancement, if one becomes a crook. The greater the crook, the greater the honor. He gets the best jobs. He must be a clever man, they think. That is so in most countries today. One country makes its crooks cabinet ministers. In another it becomes normal for a kind of crook in wheeling and dealing in terms of political and economic peculiarity to even make president. In the United States, perhaps in that kind of society, it is a little different. Though you have your clever corporate executives." Another group with the Italian flag marched along, shouting, "We won, we won." My stout old man regarded them with a big smile. "I have a little nephew," he said. "He's a six-year-old boy. When he went to school for the first time he was asked to bring 50,000 lire. He brought them. He became enrolled in the soccer program, and the first thing he was taught was to kick and head the soccer ball. Every baby born in Italy now becomes ipso facto a soccer player, as in the United States a baseball player or football player. No question about it. No case of conscientious conviction and mental participation is the problem. There you are, my good friend; this is soccer now for you to learn, and don't squeal about it. Wonderful, isn't it?" He spoke with a laughing bitterness and then turned to me with a kind of apology for such gloom. "The truth is," he said, "I am disgusted with this kind of life. I remember life before and after the war. It was still a good old world, good-natured, with a sense of peace. If a man worked hard he made a little money. If he saved it, its value seemed secure. If he did not care for saving, he spent it on giving happiness to other people and himself with a generous hand. Life then was charming, gay, light-hearted. We were not all thinking of war, rivalry, group disputes, or oil, chemicals, and poison gas.

"In the United States, for instance, where I lived for several years before you did, learning the language, working hard, going to school, and become a young businessman, it was peaceful and free and tranquil. There was liberty for liberal opinions. One could say what one liked, even if it were nonsense!

Now, in Italy, Europe, East and West as well as North and South America, who can say what he likes? Where is liberty of thought? Where is happiness?" He shook hands with me politely. "I have enjoyed this conversation," he said. "It is always nice to meet a good friend again. One can speak one's mind freely." He departed from me, leaving me a sadder and a wiser man. If he had told me the truth, and I believed him, Italy today was not as prosperous as it looked. Storm clouds were creeping across the blue sky.

I reported my conversation to another much younger friend of mine living in Italy, who laughed heartily. "Oh! To meet even one man," he said, "who will acknowledge that he is not prosperous! I know Italy pretty well. I assure you that for the majority the standard of living has gone up prodigiously."

"But will it last?" I asked. "The old friend who has just left me is convinced that people are being supported by fake wealth that is almost exhausted. *Panem et cicenses*—can a nation exist on that philosophy? Didn't its people come to grief that way nearly two thousand years ago?"

"It is nothing like that," he said, "my good friend. The Italian peasant is a hard worker. Italian youth in the factory are working keenly. The new government leaders with a new formula in politics have brought about a new renaissance. Italy is now one of the great powers, whereas she was disintigrating and demoralized, and lurching into anarchy. We already won the soccer World Cup, and as you know we are Number One again."

At this point I acknowledged some of the truth in this reassurance, but I had a doubt in my mind. It was certainly true the Italian worker was and still is industrious, at least those few who work. Had I not passed a few of them in the fields? Had I not seen them bending over a poor patch of earth on those familiar mountainsides scores of times, in my memories and on other trips to Italy? But what will happen if they cannot sell their products? What will happen if the things they made in the factories could not find new markets? How could they carry on if all the businessmen were advancing towards bankruptcy? Perhaps it was not quite as bad as that. Things are never quite so bad or quite so good as men are inclined to say when they get talking. The search after truth has to strike something of each side. I had to start to make my personal analysis from the extreme North to the extreme South of Italy (See related materials).

From the Extreme North to the Extreme South

What Is Italy Today?
(An Economic and Social Analysis of the Country)

The topic "What is Italy Today?" focuses on an economic and social analysis from the extreme north to the extreme south of the peninsula.

Understanding the answer to this question will greatly help in understanding Italy, the United States, and other countries as well. The standard of living of each country depends upon the natural resources it has and the use it makes of their resources. The things a country doesn't make must be bought from other countries, and it pays for these products by the sale of its own surplus goods. The products a country buys are called imports, and the products it sells are called exports. No country can keep on buying more than it sells, any more than anyone could keep on spending more money than received. It is necessary to find out what Italy has and what she must buy from other countries. At first look, it seems that every effort has been made by the Italians to stimulate and increase their output of agricultural products. They have been hampered in some areas by poor soil and lack of farmland, plus a lack of modern techniques and advanced technologies and scientific methods. In such a country it is necessary to make use of every bit of land referred to in studies and project proposals about specific areas of concern and to take great pains to refertilize the soil. For instance, present and past governments have spent a great deal of money and time in filling in a huge gap of zoological problems, especially in these specific areas already defined in Central and South Italy. In other sections of Italy it is easy to find corn, grapes, olives, tomatoes, lemons, oranges, hemp, beans, oats, potatoes, sugar beets, barley, rice, chestnuts, and silk culture. Milk from cows, goats, and sheep is used to make many different kinds of cheese, such as romano, parmigiano, provolone, et cetera. Consider also some manufacturing. Silk and rayon goods are made, as well as cord and coarse linen from hemp. Cotton goods are also manufactured from cotton that is imported, mostly from the United States. The automobile industry is important; among the automobiles made are Fiat, Lancia, Alfa Romeo, Maserati, and Ferrari.

With these resources Italy has, one might think she has ample resources to support her people. Yet, when visiting the many small farms throughout Italy, a very low standard of production output is found. The families living in towns or on the farms sometimes manage to raise enough foodstuffs for their own use, but they have no surplus for marketing. Because of wrong and changing policies from the many governments in power in the last few decades, as well as other considerations, many Italian families have moved from the countryside and towns into overpopulated cities and immigrated to North and South America, Australia, and to some of the northern European countries. This should have made it easier for those remaining to get a bigger share of what there was left. In addition, these immigrants send money back to their kinfolk in Italy so that they might buy the things they need.

From the above analysis it must be admitted that in general farmlands are poor, and as a result, Italy has not been able to raise sufficient agricultural products for its people. Corn has to be imported. Wheat growing has barely reached the point where their own demands are satisfied. However, the major items Italy must import are coal, petroleum, iron, copper, wool, and meat. Without these items a country cannot exist. Italy must have these products and must find a means of paying for them. It is important to see what Italy has done to pay these tremendous bills.

As has been said before, a country pays for its imports by its exports. What can Italy export to other countries? Grapes are made into wine, and Italian wines are sold all over the world. After World War II and during the present time Italy had hoped to ship great quantities of wine to Canada and the USA., but this still is mere illusion. California can supply all the wine that is wanted, and it could start exporting everywhere, including Italy. Italian vermouth, for instance, and some other special brands, however, do have a sizeable market in the United States and some other countries. Olive oil pressed from olives is exported, and the United States buys a great deal of it. Canned tomatoes and tomato paste are sold to the rest of the world, largely because the Italian farmer raises a small plum-shaped tomato that is tastier than the large round tomatoes. But again competition steps in. Packers in California as well as in other parts of the United States are now growing the Italian-type tomato on a commercially profitable scale, and of course they can be sold much cheaper than the canned tomatoes shipped from Italy, on which there is a high tarriff. Strange as it may see, some of these packers in the United States are Italians who have been shipping canned tomatoes from Italy to the United States; now the process is reversed. They are now raising tomatoes in several different regions in the United States and canning them there. In a way they are competing with themselves. All the tomatoes for the American market are grown in these regions and other states now, and thus Italy has lost another market for her goods. These Italian packers cannot be blamed for taking this step, for if they did not do it, someone else would, and they would not be able to sell their Italian tomatoes anyway. A good deal of Italian cheese is exported, plus some oranges and lemons. Of course, the United States no longer buys these oranges and lemons, as California and Florida produce these fruit in quantity. As a matter of fact, Italy must compete with the United States in other countries' markets for the sale of her citrus fruits. The United States at present still imports much of the Italian cheese, but efforts are being made in Wisconsin and some other regions to imitate and eliminate the Italian cheese at the same time. These efforts have met with relative success; if enough is produced to satisfy the demand, the cheese manufacturers of the United States will probably take over other foreign markets at will. The question is: what effect will this have on the Italian cheese industry?

Italy exports silk and finds that Japan is her strong competitor. Japan is capturing more and more of the world markets every day, because her workers are producing more at lower costs, so she can sell at lower prices than anyone else. It may be possible that in a few years this means of livelihood will be nonexistent in Italy. After mentioning all of the difficulty Italy has had in selling her goods, it will be no surprise to learn that, in the past, it has imported much more than it has exported. However, Italy had two other sources of income. One was the money received from millions of Italians who immigrated and sent money back home. Another was the money spent by tourists visiting Italy. What has happened lately to these two sources of income? With the problem of unemployment and of the economy all over the world, Italians living outside of Italy have no money to send home. For the same reason, very few people have the money for traveling.

The pressure of economic conditions all over the world makes it difficult for Italy to balance her imports against her exports. First, every country tries to keep out foreign products. It has been seen in the United States with lemons and oranges and probably with cheese and, of course, canned tomatoes in the future. Second, each country makes even greater attempts to sell its products in other countries. For instance, Sunkist oranges from California are competitive with Sicilian oranges in France, England, and Germany. Japanese silk and silk goods are underselling Italian products all over the world. What is Italy to do? Nature has not been very generous to her, and now things are worse than ever. One can only guess at some of the things that can happen. Here are listed a few of them.

1. Unless there is an unforseen change in world economic conditions, Italians will have to get along with fewer luxuries, such as smaller newspapers and fewer automobiles, new clothes, politicians, lawyers, doctors, professors, et cetera.

2. They will have to increase efforts to raise as much wheat, livestock, corn, and potatoes as they need and plan their meals entirely from homegrown products. (Proposed "'Sirente Ranch" studies already submitted.)

3. They will buy as little as possible from other nations, restricting imports to absolute necessities and buy them only from nations that in turn will buy Italian products. (A two-way traffic proposal—see material submitted, Campus of International Character.)

4. They will try to find energy substitutes, such as using methane alcohol made from fruits and vegetables and motor fuel instead of gasoline, or using new technology for oil discovery such as shale oil technology from some local rocks (See "Technical Report on Petrolic Roccioso"). Water power has been already used to a large extent in order to produce electricity. Thus, the importing of coal is reduced. (A survey done on Monte Rosa, Roccaraso, and other sites, see report and pictures to introduce "Petrolio Roccioso in Italy").

5. They will make every effort to draw out more natural resources. Italy has excellent rock deposits similar to shale oil in the United States. It may be costly to mine these rocks, but on the other hand, there are hundreds of thousands of unemployed who must be supported by the state, and they may just as well be used to

mine the rock, no matter how difficult it is. (See: Study of Petrolio Roccioso in Italy).

6. They will try to attract as many tourists to Italy as possible by offering them cheap rates in hotels, restaurants, and railroads, even cheaper than to Italians themselves. This is already happening. (See: Study Parking Garage and Tourism Projects Proposal Recreation Centers Study in Italy's Regions.)

7. They will help whatever industry can sell their goods outside of Italy by giving them money in some form. These industries can then undersell others and bring money back to Italy. At the same time, workers in these industries will also be called upon, as they have already been called up, to work for less and less money, just as is happening in Japan and in certain industries in the United States

8. They will establish more and more co-op activities or self-sustaining family farms. Life on these farm units may not be on a high standard, but it is better than starving to death in some slum of a big city.

For years to come there is no other alternative. For now, *"Tutti i nodi sono arrivati al pettine,"* which means there are no other alternatives but to work and produce.

Thank you very much for your attention.

Aspr Surd

To Whom It May Concern;

The Enclosed "Study to Introduce Petrolio Roccioso to Specific Locations In Italy" is the content from the Italian version. This material will be addressed to a Roman and Milan forum composed of a few distinct persons.

Suggestions and critiques are welcomed. Please send them to the author at the address below. Thanks very much.

Enclosures

Introduction of "Petrolio Roccioso" (P.R.) To Specific Locations of Italy

June-July, 1982

Famous Hotel "Esplanade" in Pescara where meetings and discussions related to undertaken Project activities are carried on during the course of years.

Introducing "Petrolio Roccioso" (P.R.) at Specified Locations of Italy (Glacier of Monte Rosa and other specific mountain sites)

"Until a person is committed, there is a hesitancy, a chance to draw back, always ineffectiveness. Concerning all acts of initiatives (the creativity working approach), there is one elementary truth; the ignorance of which kills countless ideas and splendid plans: that the moment one definitely commits oneself, then providence moves too. All sorts of things occur that would never otherwise have occurred. A whole stream of events issues from the decision, raising one's favor al manner of unforeseen incidents and meetings and material assistance, which no man could have dreamed would have come his way. A great lesson to have learned, above all, a deep respect for those couplets: "Whatever you can do or dream you can, begin it. Boldness has genius, power, and magic in it."

by Goethe

Introduction to the location and personal feelings. This introduction of Italy's specific areas, especially the Monte Rosa Alps, is presented here as an exercise in self-fulfillment, one's inner strength spent in daily living and daily confrontation with one's own environment, which is renewed from different sources: satisfaction, human relationships, artistic and scientific understanding, religious and philosophic conviction, personal achievement in works and professional pursuit. My own renewal certainly comes quite often from visiting these mountains, my special background. As a matter of fact, these mountains will never cease to mean home for me. These are the scenes of my first awakenings to the world of the mountain sites, of experiences that could have occurred in any range but for me occured among these familiar peaks. The memory of these mountains does not fade out; it doesn't matter how distant one may be. Consciously, any traveler will make his hills a standard of reference for all mountains that he sees. Unconsciously, one will find the proper shadows and the proper light upon all the mountainways one ever walks. It quite often helps me to remember that there is a legend in Greek mythology telling how the giant Antaneus wrestles with Hercules. Hercules succeeded in downing the strong giant, but again and again Antaneus rose to continue to fight. Finally, Hercules realized that the giant renewed his strength miraculously each time his body touched the soil. His mother was Gaea, the goddess of Earth. In the end, Hercules prevailed by lifting Antaneus into the air and strangling him there. I remembered this legend when visiting Gela in Sicily and also each time I have touched the soil of my mountains. I must admit that my own renewals come from this touch and, no matter what has happened before, I feel I can face once again the demands of life for a time after my communion with the peaks of my home mountains. I have another strong feeling, however, when I am in my mountains, the Alps and Appenini of Italy, a feeling not only for the history of the mountaineer, but also for the importance of these mountains in the history of human civilization and thus of the planet. I am reminded always that I am stepping on historical ground. So many passes are associated with names of ancient and modern events and the people who cross them, so many ruins of medieval castles survive, so many names of places and peaks have Roman roots. Some names, mostly in the valley, are said to have Arab roots, reminders of the Saracens who made incursions into Alcara, Sicily; or in Macugnaga (Monte Rosa location), on the nearby Swiss border: for instance, Piano del Moro or Passo Monte Moro, or Grotta dei Saraceni. Never was I more consciously aware of these historical places, especially from these mountain sites from the first time that I crossed and recrossed them.

Glacier Description of Monte Rosa

When I was in these locations for the first time, there was limited access to the ice and rocks. Only those related to activities in duty and commitments would force a person to "work-study" and look his way up the mountains with some "difficulty." Today, cableways lead easily to the glacier of Monte

Rosa. A cableway goes to the first stop station, from which you can see the main glacier in all its power; the second takes you to within a few feet from the glacier itself. Going up to this glacier I interrupted a climbing excursion just to take a look at the rocks surrounding the site and the bizarre ice formations. I stepped into the station platform and took a few pictures of the locations; the view dramatically changed. In the past I had seen the barren rocks in the chair lift as it ascended the wall before me. Now the dark rocks switched to the white gold of the ice laying in the sun. As the chair lift reached the top, I sat down on one of the boulders. I picked up a few loose pieces of rocks (samples) and new thoughts told me how different the Monte Rosa glacier has been since my first contact with its peaks: the jagged maze of pinnacles and spires, their serrated chasms, and how gloomy the Valley Anzasca was at the time.

There are several glaciers in the surrounding Alps and other places. Some of them are more than four miles long. Most of them move at the rate of 30 to 600 feet a year in distance. It is said that some of the glaciers can move a hundred feet a year. In recent years many glaciers, almost all in Switzerland, have regressed, some at the rate of fifty feet per year. Even in my own experiences visiting this location, I have seen from this Mount Rosa Glacier an ice character before a dry rock that appears smaller. I remember reading that most of the glaciers of this earth combined, not counting those near the Poles, makes up only 2 percent of the total. This glacier also commands the greatest errosive power in evidence. Something of the tough persistance of this glacier in smoothing the rough environment seemed to me reflected in the hardy people in the area, who wrest their livelihood from the mountain. There is no peak in this location which I have directly visited and experienced that may not be climbed with perfect safety by a practiced mountaineer with a good guide and fine weather, under favorable snow conditions, and there is not a peak in this location that may not become dangerous if the climber is inexperienced, the guide incompetent, the weather bad, and the snow unfavorable.

Glacier Sediments and Rocks

Although ice now covers only a small part of the Valley Anzasca, a large part of its surface has been glaciated. Ice moves from the high altitudes of the mountains to the lower grounds, blanketing the lowland areas with a thick cover of glacial sediments, and the land surface has been profoundly modified by erosion, especially in the upper land and the valley. Ice is armed with sedimentary detritus in its lower layers. As it moves over the land surface, it scrapes off the loose soil and rock and abrades the underlying soil and rock floor, produces striae and grooves. The latter may be several meters deep and tens of meters across and may be followed by kilometers in their extreme development. Melted waters flowing in funnels in the lower parts of the glaciers wear away the underlying rocks as they transport sand and gravel. Eroded debris accumulates on the glacier when materials fall on the ice surface from nearby slopes and when it is eroded from the base of the ice. The glacier transports a large volume of sediments, and these are deposited under the ice, or at its snout (see photos).

This sediment has very distinctive ill-sorted texture and is known as till. Individual clasts are often grooved and striated. Gravel-sized clasts show marked elongations in the direction of ice flow. These massive sediments are sometimes banded and often intensely deformed by ice moving over them to produce structures very reminiscent of highly folded rocks. Interbedded with such ill-sorted deposits are layers of better sorted, cross-stratified sands and gravels representing the deposits of englacial or subglacial tunnels through which water flowed. Wide braided plains are developed in front, down to the Valley Ossolana. This is covered with gravel and sand, and they are formed by the seasonal melting of the ice. These sediments are composed of materials resulting from reactions by the surface rock and the earth's crust, the gases and liquids of the atmosphere and hydrosphere, and the biosphere, consisting of organisms and their products.

These reactions, called weathering, produce a veneer of broken-down solid detritus (the regolith), which, then enriched in organic detritus and attached by organic agencies, ultimately produces soil. Products of weathering are carried away from the site of reactions. The process of erosion by various agents influenced by the forces of gravity; the most important of these agents are running water, wind, and ice. The products travel in a solid form as bed load and in solution as solution load; weathering and erosion lead to denudation and the destruction of the upstanding land of the Valley Anzasca. Ultimately, the products of denudation are laid down in a variety of settings, to form an accumulation of sediments in the process known as deposition. After deposition, the unconsolidated sediments are altered to sedimentary rock by diagenesis: a combination of a physical process such as compaction are complex chemical changes. The source rock, in relief, climate, and vegetation control both the amount and the nature of the sediment produced. Transportation produces changes in mineral composition. Many of the minerals of igneous and metamorphic rocks have formed at high temperature and pressure. Generally, however, it is minerals that formed under low pressure and temperature that persist when subjected to conditions on the earth's surface and that are dominant in sediments. The softer and chemically unstable minerals, or rocks, the minerals that cleave and fracture, and the rocks that split most easily undergo a gradual process of preferential elimination from the load of transported sediment.

Oil from Rocks—"Petrolio Roccioso" (P.R.) In Italy

What alternatives are available for Italy rather than importing so much oil? One general alternative is to explore and try to increase supplies of domestic substitutes, such as methane and/or oil from rocks: "Petrolio Roccioso" (P.R.). Discussions about the various alternatives have been exhausted, in a sense, and made public for difficulties connected with them. However, interest in oil from rocks (P.R.) seems to be worth considering, largely based on the enormous amount of oil from rock deposits in some specific areas visited in Italy. Another reason for interest in processing oil from rocks is that process for the production of liquid fuel from P.R. appears to be much less than costs defined in other attempts in other locations with similar processes. This is primarily because oil from rocks contains a very high ratio of hydrogen to carbon, and processing costs tend to correlate directly with the increase in the net H/C ration required. This cost advantage could be somewhat offset by increased materials handling required by rocks. But, on balance, it is expected that liquid synfuel will be produced from rocks. An interest in oil from rocks seems to be sustained also by the fact that the real cost of most oil in Italy will continue to rise, and as a matter of fact, has already surpassed the cost of producing it from rocks. Government assistance is offered to industries on the grounds that:

1. There is a public value, which cannot be directly captured by a company undertaking a P.R. venture, in resolving domestic oil problems.

2. There is need for an immediate start in order to have significant oil from rock production in place.

Oil from rocks—P.R. processing technology—is simple in principle. Oil-rock contains a carbonaceous material called *kerogen*. When t his rock is heated to about 900°F, the kerogen decomposes (this is called pyrolysis) to yield oil (raw P.R.), gas, and residual carbon remaining in the rock. The total solid residue from retorting is known as *spent rock*. Typically, "rich" rocks under consideration yield about twenty to forty gallons of grezzo P.R. per ton of rock heated. Research has been done into other ways of recovering oil from rocks; for example, by extraction with solvents or by the action of micro-organisms. No method other than heating has shown any real potential for commercial application. Oil from rocks processing currently requires about one to four barrels of water per barrel of oil produced. This water is used in P.R. processing itself, as well as for dust control, but the largest single amount, up to half or more of the total, is usually for environmentally acceptable disposal and revegetation of the spent rocks. Water availability, although a problem in some locations visited in Italy, in other specific places is not a problem without a very simple solution. Opinions about its importance as a constraint on production is significant but need not be an absolute economic barrier if institutional regulations are overcome.

Technology Envisioned

Production of oil from rocks on a large scale could provide opportunities for significant technological economies not otherwise realizable. For example: *prompt accellerated development studies, even on small-scale oil from rocks production, should be enlarged in concept and encouraged in educational endeavors in the national Italian interest.* These studies will facilitate, and may be essential to, the technological development that should occur both to reduce current uncertainties and to make informed decisions about the independence of future related industrial projects. Further work should be expedited to justify studies on a more detailed evaluation of the technological opportunities, of their potential economical consequences, and of various structural options that would encourage accelerated development studies. The greatest potential for saving and eliminating the burden cost of mining for surface retorts treats part or all of the surveyed location of Italy, to be considered as a single potential surface mine according to its natural geological configuration of rocks (see pictures taken and description of locations)—even though major aquifer disturbances and other environmental problems would have to be resolved. The largest potential for surface retorting appears to lie in large fluidized bed retorts (reactors), or Transport Line Reactors (TLR). Operations under pressure or with retorting atmosphere other than air should be considered for both fluid and nonfluid retorts, as well as TLR tests, eventually in a work cooperative Refiners faced by a large quantity of P.R. feed are apt (in their traditional way) to develop new refining technologies to handle that feed at significantly lower cost than now foreseen for brute force hydrogenation, followed by conventional petroleum refining. Therefore, it is urgent to enlarge this study of an oil from rocks industry in Italy in order to accelerate the rate of development of related technology. This increase in development would lead above all to a reduction of technical, economic, and environmental uncertainties and put Italy in a position to exploit large-scale P.R. more rapidly, as it is necessary and urgent to do so. A project study involving both the private and public sectors would help and may be essential to accelerate development studies and to seek feasible locations to introduce P.R. (oil from rocks) on the huge scale potentially desired. This is a possible model, as a mechanism for the developmental studies and implementation of the already mentioned and other technologies. An R & D study and project operation could be linked to such undertakings through a wide range of funding, programs, and administrative devices. Two types of further study will be useful for further consideration of P.R. projects in a feasible area in Italy:

1. Possible technological alternatives for a large-scale industry should be hypothesized, and the economics for those alternatives should be estimated. Studies of feasible areas or types of locations would not forecast absolutely accurate costs, but the relative cost could help identify the most promising technologies for further R & D and potential gain relative to current technologies.

2. Various infra—or tie-in structural options for a P.R. industry should be examined in these feasible areas. Options should be described in detail, with the advantages and disadvantages of each. This will contribute to a well-informed choice of an implementation mechanism that best fits policy constraints. Significant cost savings

should be certainly achievable in the mining operation in some of these specific locations already surveyed (reference Fisher assay tests and rock samples collected). However, the enormity of a mining operation moving several thousand tons of rocks per day calls for innovative material-handling approaches, by either identifying old technologies applicable to specific locations or developing new technologies for it: as an example, if labor productivity is not met at a certain demanded level of rock-tons/man-shift in mining. There appear to be no technological barriers for the development, or use, or both, of mine equipment on a much larger scale. Very large conveyors are already available at these specific locations. There may be some difficult environmental problems associated with large-scale mining operations; and it needs an "alternate" study for the required solution. Crucial problems of spent rock disposal may be eased by high-temperature retorting, which seems to reduce both the volume of and the soluble alkalis in the spent rock. Several more speculative suggestions can be made for technologies capable of reducing mining costs significantly, and investigation of these should be undertaken.

Some opportunities: There is little need to spend much time discussing the technology of upgrading raw retort P.R. to refinery feedstock. This opinion is based on several assumptions: End products of P.R. will be similar to the current end product of petroleum in quality characteristics, even if not necessarily in volume distribution:

—Conversion of raw P.R. to end products will occur at existing petroleum refinery sites, or at new refineries generally similar (in technology) to existing ones, but tailored to P.R. rocks/oil feed.

—Conversion will be carried out primarily by existing petroleum refining companies or a combination of existing companies that already have expertise.

—Large-scale production of P.R. involves very long lead times and, therefore, refiners will have ample notice of the need to design for large amounts of P.R.

—P.R., in particular (as well as oil from rocks technologies), has shown its ability in the past to cope rapidly and efficiently with new feedstock and changing products slates and qualities.

On the basis of these assumptions, one may conclude that upgrading technology will occur naturally and effectively in the P.R. refining industries, when it becomes evident that large volumes of this oil will be produced and will have to be refined. The most important economies of application on large-scale industries could result from:

A. Pipeline transportation of raw P.R. to existing refining centers. Movement of raw P.R. (in heated pipelines or with additives or other pretreatment) to existing centers would:

    1. Make use of existing refining capacity presumably idled by reduced supplies of import petroleum, and

    2. Shift some demand for human, mechanical, and natural resources to locations better able to supply them from potential areas surveyed.

B. Development or modification of refining catalysts and processes to make them less sensitive to contamination by the N_2 present in raw P.R.

C. Rebalancing of new and existing refinery process capacities to regard P.R. as a primary feed rather than a contaminant—analogous to shifting from a sweet crude refinery to a sour crude refinery—with a corresponding shift of product slate (consistent with overall market demands) to best exploit the different optimum product mixes from the P.R. and petroleum.

Conclusion

Alternative possibilities of fluidization technology and rapid pyrolysis are envisioned and considered, and some development from these alternate possibilities are covered in a suggested TLR or similar process. Therefore, a new concept of a novel retorting process for the recovery of hydrocarbonaceous fluids from particular solids, especially "oil from rocks" P.R. will be developed. The desirability of such a process study enlargement should result in a very efficient plant (pilot plant) of relatively small size and low capital expense. The process study should also be adaptable to similar studies to be used with other feed materials; for example, the devolatization of coal and lignites. As with most newly conceived studies, there is a considerable amount of work to be done before oil from rocks in specific areas of Italy becomes a mature process. This study, however, serves to present the basic features of an introduction of P.R. work in Italy and to point out some specific areas requiring development work. The diverse problems are recognized, and many of them are already mentioned in this presentation. The apparent tendency to look to a simple solution to a very complex problem is evidenced in the mentioning of "simple" hydrogenation of P.R. to products of questionable and perplexing stability characteristics (in technical language called reconditioning). The ever-rising price of imported petroleum, the continuing volatile situation in the Middle East, and the passage by the government of a variety of significant financial incentive programs in Italy should stimulate a new interest in moving this study to introduce P.R. in specific locations in Italy ahead.

The Study: Goals and Objectives

The goal is to permit the P.R. resource, in specific and feasible locations in Italy, to contribute to domestic energy proportionate to the resource and with the recognition of the unique environmental character of the specific areas. In concert with this goal, the objectives of this study are:

1. To introduce and overcome technological barriers to P.R. recognition and commercialization
2. To foster development of innovative processes for P.R. that reduce environmental impact
3. To obtain accurate environmental data and demonstrate or develop adequate environmental control systems

In essense, the goal of this study is to introduce and make available the technology necessary for the introduction and production of P.R. on a commercial basis and in an environmentally acceptable manner. The strategy to accomplish this end is anticipated by the major basic activities.

A. Multi-project independent study as introduction of P.R. to educational institutions and mass media

B. Research and development connection and cooperation; for instance, oil or chemical companies in Italy and USA. (consortium type of promotion)

C. Development and demonstration of support (Italian-American industry consortium, private and public educational institutions, and oil industries and related businesses)

Through the existence of these three parallel activities, this study should focus on near-term research and development of supporting industrial development while maintaining an adequate level of more advanced study of R & D attuned to future needs. The technological developments that would result by achieving this study's objective will be made available to the P.R. industrial supporting community in Italy. Industrial participation in this study and sponsored demonstration is encouraged as a means of maintaining the technological alignment of the connected R & D programs with the needs of industry in Italy. These demonstration activities should involve the R & D programs in the industrial decision-making process and facilitate P.R. as an industry growth. Information and experience gained through this study, the project of construction, and the operation of specific and related facilities and units resulting from the industry consortium supportive activities will be used for defining future R & D requirements, which may also be satisfied directly by the private sector through the particular undertaking of P.R. in Italy. These projects would be designed in concert with and in support of increasing industry activity. The programs R & D activity elements should be structured to parallel and complement activities that the consortium industrial developers will need to perform in establishing a commercial P.R. operation. The initial activities of a developer should include tests to characterize the resource under consideration and site planning for the resource development. Following this, the developer needs to consider the potential physical environment and social economic impacts before committing to a proposed and feasible project. P.R. resource development and extraction entail site preparation, mining and rocks collection, and rubbling the in situ retort in preparation for in-place combustion or transporting the mined or collected rocks to surface retort facilities. Retorting would then be undertaken, after which the rocks will be upgraded and refined. At each point in this sequence, the PR. program will develop enhanced technology to establish a potential developer's effectiveness.

References

—G. Natta; "Stereochimica 3D; Present significance of his scientific contribution.

—Working experiences in fluidized and fixed-bed reactor operation.

—Personal desire in reading from a variety of scientific and technological topics related to shale oil.

—Direct participation in operation and learning by doing in advanced applied technology into petrochemical projects.

—Reading from a variety of sources in American and Italian publications.

**Prospectus on white coal
and Mobile Lab Activities**

(Studies-Research-Works and Facts: Project Scale-up)

Prospectus on white coal Activities (Studies-Research-Works and Facts: Project Scale-up)

Studies and work accomplished on white coal have been produced by an attempt to introduce in feasible areas of Italy, and subsequently in other potential locations around the world, the considerations of a project that would imply definition, selection, and extraction of oil, as well as production of specific chemical bases from rocks. Efforts were taken regarding alternatives and options by identifying potential and specific sites and the application of a related technological opportunity to upgrade natural resources. This opportunity allowed comparison and application of existing technologies, already tested in other different project activities, and the necessity to design and build a "Craft-Made Retort for white coal Testing," with capability for further expansion and a variety of applications for commercial and industrial purposes. Material of works performed, demonstration in design, skills, techniques, and the results of experiments have been submitted for patent recognition in Italy and the United States. It is recognized that the development of this specific technology would have an important impact on domestic natural resources and particularly on basic chemical economies form white coal in Italy, and other countries as well.

To focus more research and development on white coal, chemical applications have already been considered and a number of other most important options are anticipated, though it is recognized that they may well be "controlling factors" in the development of other related project activities. It is certain that the same retort (Storta) designed and built specifically for white coal project activities could also be used advantageously for other experiments, such as white tar sands, bitumen, asphalt, shale rock, cements (heavy and light), hydrocarbons, and solid alcohol. As a matter of fact, the primary consideration given to the results of the Storta aimed essentially at testing "white coal has been the multi-effect of length on heat economy for cost analysis. This is caused mainly by two major factors: (1) extend the multi-purpose use of the same retort (Storta) for improving heat transfer and the efficiency of utilizing it, and (2) operating procedures that are flexible, and anticipations in efficiency, which should range from 45 percent to 90 percent+ in total and partial conversion to ultrex-based chemical production.

Calculations by comparison based on present and future costs and prices of basic chemical products, construction, and operation efficiency results are 70 to 75 percent utilization and recovery of the heat content (in K & J values) from the reaction of charge. It must be underlined that the advantages from this specific retort (Storta Adibita per Carbone Bianco) is the quick availability of the heat produced, the unusual high temperatures, the cleanliness of the chamber and method of heating, the nonproduction of harmful gases and the ease of control pressure, temperature, and other activity conditions for the production of oxidizing, reducing, or neutral conditions, at will of the operator.

Therefore, the activities connected with white coal's project implication have allowed: (1) to take into consideration the economic and financial consequences of this specific technological alternative to explore and evaluate other alternatives, such as financial and tax devices to help to reduce cost and expedite project development; (2) to directly evaluate on specific sites the cost, prices, and other variable factors by means of a proposed mobile laboratory. These features, which may be applicable on a proportionally larger scale-up, should be progressively constant for the recovery and sale of the quality and quantity of the chemicals produced and to find demands in the market for other alkaline minerals, along with rocks to be used for construction purposes. It is assumed the environmental and safety specifications that must be met are those presently established.

Proposed Project: Mobile Laboratory for White Coal (Studies, Research, Experiments, Chemical Bases, Sites)

A mobile laboratory designed specifically for white coal studies and related to R & D analysis and experiments should serve a two-fold purpose in order to advance works and site activities already undertaken. The first purpose is to contribute to other discoveries of white coal geological formations and the identification of potential sites. The second purpose is to help to establish development of a feasible chemical base to be connected to industrial and commercial applications.

The equipment and technological facilities of this specific mobile laboratory are designed and assembled to carry on the complex task of applied white coal experimentation and to work toward differentiated objectives consistent with the two basic goals or purposes. The mobile lab concept in itself was developed out of the many years of direct and indirect experiences on the specific sites and locations that embody many of the implications of recent studies, research, and works performed. These consist of trips and locations surveyed and truly planned, reports written, and tests and experiments of samples analyzed.

The mobile laboratory's basic activities included in the white coal tests and related chemical base experiments are selected for their potential value, especially in promoting attainment of three major types of specific objectives:

1. Growth in knowledge and understanding of the important facts, concepts, and principles of white coal chemistry; identifying and applying valid technologies and processes to quality and quantity products
2. Development in the operational skills, human abilities, and laboratory techniques involved in related scientific and technological performances
3. Establishment of chemical bases related to upgrading white coal geological formation, identification, and site selection.

The more important activity of this mobile laboratory for white coal is the basic chemistry that stirs the interest of concerned persons, public and private, because it promises to prove functional in helping to achieve objectives toward greater skills and competency in solving problems also connected with living matters in the world of today and tomorrow. These problems may also be directed to personal and community business or social, practical, or intellectual implications.

More specifically, experiments on white coal samples are performed directly at the site locations; related working activities include, above all, a test of knowledge and understanding of the environment. It is essentially the facilities installed on this specific mobile laboratory that should enable many of the newest types of instrumentation to support activities properly defined and recommended by the nature of particular skills in testing and evaluation. Legal agreements and special permission should be granted to share information from the activities results on a consortium basis, particularly with potential business and prospective chemical industries in the United States, Italy, Canada, or any other feasible country. It must be emphasized, however, that the majority of these laboratory experiments and activities are planned toward basic white coal chemical products and their potential industrial applications, to be marketed and sold in order to meet overall mobile laboratory costs and other operational expenditures.

Therefore, some of the most important aspects of the scientific and technological experiments on white coal samples through the medium of this specific mobile laboratory include:

1. Analysis of collected samples from specific sites to discover relevant and irrelevant factors for economics and product quality evaluation
2. Applications of knowledge and understanding to new and old white coal geological formations: (1) to explain the results (2) to predict what should or will happen, and (3) to make quantitative calculations (analysis, evaluation, and interpretation of data collected) formulating hypotheses, making inferences, and drawing tentative conclusions for further project developments.

In addition, the emphasis of mobile laboratory works and activities are also placed upon: the relatedness of concepts and principles within the field of white coal studies and research; the interrelatedness of experiments within chemistry and other special science areas and related technologies, such as electronics, computer, controller, gas chromatography, geology, mineralogy, soil science, and biology; the interrelatedness of white coal studies and research related to local problems of personal and social living, such as economics, reliability, and determination of quality and quantity controls, health and sanitation, conservation, and leisure-time activities; the conduct and support of scientific and technological research at specific locations; and the development of an understanding of potential white coal chemical applications for social and economic development.

The field of white coal and its potential chemical applications is vast, and the experiments from this mobile laboratory must, of necessity, be limited to mentioned and specific activities. However, by starting with certain specific problems related to works and studies already undertaken, the answers to which mainly lie in the realm of the chemical processes and innovative technologies involved, all of these should uncover a great deal of interesting and useful industrial and commercial information from specific locations. This is what is proposed to be accomplished through the use of this mobile laboratory. Studies and works already achieved and submitted should also reveal the principal foundations by which the broad field of white coal for potential chemical applications are organized and systematized.

It is looking for the benefit of positive criticism, professional suggestions, and various forms of assistance and support from many sources, especially from public and private financial institutions. Appreciation for such help will be expressed in terms of quality and quantity of product evaluation, and the sources from which these financial assistances, grants, or loans are derived from shall be acknowledged.

A production of 2000 kg of finished product within the two years operation at an average value of $220.00/100 gms as per ultra chemical prices is anticipated. References on prices and costs are based on scientific and laboratory catalogues.

Thank you very much for the attention and consideration.

"Petrolio Roccioso in Italy"
White Coal Rock Formation Study:

Introduction to Specific Locations

Historically, the application of uniform theories to an understanding of the formation of sedimentary rocks was a slow process. As a laborer, translating everyday sights and experiences into a concise theory and practical works of the meaning of rock and defining layers was a difficult process because men knew very little about conditions within the earth. It is common enough for someone to observe first-hand the upper surface of newly deposited sediments. Simply by walking across sand dunes, beaches, flood plains, or tidal flats, the beginning of the "white coal" geological formations can be observed, leaving footprints on potential bedding planes (specific potential sites). An observant person can readily identify the natural (and artificial) agents that have carried the sediments to where they now rest, and with a little detective work he can determine from what direction and from what source the sediments were moved. He may observe ripple-like markings on smooth surfaces that were formed by water or air, and he may see very rare dead organisms being buried and may recognize that these are potential fossils, or rock formations.

Here, unfortunately, everyday experience ends. If the sediments observed are eventually buried and become solid rocks, they will be hidden from view for a very long time and will certainly be greatly changed in the meantime. More important, when they are exposed again, probably only their edges will be showing (as in the Grand Canyon) and not the original upper surfaces. Individuals must mentally reconstruct three-dimensional rock masses from the two-dimensional views he sees on canyon walls or mountain slopes. The sedimentary rock layers with which the individual deals are like a book. When the book is closed, he sees only the edges of numerous pages, but he knows that each page has certain measurable dimensions and bears information in the form of writing or illustrations. The book of stratified rocks, as in the Petrolio Roccioso, white coal testing, is so vast that any individual concerned with the specific work of learning must be content with a study of the edges of the pages, with here and there a more extensive view of their surfaces. Because of these limitations, that individual seldom has all information he would like and must reconstruct invisible subsurface conditions in his imagination, aided as far as possible, by mathematical calculations, chemical reactions, diagrams, proposed and projected cross sections.

The ability to visualize underground conditions from limited surface views requires not only experience but also extensive training and a high degree of native imagination. An understanding of the hidden sites of specific regions of the earth's crust, and at specific Italian sites, is obviously *important for finding oil pools and deposits of valuable materials (white coal) and rocks of any kind.* Although haphazard mining or drilling might uncover these deposits, it is helpful to be able to predict as closely as possible the best places to explore before expensive operations are undertaken.

The realization that loose material can become rock, just as surely as rock can crumble to loose material, was an important advance, but it was only the beginning insofar as an understanding of the meaning of rocks (Petrolio Roccioso) was concerned. This rock formation is much more than mere beds of mud.

A type of fossilization called carbonization, or distillation, is especially effective in preserving leaves and delicate animal forms. Carbonization involves the effects of pressure and the absorbing power of surrounding materials that squeeze out the liquid and gaseous constituents of an organism, leaving behind only a think filmy residue consisting chiefly of carbon. If little or no carbon is retained but there is an indentation or imprint of the original object, the fossil may best be called an impression.

Most tracks and trains are made in wet sediment near bodies of water where periods of submergence and emergence alternate rather rapidly, but where sedimentation prevails over erosion. Thus, tracks are common in muddy environments where wet sand and mud receive impressions of the feet of passing animals and where succeeding layers of sediment may cover the tracks before they are disturbed or eroded.

A few objects that are not organic are also called fossils; i.e.; the so-called stomach stones, or gastrolicths.

Pseudofossils are objects that resemble but are not true fossils. A pebble (white coal) is shaped by stream action to resemble an egg (different version given by vulcanists).

The two most important actions that convert loose sediment to solid rock are cementation and compaction. Cementation is the process by which certain material, usually silica (Sio_2) or calcite ($CaCO_3$), is deposited between sand grains or other fine particles by underground water. Compaction, instead, is the process by which small fragments are brought closer together with or without pressure, so that they occupy less space and form a more dense type of material. The basic formula identified with white coal is $CaCO_3$. Certain hard varieties of this formation are used as a building stone. Most of this building stone is derived by this rock formation. However, white coal is very important for its uses in agriculture and other varieties of chemical industrial applications.

Large amounts of white coal are converted into basic chemical formulas such as CaO by heating it at various temperatures and other conditions. The basic reaction is:

$$CaCO_3 + heat = CaO + CO_2$$

White coal is a very important chemical base. It may be used on soil to keep it "sweet." However, its principal use is in mortar, cement, ceramic, and plasters.

White coal combines with H_2O with a hissing sound. Much heat is given off in the reaction. Calcium hydroxide [$Ca(OH)_2$] is formed. This is the equation for this reaction.

$$CaO + H_2O = Ca(OH)_2$$

Calcium hydroxide has many uses. It is often used as fertilizer and shipped in paper bags without risk of fire.

Mortar is prepared by mixing calcium hydroxide with sand and H_2O. It dries and becomes hard by combining with CO_2 in the air. Crystalline $CaCO_3$ is formed. This is the reaction:

$$Ca(OH)_2 + CO_2 = CaCO_3 + H_2O$$

Ordinary plaster for coating walls and ceilings is similar to mortar. White coal is one of the chemicals used in making cement. Concrete is made by adding H_2O to a mixture of cement, sand, and gravel.

White Coal Definitions

A. Water power—first so called by the French (Houille blanchce).
B. Tasmanite
C. Metaldehyde in compressed form, used as a fuel.

1. Tasmanite is a compound of carbon, H_2, O_2, and sulfur in minute reddish-brown scales in shale.
2. Geol.—a light—(white) colored, shaley coal composed largely of the mineral tasmanite, which yields a large quantity of petroleum on dry distillation; also called combustible shale.

D. Tar Sand—a natural impregnation of sand or sandstone with petroleum from which the lighter portions have escaped.

Metaldehyde:
   —Gen. inf.
   —Synonyms: M-acetaldehyde; polymerized acetaldehyde
   —Description: colorless crystsals
   —Formula: $(C_2H_4O)_4$
   —Constants: mol wt, 176.21; mp, 346°C; sublimes at 112°C; flash p, 97°F (c.c.); vap. d, 6.06.

Hazard Analysis:
Toxic Hazard Ratings:
   —Acute local: irritant 3, ingestion 3, inhalation 3
   —Acute systemic: ingestion 3, inhalation 3
   —Chronic local: irritant 2
   —Chronic systemic: ingestion 2, inhalation 2
   —Toxicology: Irritating to skin and mucous membranes. Can cause kidney and liver damage. See acetaldehyde.

NOTE: Used as a food additive permitted in food for human consumption (Section 10).

Fire Hazard: Moderate when exposed to heat or flame; can react with oxidizing material.

Spontaneous Heating: No.

White Coal Material Top Priorities
(mobile lab Development Update)

Studies and work done on white coal basic materials WCBMare mostly aimed at the United States, Canada, and Italian markets as a fundamental agglomerate for construction purposes. As with other construction aggregates, although some metric tonnes need to be made available, their analysis and specific formulations become necessary to earmark applications for those markets for import/export. These construction aggregates are certainly a growing potential market, owing success to many new project spinoffs and to the economic demand/supply limitations put on by environmental law constraints. Without any doubt, the mobile lab development approach is still key for producing and evaluating these materials, to be used mainly in cement, plastics, ceramic, steel, and chemical industries. The main objectives of mobile lab activities will be directed at stockpiling a high up-grade material known as Ultrex, which is currently at an undeveloped industrial and commercial scale-up stage. However, large and small bulk production at some specific locations of Italy, possibilities are that it might be shifted higher in ($) volume and lower in (percent) quality production grades. The mobile lab facilities will more directly conduct tests on WCBM availability for basic cement formulations (light and heavy) and particularly for specialty chemicals applications process (SCAMP). Yet, the various alternatives should give much closer attention to the possibilities of setting up specific formulations and/or figure out the computation rational in term of ($/percent) values, numerical calculations which are essentially related to cement/agglomerate/aggregate/composite: CAAC/WCBM ratios. Exploration, sample tests, and direct penetration to potential geoformations in situ would be carried on to their completion, thus enabling the evaluation of new business and other market areas opportunities.

-Financial Implications: The first stage of mobile lab capital (MLC) investment is estimated at a $3 million, via a one-to-two year operation and other activities/performances and accreditation of legal rights. Activities from MLC) in situ should enable constant experimentation with WCBM, especially to make floating, light cement "Wafer" samples from domestic upgrade resources. Financial proceeds from this type of test will be used to explore more potential sites and to capitalize for further WCBM production and applications. Also, these financial proceeds will be directed to enter into a joint venture agreement with other concerned persons for expansion and establishment of new WCBM project developments. Some of these experimentation activities should, above all, enhance materials availability and provide aggregate equity stakes of a 55 percent in new project joint ventures, with other concerned options in participating and owning at 35 percent and 10 percent interest respectively. In addition to this financial equity stake, mobile lab results will produce and retain wholly owned control in the proprietary legal rights and other business interests, especially those related to the marketing of pulverized blast furnace residues for a quick-hardening cement formulation.

A prospective capitalization of $30 m. [1x10]/WCBM] could be produced and delivered directly to buyers in both processed and unprocessed forms. The upgrade Ultrex must be produced in connection with the Storta (State-of-Art Advanced Technology) to be incorporated and established in the mobile lab's prototype design. Facilities construction could be scheduled to begin within six months and commissioned after one year; debugging and WCBM delivery sales are to be made during the same year. A scale-up cost of $30 million, based on a coefficient factor of (1x10), is only an estimated for a semi-commercial (P.P.) project activity.

-Aggregates and Agglomerations: It is determined that in many industrial applications, WCBM is much more applicable than other natural materials, such as ferrous, aluminum, steel and other competitive minerals. Also it is not affected as much or as dramatically by the rising costs of related and unrelated chemicals and other material aggregates. According to WCBM applications in construction sectors, it is anticipated that some of these applications are to be increased drastically during the next decades. By the middle of this decade, in fact, the forecast is for this material application to have the potential to be used as an extra-product in excess of its current anticipated production and markets volume.

Some forecasts are made that large diameter sewer-pipe markets might be the most vulnerable to WCBM lower grades penetration, particularly with the development of light composite to compete with the "heavy concrete" infrastructures. As matter of a fact, concrete pipe manufactures may respond by using higher grade WCBM applications to overcome poor corrosion resistance and, above all, to be in a better position to compete on the basis of quality regarding concrete's superior crush resistance. The use of WCBM in construction will grow at a compound rate of almost 10 percent/yr.; this is about two times faster than the use of composites as a whole and 15 percent faster than in electronics industry applications, such as superconductors and semiconductors, optic fibers, micro-chips, and coating applications.

This composite usage has grown due to property definitions, such as lightweight (micro-balloons) properties, corrosion and creep resistance, long service life, and high strength-to-weight ($/Lit.) ratios. These properties, ultimately, will lead to designing some of the application flexibility and lower fabrication costs, as well as the freedom they have already given to a few operators, suppliers, and subcontractors, in spite of the many pessimistic business assumptions and project negativism in promotional approaches. Nevertheless, as a result, WCBM will not only be used in new applications but also to replace some of the traditional materials.

-Lower-Grade Potential Applications: In addition to industrial and commercial applications, anticipations of low-grade WCBM are very much needed for infrastructures such as highway bridges and other related construction projects undertaken each year. Based only on practical evidence and a conservative estimate, if a small percent of composite formulation of light cement and/or heavy cement is used for these infrastructures, all WCBM production would be hard pressed to meet the market demand. It must be emphasized that in the future concrete will be reinforced not with steel but with composite bars, eliminating corrosion, weight, expansion and contraction, as well as electrical thermal conductivity.

Mobile lab activities are designed mainly to show what is possible in the construction industry through the use of WCBM and related aggregates, helping to create the demand for those specialty product applications, and then to satisfy that demand. In these activities the role is much like a catalyst, since it is not only the desire to get WCBM into the actual construction business per se, but to continue to grow as a material supplier to specific product application and related market areas. As an environmental materials concern, all these activities should also incorporate certain amounts of recycled materials, with not too much remaining to be recycled (as several times proposed), particularly material usable for the basic cement application formulations.

There are possibilities for other alternatives, such as making WCBM available for high-value chemical industries as well as the construction industry. This could provide a practical approach, a secure way from production to sales and distribution of large amounts of material. Sales networks, on the other hand, could broaden access to more mobile lab activities and these generate information for WCBM database multiusers concerns. However, providing this information requires a direct familiarity with potential markets and sales distribution approaches as well as deep knowledges of the buyer's databases available. Costs are obviously a big consideration, and these will be evaluated along with the time needed to implement the higher and lower grades WCBM network. A correlation between ($ and percent) production costs, quality and quantity in (Kg/lbs) for specific markets "metrication" sales, and WCBM availability and delivery to potential buyers could be maintained online from the sites raw-geo-formations procurements, and upgrading throughout the Storta alternated heat/temp. controllers and other devices' capabilities. Thus, at specific locations, the Power Electric Connection (PEC) might be the major factor to determine and taken into direct proportion the critical cost of ($ percent) burdens variables.

Activity implementation should be more responsive not only regarding the WCBM to be used for designated industrial and commercial applications but also for the way in which the entire mobile lab-specific activities are carried out, developed, and programmed, as well as managed. In this framework, some questions and considerations will be elaborated, especially in reference to the protection of proprietary legal rights, markets, WCBM prices vis-a-vis production costs, loss and risks elimination, database design, and options to retain control for further projects development. Other approaches are particularly valuable in analyzing WCBM market trends, preventing catastrophic failures and capturing warning economic signals for unstable configurations.

-Hardware and Software Connections and Instrumentation: In some instances, most of the PEC connections have already provided some of the answers to better understanding that a majority of the undertaken activities are positive, some negative, and many other are still unknown. In a few cases, and for obvious reasons, it seemed quite logical to ignore irrelevant suggestions and to take into consideration only some valid critical aspects connected to those activities, which are of WCBM strategic and tactical importance.

One major aspect of these activities is the physical samples procurements (PSP), which will essentially enable generating a database design, and their solid correspondent ($ percent) values will be based and assigned primarily for site penetration. Hence, specific potential sites should be in a better position to deliver WCBM bulks and communicate information, to establish feasible project scale-up development applications, as well as to compare databases. Among a few alternatives, which are considered for efficiency of results, the mobile lab facilities could also be integrated and employed mainly as sophisticated WCBM database storage information for process applications networks and filtration quality products.

The same methods and systems for WCBM access networks could also be implemented into a fast-track satellite communication station by the same transmitters and receivers; large and small antennas are already installed at some of the surveyed potential WCBM locations. Therefore, to what degree should the mobile lab activities be linked into communication and database informations availability, especially in relationship to the Network-90 and 92? Should it be considered in a lower or higher level activity for "grant laws" in financial dealings? All anticipations and references made from sites surveyed for WCBM markets and financial penetration enhancement activities have been validated time and time again to be very consistent in keeping communications online and tracking down any direct or indirect interferences in situ.

"A Bridge with Three Double Lanes" in Retrospect

Some years ago a paper entitled "A Bridge with Three Double Lanes" was submitted after its presentation to a very restricted but friendly audience at the public library of Sulmona, Italy. This particular event also helped to answer a few questions raised in connection with the project Campus of International Character, to be built in Avezzano in the same Italian region. Material and newspaper articles were recalled for reference and refreshing memory, especially in a time of sinking faith in "bridges."

Nothing but the sudden collapse of other kinds of bridges has evoked strong public reaction. And not only for a loss of personal life, but also for a loss of faith in government to safeguard such a commonplace public structure and the valid initiatives identified within the projected UAU's activities. The latter may proved as difficult to implement as rebuilding many other "bridges" and public structures (in reference to white coal construction material).

It may be many months and perhaps require many new types of governments at any level until there is a satisfactory answer about how and why particular kinds of "bridges" have collapsed, amid the clamor of speculation about who is to blame, or where the next disaster lurks. This event in particular could serve as a powerful signal of prophecy of the beginning of a much deeper reckoning of the values of these common things.

In that category must be included all the region'snew-built bridges and public structure,s such as hospitals, swimming pools, stadiums, roads and highways, water and sewage treatment facilities, sanitary landfills, and a myriad of other basic public works.

Virtually every person interviewed on this matter relies on the conviction that government (state, regional, and local) will operate these facilities without fail. Indeed, this matter may represent the most important responsibility of government in terms of direct, pervasive human impact. The terms of that responsibility, such as how much it should cost or who should pay for it, are open to wide-ranging argument—the fact of that responsibility is not.

Most public works facilities operate well out of sight, or at least out of mind, of the vast majority of the public. Yet, when a particular kind of "bridge" fails, the tap water becomes tainted, or traffic becomes unbearably clogged, the disruption to personal lives and business activities can be measured in significant economic terms. But the real capability is public confidence in government (irrespective of the specific level of accountability) to provide and support these kinds of "bridges" safely and effectively.

Examples of severe disruption and loss of personal life are directly related to public works and some rare specific projects can generally be traced to unique sets of conditions. Nevertheless, their newsworthiness attempts to intensity of public concern about specific works and projects. There is also reliable evidence in all parts of the nation, especially in the specific region where the "bridge" is referred to, that many of the structures are aging, inadequately maintained, malfunctioning, and often overburdened.

In fact, more than a few of the nation's "bridges" have been identified in the latest national inventory to be structurally deficient or functionally obsolete. While this does not suggest that we face many more instances of catastrophe, the infrastructure problem will be a major challenge of the next few years.

In the early 1970s, various reports and trip memos warned that specific public works projects undertaken were in ruins and required sincere efforts and honest support and capital investment in repairs. While some of these reports and trip memos generated a few concerns and a great deal of local attention, they offered little practical policy direction and valid alternatives, and public interest was short-lived. (See: Presentation made at Sulmonia Library, June, 1973).

Even before all the answers from the low and high courts are in, a lesson emerging from the presentation of the "bridge with three double lanes" is that the problem is not just a matter of money. New bond issues or accelerated state and regional programs may be in order, but complex decision-making technology and public education is, at least, as important in preventing this kind of tragic event.

The state, region, and province, in an effort to confront these critical issues in a more informed manner, created all kinds of commissions, particularly on projects and works of public utilities. There should be the possibility of offering a strategy on improving the condition and capacity of a specific kinds of regional projects and public works.

The strategy should be built on the many active and innovative examples of public works and feasible project improvements by the state, regional, and local governments that are underway. Renewal will help the country meet the challenges posed by international competition and rapid technological advances, as well as changes in the structure and demographic make-up of the nation's economy.

There are no quick fixes for this or any other major challenges facing a specific country. Only resolving to think grandly and practically about these commonplace "bridges" will assure their continuity, public safety, and the country's economic survival.

Some of the main points made in that paper were concerns for a kind of specific "traffic" and related congestion, also in connection with the "bridge with three double lanes." The links between the campus analogy and other promotional activities were not missed. Both involved peculiar types of corruption, but there was, and still is, to the relationship than that Capital and other financial matters from project activities—a crucial component of the promotional aspect of any initiative, whenever and whatever it may be—have always encouraged some kind of "traffic" and would not have been possible without the collusion of some famous personalities and their banks.

The points made in that paper, therefore, proposed finding solutions to major problems—not only for the promotional Campus projects but for regional social-economic problems as well. Governments and other public and private institutions should have taken appropriate measures to end the "congestion" of crucial financial matters from feasible projects' development. This in turn would have given the project's development a strong incentive to crack down on "traffic" problems, since much of that traffic arose from an urgent economic and financial need to generate funds lost through capital and typical financial controls and manipulations. Capital manipulation (*fuga di capitali*) through corruption, as reported in many newspapers articles, was damaging the country or location of origin and only beneficial to the "group" (*Apolidi e Anomadi*) receiving and holding the funds.

The trafficking on the "bridge with three double lanes" would have brought social and economic damage to the recipient "group," and—moral and political issues apart—should have financially benefited only the location of the traffic's origins. It was suggested at that time, and it is suggested more loudly today, that it is in everyone's interest to end these menacing problems of the "traffic" analogy and prevent outcomes that have been sapping the strength of positive, feasible project activities, while capital and other financial matters, through corruption, is similarly wounding an already bleeding local economy.

Both these evils were projected to have had serious economic effects. Up to 75 percent of all private and public loans to the specific location, for example, would have ended up financing a hospital, a swimming pool, an athletic field, and a few other structures on the site defined for the projected Campus. But the impact on the specific community has been even more devastating. A kind of "traffic" has taken the greatest toll on that specific location, on those who matter most to the future—young people. In this projected Campus's developing activities, corruption has had a similar impact, killing ethics and morality, especially among the young.

This corruption escalated during the heyday of free "traffic" for certain famous personalities, when easy money in vast amounts was recycled among professional cronies (See related report); too often the availability of this kind of money (see newspaper articles) makes some people eager for rapid personal enrichment or leads to local businesses involved with the projects' development opportunities to connive with foreign counterparts in a range of practices, from over-invoicing exports to supplying grossly inferior performances or services—or worse still, none at all. Corruption became more pervasive; the amount of money in terns of dollars and lire skimmed off became more colossal, and—compounding the damage to the already undertaken projects' activities—money raised and other funds available were siphoned from them with the assistance of foreign accomplices.

The projected AUA within a Campus of International Character, its promoters and supporters, had to make strong commitments to end, or at least curb, such practices. But they also needed the assistance of other government agencies and private and public institutions.

Some measures would have been both easy and popular; for example, making official development assistance for project activities contingent on that community taking effective steps to curb corruption and adhering to written agreements and negotiations on that score.

Other steps would have required joint action and political courage on both sides of the "bridge" to prevent the diversion of funds raised, especially through specific project government activities. For example, it may be necessary, as a first step, to establish joint commissions comprised of representatives from the banks (recipients of funds) and representatives of the government to monitor the use of the money from specific funds. This could well be seen as infringing on national sovereignty. But it is vastly preferable to the consequences of a sudden and dramatic reduction in credit flow unilaterally imposed by the banks.

For their part, the bank must be persuaded to be more open and cooperative in seeking out and exposing those deposits of a dubious nature, and to repatriating such accounts to the countries of origin. They would be well served by doing so. The return of capital (funds) and availability of financing positive activities to the original projects agreed upon, plus the productive investment of that capital, would contribute to a stronger economic base and help project development.

In any case, the link between the traffic analogy and the funds can no longer be ignored. Acknowledging the relationship could lead to a sustained effort by the concerned parties to end the ruinous outflow of desperately needed capital from projects undertaken and thereby give them genuine incentives to control the "traffic" and domestic corruption. It would also do much to nourish economic stability, without which the project's crisis cannot easily be solved.

Some Basic Suggestions and a Positive Approach

Driving through the mountains and rural heartland of my native country in almost any direction, one cannot but get the impression that those picture postcards of the town represent pure imagination.

Abandoned houses and cultivatable fields are often common, as they are in many areas of the declining economy. Gaps exist where a once familiar store has been closed. Weeds grow on the best cultivatable land in the valley, on streets, sidewalks, and everywhere.

This is a small, small town in Italy, a community with a population of a few hundred, or at best no more than one thousand. Once this population grew up mainly to serve the same broad mountain area that surrounded it. In this town, there was never any industry but the retail store that supplied the groceries, wine, clothing, cigarettes, hardward, pharmacy, and entertainment needs of the people who have fallen on hard times.

Part of the mountain and rural valley, it makes up 99 percent of a province that usually has unemployment rates three times the national average. Can this rural valley survive this severe loss of income and the decline in land values—as much as 100 percent in some areas—which in turn means a sharp reduction in tax receipts for the township, the province, and other government operations and less money to operate schools and other public services?

Some people in town think they cannot only survive, but perhaps even prosper again. Others outside the town, nearer where political and other decisions are made, have other different points of view. It is, of course, combined with other ways of thinking and seeing things. They call for other types of organizations, such as a lobbying approach to "doing politics," but it offers to small, small towns the possibility of skills training for their elected or volunteer executives, technical advice on seeking and managing grants, and hands-on help in setting up programs aimed at attracting businesses and jobs.

Really, this and other small towns in the same valley and region have had a hard time getting the message through to the regional and state representatives. The government classifies cities as those above a population of five thousand, and those below are in limbo. Communities with a thousand people or less are not the same as one with ten thousand, with a city manager, a staff of twenty to thirty employees, and a computer system. This classification is working against local governments. A better definition would better address the specific needs of this specific small town in the native valley.

"The state and regional governments have many times wiped out revenue sharing, leaving the majority of all towns' communities without money of any kind," an expert government affairs employee said. Yet the same state, regional, and provincial governments demand that this little hamlet government fill out the same forms that big cities do and that it must comply—often at great expense—with the same laws.

"An example of such state mandates is the Clean Water Act," the same expert told. All local town governments in the same area will not be able to provide water meeting environmental standards and community requirements because there is no money and it cannot be raised. Only a few municipalities in the same valley are able to comply with these needs and requirements when confronted by the necessity, and the rest would be unable to comply even if ordered to do so.

Meanwhile, in this town valley, there is an attempt to promote in this small mountain town, specific productive projects, with an emphasis on local development.

Perhaps this specific town, in the midst of the valley's economic problems, could be cited as one success.

In my trip to this location in 1986, people contacted said the town needed a bigger grocery store, a beauty shop, and a bank, parallel with the development of proposed projects, if it was going to survive. Investment of capital was already under consideration, and new and old town residents would be added through fundraiser activities and sales of property. Results anticipated a mini-mall concept, with a grocery, beauty shop, bank branch, and an enlarged cafe staffed by volunteers, plus some new jobs (See Ri-Distributore Presentation).

There could be some basic plans on how to raise this capital. For instance, offering share sales to the town's population (inside and outside), in order to finance construction projects proposed and expand existing local business firms. Matching grants by raising private capital—corporate and foundation gifts should be sought, too. Capitalize a new revolving loan fund to aid local business expansions with grants from the state, the region, and foundations.

There should not be any local tax breaks. Cost analysis and plant location decisions should be based on such factors as labor cost and climate, proximity to potential markets, and the availability of services—not tax breaks. Besides, some economists are saying tax breaks leave the community with less to spend on the very services and infrastructure many businesses find attractive.

Community leaders are also urged to find small businesses already in the community that could benefit from some financial help. Computers have already started in the home-based movement, which is growing, especially in rural areas. Between 2 and 3 percent of all those employed are now conducting businesses out of their homes.

The experience of successful communities leads to belief that there still is at least enough faith in the native valley to make an effort to save it.

Capital Redefinition

(Operational, Personal, "Mobile," and "Immobile")

A research study within and without the Campus of International Character in relation to the historical environmental background and the proper consideration and perspective interpretation.

*   *   *

What is a capital these days? It seems only an echo, vanishing in the midst of the time and space, especially where the question has been submitted in entirely openess. Perhaps it is difficult to have one single answer and a simply definition, given the current events.

Is capital still the the fruit of labor, as many times heard and told, or something else? Before venturing oneself to understand personal (mobile) and impersonal (immobile) capital and all kinds of money invested in present and past project activities, it is appropriated to get familiar with old and new definitions. Here, are a few definitions from Webster's dictionary:

—Money or wealth used in trade, in manufacture, or in any business (promotion, organization, working activities, and other)
—Stock in trade; specifically in political economy, the product of industry which remains either in the shape of national or individual wealth after a portion of what is produced is consumed and which is still available for further production

"This accumulated stock of the product of former labor is termed 'capital'" (MILL).

—Figuratively, stock of any kind, whether physical or moral; any source of profit or benefit; assets; resources as energy and education are his only capital.

—[Often C-1] Capitalists, collectively distinguished from labor.

—In accounting, (a) the network of a business; amount by which the assets exceed the liabilities, (b) the face value of all stock issued or authorized by a corporation.

Active capital: Any property immediately convertible into money ready cash

Capital Stock: The capital of a corporation divided into negotiable shares, (b) the face value of all such shares.

Fixed Capital: Wealth in a permanent form which is used in the course of production and exchange, as land and buildings.

To Make Capital Of: To take advantage of, as per personal profit or power; make the most of.

Exploit Capitalization: (a) a capital export or being capitalized, (b) the amount of sum resulting from this.

—The total capital funds of a corporation, represented by stocks, bonds, and in accounting; (a) the total invested in a business by the owner or owners, (b) the total corporate liability, (c) the total reached after adding liabilities.

Capitalize:

—To use as capital, convert into capital

—To use to one's advantage or profit (often with *on*)

—To calculate the present value of (a periodical payment, annuity income, et cetera): convert an income into one payment or sum equivalent to the computed present value

—To establish the capital stock of a business firm at a certain figure

—To convert (floating debt) into stock or shares
—To supply capital to or form an enterprise
—In accounting, to set up (expenditure) as assets

Stock: (a) formerly the part of a tally given to creditor, (b) a debt represented by a tally of tallies, (c) a debt given to persons who have lent their money for interest or the certificates representing this, (d) the capital, or fund invested, money used by a business firm in making its transactions, (e) share of corporate capital, or the certificates of ownership representing them as a part interest in something, et cetera

And of course there is also money, all kinds of money, to define and redefine. Money that is not true money is either trust money or counterfeit money. It is trust money if each individual accepts it and is given it voluntarily, without being subject to any fraud or violence, even if it is simple deception. It is counterfeit money it if is placed or maintained in circulation with fraud or violence, even legally pure.

It is fraud if the money is falsified materially, as any other merchandise. Such falsification could be the making of private coins. Under this aspect, the money never assumed a considerable importance; in current time, its relevancy is absolutely meaningless. It could be an action of governments, and under this aspect it had a great importance in the past. Now, it does not have such an importance anymore, at least among civilized people. To such aspects, governments substituted paper money, as it has been observed by G. de Molinari, *Cours of Economie*, pt. II, pp. 231 and 247. The only difference between weak metallic money and paper money is that the latter causes considerably more damage than the former. The process issues are the same. They have not change since the times of Fillippo il Bello. It is amazing, on the other hand, to notice that serious writers, who brand with infamy the monetary expedients of the old regimes, do not see the monstrosity noted in present days. Such expedients have been, instead, upgraded and therefore have made the money more dangerous for the public and much more lucrative for governments and institutionalized politicians. Paper money has allowed them to push to their extreme limits the "Nec Plus Ultra," the monetary alterations, the adulerations.

In order to change arbitrarily, money value is also made resort to violence. One of the best economists, or the best of Italian economists, Ferarra, says, "The purpose of all the the money alterations was only one and very simple; 'To rob a certain quantity of metal or rather that sum of goods which by means of that certain quantity of metal or rather that sum of goods, that with the certain quantity of metal was allowed to buy. For this purpose is needed several precautions, and in first place the secret . . .' Primarily notable are the words cited by Promio (Monete di Savoia, I, p.95), which are located in the Monetier bonaccorso's account, where, mentioning 826 double blacks, it is adding that *'de lege et ponder nihil declaratur hic de mandato domini.'* Here is the fraud. It was needed, in the second place, the violence. The Prince would not have reached his goal if he had not commanded that the sums to be paid to him must be paid in a certain kind of money, different from that he paid his creditors."

Only with the aid of the law in general is it possible to practice this kind of violence, which, in the words of several persons, is not for that reason mostly reprehensible, because the laws should repress as a main objective, and not favor the violence and the dispossession.

Account money is money that does not exist materially and that is needed in the account. It is, therefore, a numerary. If the exchanges in the account money are entirely free, such money is a true numerary, such as, in England, the guinea. The guinea does not exist anymore, but this terminology indicates a certain gold weight.

Auxiliary money is almost never true money. For the most part, it is trust money and sometimes false money.

Circulation money enables and facilitates exchange and production. The services yielded are of two kinds: (a) it allows arbitration among different goods, and (b) it serves for transformation of present goods into future goods exchange.

It is possible to exchange any goods with any other goods, by means of money. Every exchange operation is resolved into two transactions, a sale and an acquisition. The money used for these transactions could be true money, trust money, or counterfeit money: This is absolutely indifferent until the general services produced by the money are considered. As for the goods arbitrated, it is possible to obtain the same results using gold (or silver); money is substituted by much less expensive means, and it is evidently profitable to use such means as much as possible. From this verification to the authority imposed by the government, there is but one single step. If the government (state in Italy) will issue false money, and if it is accepted by everybody, it shall yield precisely the services expected. Even if it is taken into consideration on this specific point of view, quite an important historical fact must be noticed. All attempts made by the state government in the mentioned imposition ended with some disaster. Instead, it has only been the private initiative that has generated the banking transfer of account, the clearing house, the warrants which arrived to save in major part the specie (metal money). Governments, so far in favor this evolution, have instead placed some obstacles for submitting the travelers checks, hitting them with fees and other kinds of similar measures. This comparison between the state government's money production and the production in a regime of free competition presents a certain interest.

It is a matter of the risk that insolvency or bad faith of some free traders could derive from political mistrust. The transfer accounts from a banker should substitute those risks which take place in relationship to the free trader and those circulated in relation to the banker, and these last risks are much less. The travel check system, completed with the institution of the clearing house, furthermore minimizes these risks. They are almost null with warrants. As a matter of fact, a warrant possessor is almost certain to have the goods the warrant represents. True money completely eliminates these risks. Trust money, which after all represents true money, does not let subsist more than generally quite light risks. As for counterfeit money, instead of minimizing the risks, it often tends to increase them.

There is, in fact, another kind of risk whose origin is much more hidden. Such risks derive from the political prices expressed in counterfeit money exposed to severe causes and frequent disturbances, which are added to much less important disturbances (perturbation) of price expressed in true money.

It is necessary, also, to observe that the cause of penury is neither the goddess's will, nor manifest in the causes of calamity, misfortune, and the citizen must avoid it. An historical interpretation of past events seems to be timely to understand present and future phenomena, especially when political monetary policy is under scrutiny.

Since men abandoned themselves to ostentation (magnificence), greed, and nonchalance, not marrying, nor marrying to have children or bringing up only two to allow them comfort and maintain them in luxury, the hidden evil is thus increasing. The evil is also derived from social problems like continuous wars and then, of course, from the ravages of Roman soldiers. Many men were killed or reduced to slavery (Strabone, VIII, 8, 11). The most famous cities fell without leaving traces of themselves, as a consequence of continuous wars. Hence, the Arcadia has been subject, and some countryside has stopped being inhabited and cultivated after the megalopolis has absorbed much left over from the old cities. (See VII, What Strabone says of Corcira). Thebes had kept, as its time, the appearance of a great village. IX. Describing the Dalmatia, a number of cities are cited as destroyed by Romans. Referring to other populations, it is added (VII; 5) that all started with becoming weak. And the Macedonians and Romans finished crushing them. Modern moralists give sermons on the decaying family spirit that led to the depopulation of the Roman empire. Wars, savage people, and oppression were the first causes. In our time, instead, excessive expenses affecting the balance sheets prevent the inhabitants of the specific community (and, of course, some other specific communities on this earth) from being more numerous and more prosperous. To the causes that prevented population increases in the Roman world must be added the destruction of personal capital (mobile).

It must be underlined that under the empire, evil seems to have become generalized in Rome. Tacito (Annuali, III, 25) says in connection with the Papia-Poppea law: "*Nec ideo conjugia et educationes liberum frequentabuntur, praevalida orbitate.*" It is suggested by other authors that Tacitus had copied from other authors. However, such an argument deducts little from the value of the findings. During our days, the attempts are much notable and are made by zealous defenders of the ruling classes to minimize, and also to legitimize, the crimes of the Roman Empire. When the bourgeois, the middle class, fought against the absolute monarchy and made use of people, they help to admire Tacitus and invade against the "tyrants." Now that they are at power, it is realized that these tyrants had something of good and almost in disdains sometime to imitate them.

Histoire des Romoins, V, pp. 654, says: "We are rightly proud of the elegant and noble society which surrounded Louis XIV." This is said under the point of view of the ruling classes. It is possible that the people who at the time died of hunger must have been of an opposite opinion.

II Leon de la Fontaine observed: "*On vous domme donne ici la victoire, mais l'ouvrier vous a de cus; il ava it liberte de feindre. Avec plus de raison nons aurious de le dessus, si mes confrerer savaient peindre.*"

The maximum of the ruling classes' benefit, above all when it is considered luxury, is always opposed to the maximum benefit of the poor classes. These are the majority of human beings, and the benefit does not coincide with the maximum benefit to nation or human race. Similarly, it could be said of labor classes and their maximum of benefits or of whatever social class is considered.

It must be added, on the other side, that of the ruling classes have often personally burdened upon the people. It is thanks to the efforts of a few individuals who left such classes that we have realized all the progress of society. It often happened that, under the impetus of powerful moral or religious sentiments, a number of individuals separated from the classes to which they belonged. They were guided quite often by altruistic sentiments in pursuing the well-being of the entire population.

One of the main causes seemed to be, first of all, the systematic destruction of personal (mobile) capital. Then, certain phenomena were evidenced, as seen during our days; for example, during economic crisis. It could be possible to review such intense phenomena as those produced during antique times, whenever a socialist, capitalist, or organization attempted to destroy personal (mobile) capital in our society.

It must be kept in mind that during the Roman empire, wealth was not only destroyed by the lunatic expenses of certain emperors nor by the expenses to nourish the Roman plebes. The most considerable destruction was accomplished as the result derived by offices similar to the Athenian aristocracies by the fiscal burdens imposed on the wealthy classes.

It is beyond imagination how much was permitted to be spent on luxury, on public feasts, and so on. Countless inscriptions tell us of generous donors' merits. Gaston Boissier (*L'opposition sous les Cesars*, pg. 44) noted that the Honoraria Summa was the sum of money that those elected to the municipality had to pay on the act of nomination in recognition of the honor made to him. It is added: "Such sums, which varied according to the city's importance, were the minor expenses that the magistrature amounted to." The expectations were quite different from those who received citizens' votes. The less rich in the municipalities offered to the electors hot wines and pastries. From morning until the evening, the poor people had the rights to enjoy this kind of generosity at expense of the "edible" or their "dunmivir." An inscription states: "My friend, ask for pastries and wine and these will be given to you until the evening. Don't blame but yourself if you arrive too late."

Twenty sestertius were given to decurions, ten sestertius to members of certain religious and commercial associations, the augustales, the mercuriales, and eight sestertius to all other citizens. As far as any kind of games that were available and paid for, the people showed more interest than in any other activity that was offered; such generosities among other things were not enough. The people demanded such meals, and such feasts were connected to the most durable and serious benefits: It was almost always that the "magistrate" undertook public works on his own expenses.

It is uncommon that authors who have spent some time on this subject did not exclusively pay attention to the transfer of wealth. Thus, writers without being aware of this problem, it is translated into destruction of mobile capital and set a sure collapse of the Roman Empire.

G. Boissier adds (page 46): "The major part of monuments which ornamented the provinces of that time . . . were thus erected with costs neither for the State nor for the municipality." It is true, they did not cost the government anything, but costs were very high to the society. They would have destroyed the wealth; they set the stage for downfall.

The emperors with all their power encouraged these generosities, and thus the empire covered itself with sumptuous monuments. The public administration which it inspired to certainly increased patronages and other kinds of privileges when it was thought that to build them was private. There is nothing to admire in a system that has ruined an entire population (the people).

Then to such expenses were added the fees paid to the barbarians to acquire peace. When the curiales of the low empire also had to support the (always) increasing weight of taxes, their position became so intolerable that it came to the point of condemning the people to be *"curiales loco supplicii"* (Codex Just. X. 32. 38). They were not permitted, above all, to abandon their order (class). Those who found refuge in the churches as in the Code Teod (IZ, XLV, 3) established the curiales in the worse company: *"Si auis in posterum servus ancilla, curialis debitor publicus, procurator, murilequlus . . . ad ecclesiaim confugiens vel clericus ordinatus vel quocunque modo a clericis fuerit defensatus nec statim conventione praemissa pristinae conditioni redditur, decuriones guidement omnes, quos solita ad debitums munus functio vocat. vigore et solertia indicatum ad pristinam sortem velut mammox iniector revocentur."* Is it necessary to make similar laws against the manners and political manipulation of our society? If introducing mandatory trade unions and other socialistic institutions of such (generous) kinds is continued, what is the real definition of money and capital? To avoid being curiales, people took shelter with the barbarians or became peasants. *"Nov. major, VII, nt. multi patrias deserentes natalium speldore neglects, occultes, latebras et habitationem dedecoris addentes, ut . . . colonarum se ancillarumque coniunctione pulluerint."*

At this point, in the proper perspective and consideration, is there any economic idea as wrong as of those individuals who could imagine that it is possible to make people progress by destroying its wealth, classes, and by destroying also their personal capital? Unfortunately, modern people are troubled much more to change the tax structure than reduce their total by cutting down the expenses. Protectionists around the globe destroy immense sums of wealth, while others with more considerable sums are dissipated in all kinds of frivolous trip expeditions and project R & D, in the name of venture capital, and nobody is able to understand their objectives and profitabilities. Such procedures would have already ruined for some time an entire country if there were not present the admirable faculty of the people to work and to save in a variety of productive activities. These activities are always endured by capital that reflects the main people market needs, not greed.

If, for no other reason, these historical events, put in the right perspective and with proper interpretation, should help understand and redefine present and future capital and money for specific activities.

Thanks for your consideration.

Freeze and Not Freeze Procedures

(Banking Accounts in US Project AUA's Invested Capital)

The verdict against the city hall of Avezzano could have enormous implications as far as law #43-1956, Investment of Foreign Capital, a Treaty between United States and Italy, and connected Italian banking accounts. The reputation of a specific Italian banking account in United States, as it is claimed, could be sequestered as violating the RICO laws by conspiring and obstructing justice related to Project AUA's local court case. The civil suit findings from the verdict state very clearly the fraud, cover-up, conspiracy, and fictitious contractual land sale deal from the city hall of Avezzano. Along the course of negotiation for the Campus land acquisition with city hall of Avezzano officials, documents show evidence of bribery, theft in public office, kickbacks, and deceit, especially examining the content of specific deliberation. Also, from a personal inquiry, it is quite evident that some of these city officials, in connection with politicians, have provided false information, especially to a local Newspaper, *Il Tempo Pagina Marsicana,* to have produced articles with distorted statements.

The summons originally filed in the local tribunal of Avezzano could have also been filed in US federal court to recover the invested capital for Project AUA's Campus activities, mainly to freeze a target Italian bank account in United States. In claiming that the city hall of Avezzano has violated the Racketeer Influenced and Corrupt Organizations (RICO) Act, Project AUA's concern has sought proper reevaluation of the invested capital and/or the correct value in US dollars of the sum determined in the verdict for damages that would bring the total to over one hundred— million US dollars, plus court costs. The competent authorities in the United States and Italy are asked to look very closely at the evidence and facts for RICO law violations, which might expose connections with a specific target bank account in the United States, the whole within the framework of law #43-1956, already recommended.

As a general principle, it is proper to present the law violation to the government authorities, to ascertain specific facts and recurrent events before the RICO Act is enforced. Without any doubts, this case could also have repercussion for other foreign capital investment directly and indirectly related to Project AUA's activities. The crucial problem is that the competent authority so far has not given the proper attention and consideration to the mentioned law violations. In fact, the capital invested on behalf of Project AUA's activities has not received the degree of protection and guaranty defined by the law. Since the petition to review the findings from the Italian court verdict was submitted to the competent government authorities, there was no follow-up, and it seemed that the file itself was somehow misplaced. In any event, the RICO suit in US federal court could be the continuation of the civil suit started at the tribunal of Avezzano. For several years, there were attempts to settle the case and/or to resolve the entire matter through an arbitration process, but the city hall of Avezanno has maliciously and repeatedly refused to do so. New evidence could allege that the city hall of Avezzano with the aid of "Obscure Forces" has engaged in a planned conspiracy against Project AUA's Campus program objectives and development activities.

There is clearly a pattern of recurrent events and persistent wrongdoing on the part of the city hall of Avezzano. It has been alleged several times that these wrongdoings are outrageous and should be investigated by competent authorities in United States and Italy. From this investigation, it is very easy to discover elements of bribes, public official kickbacks, and corrupt practice under a form of property right alteration that is another form of bribery. But the years of litigation in the local Italian court rooms have focused more on the technicalities and breach of contract, rather than paying attention to these allegations. Only recently the reelected mayor of Avezzano and city administrators have been forced to turn their attention to the rezoned campus land sale negotiation and connected capital investment in US dollars and the RICO Act implications as per law #43-1956. A cost reevaluation and an analysis of the capital investment for Project AUA's Campus development activities have been performed and accordingly examined by scholars and professional specialists.

Therefore, after competent authorities in the United States and Italy have acknowledged and examined such a capital investment determination, there is no other alternative but to seek a judiciary avenue to freeze an Italian target bank account in the United States and Italy as well. It is evident now that the city hall of Avezzano has maliciously and deliberately manipulated the Campus land deal to an exorbitant multi-million market price to exclusively benefit a new private ownership. It is clear now why the city hall of Avezzano has refused to disclose key documentation so the public and other concerns could forget why the delivery of the property title to Project AUA had to be modified for reconsideration by previous administrations. The whole might explain whether the Campus key documents and deliberations are still classified as a sort of confidential work-paper or top-secret agreement. It might explain also that in the request for such a key documentation, the city hall of Avezzano officials have refused again and again to verify facts, events, and deeds. Certainly this kind of conduct has abused the disclosure of public record laws by advocating such secrecy and denials, when related Project UAU documentation should be made public.

In other information provided about this kind of secrecy and denials, it is stated that the city hall of Avezzano's behavior is to keep secret the entire matter, and to be more explicit because of the many political crises and changing administrations, the subject matter is considered to be immaterial and irrelevant from any previous written agreement and commitments. This is the logic behind and the main reason why the city hall of Avezzano officials choose secrecy and any kind of expedient in denial of evidence. But acknowledging that such expedient and legal evidence effects millions and millions of US dollars for promotional and organizational activities, along other particular aspects of the Project AUA Campus program development, the subject matter is too important to be ignored or forgotten and should be reviewed by competent authorities as soon as possible. It is now time that the city hall of Avezzano officials start to release more detailed information and convincing explanations about the new Campus land modifications and Project AUA contractual agreement. It is time to call for action; freezing an Italian bank account in the United States is the most and secure alternative to be considered by the competent government authorities.

The City Hall of Avezzano, Office of the Mayor And Vice-Mayor in the Campus Land Sale Deal

There is no doubt that after so many meetings and discussions held at the mayor and vice-mayor's office of the city hall of Avezzano, Italy, in connection with Project American University of Avezzano's Campus land sale deal, the conclusion and evidence derived might show anything but a pattern in deceptive sales practices. Those responsible city hall officials seem to ignore that international laws, particularly in the United States with the Federal Trade Commission and statutes in most states make deceptive sale practice unlawful. Historically, the Campus sale deal is an act in which, during the course of years, the Avezzano city hall officials main purpose was to deceive and to manipulate written contractual agreements. A more recent reformulation of the marketable Campus land sale price may also define a deceptive act as one which is likely to deceive new prospective buyers acting reasonably in the circumstances [See, e.g. Mass. G.L. e.93A, §21(1); 15 U.S.C.A. §45(a)(1)].

The last news is that the city hall of Avezanno must be part of the American University of Avezzano, Inc. ownership to give validity to the provincial prefect's "Decree of Public Utility" for the approved project Campus program. But when everything seemed to be agreed upon, differences resolved, and some of the controversy (legal and non-legal)worked out over the Campus land sale issues, another more critical problem of very critical importance to the specific location has emerged that might threaten further delays in Project AUA development. Early deliberations from the city hall of Avezzano are the most important legal documents for Project AUA's Campus program development and the initial deceptive act from the city hall administrators. Based on specific deliberations and related agreements, a sale contract was signed by the Project AUA's concerns and a check was cashed in for the land payment as requested by the mayor pro-tempore; new proposals and modifications were forwarded to delay the title to the property, and other deceptions followed, mainly to cover up the real issues concerning the Campus development: fraud, stealing, project property alteration, obstruction of justice, and many other wrongdoings in violation of civil and penal laws.

Some of these violations, as they are analyzed by competent authorities, should be reviewed in light of the work that has been done—the capital invested in US dollars for specific project activities; the loss and damage caused because the Campus land sale's legal controversy remains so long unresolved. But other recent experiences with the city hall of Avezzano should not be underestimated and must be taken into proper consideration, especially in light of the evidence that the main city interlocutor is trying to evade very serious financial and legal responsibilities by avoiding open scrutiny. Although it is true that the re-elected Mayor, as explicitly stated, supports Project AUA's Campus Program development, the enormous problem attached to the last meeting held with city officials concerns not only conflict of interest but the deceptive sale practice still being carried on. Before any further futile meetings or discussions, what the mayor should do is to make sure that city officials make a full and open disclosure of the entire matter by providing access to the original Project AUA file and the requested documentation accordingly submitted.

Also, it is imperative and can't be stressed too strongly that the mayor of Avezzano's apparent interest in proceeding with the Project AUA program in no way relieves the past city mayors and administrators from those obligations or to being available for questions on the matter of deceptive Campus sale practice. The entire matter will reveal a prevalently fraudulent intent to essentially benefit a third party, in the meantime misdirecting the course of the contracted land sale stipulations; that makes the attorney legal representation which one knows to be false and which is believed not to be true. There is a fraudulent misrepresentation of facts and of defined agreements among concerned parties. Of the entire Campus area defined in related deliberations, at least 90 percent is owned by the city hall of Avezzano and leased to private parties for farming purpose. Prior to the rezoned Campus program and the city council's unanimous approval, the remaining property would have been reclaimed by the city hall of Avezzano to be sold to the "American University of Avezzano, Inc." for a price not more than 250 Italian lire per square meter, as negotiated. In the event of problems with tenants in releasing such property, about 180 thousand square meters, procedures for public domain expropriation would have been carried on by the city hall of Avezzano.

It must be pointed out that evidence and reported information related to the rezoned Campus land revealed manipulation of property titles and illicit political maneuvres to boycott the fulfilment of contractual obligations. In fact, the whole recent "new modifications for the Campus land development" is another ugly decision in spite of good intentions. Such a tactical position by the city hall of Avezzano, in the past and present, usually involved offering a piece of property at a low price to lure a potential project; after pirating the relevant documented information, they then created concerns about buying at higher price per square meter, even though such practice is prohibited by statute in most states (See Model Penal Code §224.7(5)). Land acquisition of parcels of the "rezoned Campus" by the Vice-Mayor of the previous administration under false pretense, during and immediately after the Project AUA program was submitted to the city hall of Avezzano, are not coincidental or casual (See: Report and Memorandum of Transactions).

But if the current vice-mayor at the city hall of Avezzano is not allowed to do a "reversible transaction" of the original title to the ownership of the "Zone Campus," what is the point of having my attorney also in charge of the public work? It must be remembered that the position of vice-mayor was held by a community real-estate tycoon now known as "the landlord of the current campus modifications." Certainly, the vice-mayor at the city hall of Avezzano is very important not only for advising the current administration on the previous mayor's land dealings but perhaps on other more lucrative business transactions as well. Evidently, it is not too difficult to explain conflict of interest, but it becomes problematic when justifying specific transactions. This kind of buying and selling of titles to the Campus land property and revolving urban affairs development in the city of Avezzano, Italy, concerns almost everybody contacted on this crucial problem; it is believed to give too much leeway for spending more time and money for additional court litigation. A situation such as this is susceptible enough to think at least twice without giving a blank check impression.

Project AUA and the "Obscure Forces"

It is not a surprise, and neither is unexpected, to realize that verdicts related to the Project American University of Avezzano (AUA), Within a Campus of International Character, are less than frivolous. Coverage in the newspaper *Il Tempo—Pagina Marsicana* includes stories and behavior in which the plaintiff maintained, and still maintains, that the city hall of Avezzano and connected "obscure forces" are mainly responsible for the damaging results of negligent actions; the "P.Q.M." in the verdict findings seem to be anything but the basis of a frivolous lawsuit as well. It has been discussed many times that the responsible city hall administrations should have been aware that when a settlement of this nature comes to closure, the awarded amount of the damage stated for "ISTAT" revaluation, related attorney fees, court costs, and miscellaneous expenses must be incorporated into the total cost of the Project Campus final decision. Any other additional costs, obviously, must also be passed along and assumed, for whatever purpose and reason the final decision is made. There is no surprise in realizing that any consequence of this decision regarding the Campus land deal dispute might add fuel for other lawsuits.

It is unfortunate that for this particular "frivolous" lawsuit, the city hall of Avezzano did not follow several suggestions to settle out of court rather than be subjected to media publicity, even though some of its politicians might eventually have been implicated in some improprieties by the local court of law. This long litigation burden, together with the "asinine negligent behavior" of the same city officials, has affected almost all concerned parties. When money in this specific community is considered for "bribes" as a purchasing strategy and is relinquished to cover some irresponsible individual's ill-conceived action against Project AUA development and personal efforts, conclusions about the outcome should not be too far. The responsible city hall administrations should have had a moral duty and obligation toward Project AUA's concerns. Activities undertaken for the Project should not have been held hostage in the Italian courts for a "frivolous verdict," the result of inept and negligent actions on the part of those opportunistic, corrupt local individuals. It must be remembered that recourse to the local court was suggested and recommended to curb such abuses and to comply with contractual agreement and land title delivery.

There are assumptions that external pressure from "obscure forces" were also applied to the local courts in Italy to define a kind of guideline as to whether the lawsuit should have been accepted or not and whether it should be pursued against the city hall of Avezzano and its related responsible officials. Once the case was finally accepted by the local tribunal of Avezzano, which decided in favor of the plaintiff, a guideline of the compensatory damage, as well as the entire amount of the investment in US dollars, as applicable to foreign capital investment in Italy (Law #43-1956), was submitted accordingly. The local courts, in fact, have concurred that Avezzano city hall was knowingly negligent. The punitive damages and the capital investment were to be assessed within the "ISTAT" guideline sum reevaluation (See related Sentences and Documentation).

Law #43-1956, Investment of Foreign Capitals in Italy, as suggested in substitution of a "Letter of Intent," seems to alter a system intended to discourage fraud in the investment aspect of Project AUA. Because concerned potential investors could have directly sued those city hall of Avezzano officials, arguing they were misled by a growing number of wrongdoings, the same city officials have often avoided the release of much of the meaningful information related to Project AUA's legal documentation. This specific law should have provided a "safe harbor" to protect those potential investors from misleading obligations, especially from the local government officials. Instead, an outpouring of misinformation, analyzed and investigated, was followed by an avalanche of wrongdoing and fraudulent actions supported by the "obscure forces." Such investigation and information has not come easily. One of the reasons for the lengthy findings is that there is little understanding of what the suggested law #43-1956 really calls for. It is not clear what the affects of the substitution of the "Letter of Intent," a meaningful obligation in international legal contests, for law enforcement is, although a description of the law itself and attachments clarify how much protection it will provide for foreign capital investment in Italy. Another lawsuit should be filed against the city hall of Avezzano for having released false and misleading statements in the contract land dealing, while at the same time using Project AUA's materials for the rezoned Campus land development. It is evident that the "obscure forces," in and out of Avezzano's city hall, have applied pressure to alter the Campus program objectives away from the land use deliberations.

In addition, the specific law #43-1956 appears to shift the lawsuit to the Security Exchange Commission (SEC) Law Enforcement Division in the United States, where obstacles to filing are not as high, in lieu of the "obscure forces" tampering with the Campus property rights. However, this action might force a continuing threat of litigation, which certainly could make the city hall of Avezzano even more stringent in the cover-up to release the relevant information still in its possession related to the file's project materials. Locked in litigation since the early seventies, as recommended for the delivery of the land title, the legal dispute has languished in the local courts of Italy for decades, further delaying the Campus Project development and pushing away potential sponsors and investors. It is obvious that early negotiations to steer the case out of the court were apparently superfluous and in vain. Enormous amount of money, time, and expenses have been diverted to the litigation and frivolous verdicts. It is not a secret any longer that stakes were and are too high for both the city hall of Avezzano and connected "obscure forces." For the local community, the land represented its best shot, not only for conflict of interest, but for the investor(s) The bottom line is that since city hall of Avezzano officials changed their minds, and the Project Campus development activities were put in limbo due to litigation because the rules of the game changed many times. As a result, it is going to require an investment of capital at least ten times or more than anticipated in the early days of the project presentation. The fact of the matter is that after all these years of courts exhibitions and manipulations, there are any longer funds to be made for such an alternative project in the rezoned Campus acreage that will make somebody in the community rich. It should be pointed out that it was the city hall of Avezzano, not Project AUA, that halted Campus Program development years ago, when construction could have started at no charge to the city budget.

At present, a resolution of Project AUA's US dollars in capital investment claim by arbitration is good for all concerned parties. This resolution means that development of the Campus area property can be made with potential benefit to the community at large and to the treasury of Avezzano city hall. Otherwise, alternatives do not seem nearly so feasible in the near future, as other litigation is expected to last months, perhaps years, costing more and more in legal fees. Not too long ago, there were signals that the city hall of Avezzano's new concerns were ready to accept a settlement (See Memo-Trip-to-Italy; May-June 1995), but it took no time to realize the same pattern of strange behavior in those discussions, thus to elapse the general understanding to writing. Many personal efforts have been reduced and complicated by longstanding political fights and antagonisms among the community parties, particularly between those not-too obscure forces, evidently full of conflicts of interest. In the end, it must be said, those personal efforts must be commended for at least trying to put animosity aside and for searching for something that would benefit the community as well as the concerned parties. It is still believed that the Project "Campus of International Character" should be revived, and certainly it should, because the Project's entire activities are too important to lose any valid opportunity for making it a success. (Suggestions and information pertinent to the "obscure and not-too obscure forces" have been discussed more than once with proper sources during the personal efforts undertaken.)

A meeting with a representative of the Security Exchange Commission (SEC), Division of Enforcement, was previously requested to follow up on the "E-Mail Petition and Memorandum" sent to his office in Washington, DC, regarding the litigation and other disputes against the city hall of Avezzano. The SEC enforcement agent agreed to meet with an agent of the SEC Education Division in charge of this matter and in a better position to directly discuss any aspects pertinent this case. It was agreed that the meeting would take place on Nov. 14, at 1430 hours, at The SEC Education Division's Washington office. Certain documents were submitted and a few related points were elaborated during the course of discussions. Reference was made to law #43-1956, cited in substitution of a "Letter of Intent," a major point of interest and guarantee of capital investment in Italy; a fundamental law of the treaty of capital investment between the United States and Italy.

Other issues and specific topics were also tackled in reference to the educational aspect of the material related to Project AUA's Campus of International Character. Relevant documents researched from specific files and personal inquiries related to Project AUA's campus activities were called to their attention for the possibility of a publication proposal, such as "Fight City Hall," determined to be valid and relevant for pursuit of an international education project. After questioning and examining the submitted documentation, a few suggestions were provided by the SEC Education Division representative, and further recommendations were made available for consideration. Some possibilities have been mentioned to perhaps link to support from other government agencies in the United States and Italy.

A meeting was held afterward to mainly review some aspects of the SEC meeting and to elaborate on the conversations held by phone and/ or fax. There were difficulties discussed, especially regarding the political machine of the city hall of Avezzano without ruling out the many law violations and other wrongdoings related directly and indirectly to the verdicts issued by the local courts. The first step to follow is the "ISTAT" reevaluation of the capital investment costs, subsequently pressing for Project AUA's Campus property rights vindication. Proposal alternatives for liquidating or continuing with the Campus activities in Italy were analyzed once again. The prospectus presented was examined in detail, especially the feasibility study in-situ and the potential for financing sources for the activities. It was suggested to wait until a meeting is held with my attorney in Avezzano before making any decision regarding new and old proposals. At the meantime, it is worth organizing the several points of discussion and information for "Fight City Hall." Thoughts, notes, and personal views from this and other meetings certainly will contribute another chapter to the publication.

Also, it is imperative and can't be stressed too strongly that the mayor of Avezzano's apparent interest to go on with Project AUA in no way relieves the past mayors and administrators from those obligations to be available for questions on the matter of deceptive Campus sale practices. The entire matter will show a fraudulent intent, essentially to benefit a third party, in the meantime violating the contract stipulation against making legal representation that one knows to be false and that is believed not to be true. There is a fraudulent misrepresentation of facts and of defined agreements among concerned parties. At least 90 percent of the entire Campus area defined in related deliberations is owned by the city hall of Avezzano and leased for farming purpose. Prior to the city council's unanimous approval of the rezoned Campus program, besides the deliberated land for sale, the remaining property would have been reclaimed by the city hall of Avezzano to be sold to the "American University of Avezzano, Inc." as negotiated for a price of not more than 250 Italian lire per square meter. In the event of some problems with the tenants for releasing such property, about 180 thousand square meters, procedures for public domain expropriation would have been carried on by the city hall of Avezzano (See letter and Decree of Public Utility).

It must be pointed out that evidence and reported information related to the rezoned Campus land stated manipulation of property title and illicit political maneuvres to boycott the fulfilment of contractual obligations. In fact, the recent new modifications for the Campus land development is another ugly decision, in spite of the Mayor's good intentions. Perhaps the new mayor and vice-mayor should re-examine this kind of "bait and switch" in deceptive sales practice. Such tactical positions at the city hall of Avezzano, in the past and present, usually involve offering a piece of property at a low price to lure a potential project and then, after pirating the relevant documentation, inducing the concerns to buy at a higher price per square meter, even though such practice is prohibited by statute in most states (See Model Penal Code §244.7(5)).

There is a lot of blame to spread around that municipality, including some prominent local real estate and financial speculators who are now loath to use public funds to devise a get-rich-quick scheme since the Campus land for sale fraud. There is still a multitude of advisers for this land transaction and suddenly other rezoned modifications (Modificazioni al Piano Regolatore), updated new price deal makers, and famous local politicians who allow the scheme to continue. In fact, from this "land for sale" scheme, it is is possible to show that at the city hall of Avezzano there are still the same people (directly and indirectly associated) that somehow pretend now knowing the project Campus legal matter (See Council Deliberations and related documentation for reference).

-Domestic Market Wrongdoings and the Rico Law Act: After consultation with RICO specialists and considering and weighing the substantial costs to continue litigation against the city hall of Avezzano, it is determined that it would be in the best interest of all concerned to resolve the entire matter as soon as possible through the United States federal judicial process. This should be much more part of the city hall of Avezzano's history than its future and also the last chapter of a remembered ugly story. The damages and loss of the capital investment for Project AUA's Campus development are submitted for US dollar evaluation and verification by a certified public accountant (See Reevaluation and Economic-Financial Prospectus). It must be pointed out that in recent years the municipality of Avezzano has spent all kind of money to provide services and infrastructure to its community. It has been rocked by a series of scandals, often involving cozy political arrangements between local city hall officials and local individuals. For years these arrangements have been considered the "holy water" of community projects financing. And, because it operated as a cluster, with a very low profile, with less celebrated Campus land deal-makers and less glamorous personalities, many of the law violations are suitable for RICO consideration.

The Campus land deal-makers, however, wanting lucrative municipal financing arrangements, quite often eagerly wrote big checks to cronies and politicians able to hand out specific favors. Evidence will show that those poorly informed local financial officers were easy prey for these politicians, who quite often were peddling risky and wildly inappropriate favors for the recent Campus rezoning modifications. But, in the summer of 1992, just when the city hall of Avezzano technical office's famous celebrities and mayor ended up beyond a prison cell, also very much part of the same municipal history, concerned government agencies began a serious effort to clean up the domestic market wrongdoings. At the end, the personal abuses and RICO law investigations should yield the best perspective on how to enforce law #43-1956 regarding foreign capital investment in Italy, and to clarify when the specific law calls for the substitution of a letter of intent, which must offer the most solid security.

Meetings and personal discussions have been carried out, directly and indirectly, with persons contacted to share views related to pertinent

Project AUA activities. It is a common understanding that problems with primary target development activities still essentially derive from the unresolved legal dispute with the city hall of Avezzano. Project AUA target developments have fallen through because the concerned principals could not get a signed agreement on the final land sale contract from the several mayors of the city hall of Avezzano to go ahead with specific Campus programs. Without that signed contractual agreement, promoters was not in a position to make further personal commitments, especially considering the financial burdens from previously invested capital and other related legal matters. Project AUA's Campus program development and legal commitments have been attached, and still are, to the letter of intent, which was acknowledged within the specific law, the treaty between Italy and the United States, local government deliberations, and, above all, binding legal documents.

To go ahead with undertaken activities before the entire legal matter with the city hall of Avezzano is worked out would mean facing another unknown dilemma. Many of these people, as well as the municipality's officials referenced, have been unavailable and could not be reached for comment. There is also a persistent thought to criticize these municipality officials. But in time, there have been some suggestions that it is better "to first resolve the problem with the city hall of Avezzano before going forward with the new proposal and alternatives." It must be recognized, however, that these proposals and alternatives need time and contemplation, and of course sincere cooperation from concerned people of that specific community is needed.

Nonetheless, the undertaken Project AUA activities have been recognized to be very much valid and relevant as far as the Campus program is concerned. The promotional and organizational efforts have also been alive and well for continuing not only in the defined Campus zone but anywhere it seems to be appropriate and wanted. If there is an opportunity to go on with Project AUA's activities, it is quite certain new proposals and positive alternatives will appear in due time. What is really needed at this point is verification from a valid authority, such as the US Embassy in Rome, that is willing to cooperate and to complete the dealings which were initiated at the beginning of the projected Campus program at Avezzano.

-Vindication of Project AUA Property Rights and Capital Investment: Before the letter of intent was requested and related guarantee law provided, capital was already invested for undertaken activities, especially for promotion, organization, and Project AUA materials submitted to the city hall of Avezzano and other connected government agencies in Italy and United States. The complete materials and designs submitted for the Campus program in Zone-Barbazzano speak for themselves. In fact, there have been displays and public exhibitions of the project designs, program objectives presentations, architectural renderings and futuristic concepts, economic-financial plans, and many other feasibility studies, together with research and development for endowment purposes. But, it is necessary to recall once again what happened to those materials, designs, and documentation submitted to the city hall of Avezzano.

It is evident by now that after all Project AUA material files were duly reviewed by the competent city authorities and properly validated by other government concerns, all of sudden the Campus land deals were no longer carried on with the same project principals. Instead, the city hall of Avezzano officials dickered with the Campus land program with another unknown developer, as reported in the local press. Now as before, the question to be asked is: Who is the developer believed involved in the planning of a Campus complex at the same location that was already under contract and payment for it already accepted? Have they also presented the required information through the proper channels with specific government authorities? It is fair to say that there is enough evidence to demonstrate the unethical behavior of Avezzano city hall public servants. The recommended undertaken litigation and the local court legal processes are very well known. What is not known as yet is who is behind the new Campus land modifications, now rezoned for the construction of a luxurious hotel.

However, a very important deliberation on record should help to identify the originator of such a proposal to build such facilities for a hotel instead for the Campus program. There has not been any single attempt by the city hall of Avezzano council to ask for an investigation of the entire matter related to the circumstances of the Campus development. Even though this community is still interested in the Campus program development project, it is very important to claim property rights to the whole project material. Somebody in town said quite openly: "I am just glad that there is still wherewithal and patience to develop those projected Campus plans, which were submitted thirty years ago," and "It is like bringing to light an old bottle of prestigious local wine and drinking only a sip." Previously, city hall of Avezzano administrations have demonstrated only contempt for that spirit in their repeated, tedious contention that only the Council of Avezzano determines what business is public. But the minority of the local council said it is wrong The common man on the street said it is wrong. Old, young, and disabled everywhere said it is wrong. The tribunal of Avezzano and the court of appeal in L'Aquila said it is wrong. It is good to see that at least some in the community have risen to agree, and also that new members in the city hall now in charge have acquiesced.

-Appointment of a New Lawyer: A new lawyer hired to look very closely at the Italian Court verdicts needed a new power of attorney, and this had to be done after consultations held with other lawyers familiar with the city hall of Avezzano's past and present critical problems. The new lawyer, from L'Aquila, has taken the responsibility to carry on the legal matter by representing Project AUA's concerns. It has been vividly recognized that the sum awarded in the verdicts should be enforced immediately, while related claims addressed to the SEC Division of Enforcement and European Court of Justice will take a couple of weeks to realistically evaluate the entire situation. Some considerations, however, have been made whether there was negligence or simple lawyers' malpractice in handling previous local court litigation. Malpractice court procedures might also have occurred out of a lawyer's neglect to file the summons and/or to notify of the verdict in time, thereby probably allowing the statue of limitation to run out on enforcing specific verdicts.

Therefore, there are indisputable indications that a few individuals, directly and indirectly connected with the city hall of Avezzano over the course of years, used bribes, corruption, and illegal favoritism of a different nature mainly to boycott Project AUA's activities for personal profit and/ or to direct profitable project work material to friends. It would be quite easy at this point to understand that the beginning of the corruption was costing the projected Campus program millions of US dollars and Italian lire per year; now the price tag is at more than a hundred million US dollars. More than a few circumstances involve individual efforts, and those questions could be very important in enabling the resolution of Project AUA's collateral activity problems. One of the most important questions is the "Foreign Service Process" for the acquisition of jurisdiction by the federal district court in the United States. According to those rules and principles, there are certain legal proceedings that have been established in the system of jurisprudence for the enforcement and protection of private rights.

RICO (Racketeer Influenced and Corrupt Organization Act) laws and the malicious abuse of legal processes have been also considered. This involved willfully misapplying a court process to obtain objects not intended by law. The willful misuse of misapplication of process was accomplished for a purpose not warranted or commanded by the writ. In fact, the tort requires a perversion of court process to accomplish some end the process was not designed to accomplish and does not arise from a regular use of process, even with ulterior motives. There were also questions regarding wrongdoings, such as fraud, which consists of an intentional perversion of truth for the purpose of inducing another in reliance upon it to part with some valuable thing belonging to Project AUA and/or to surrender the legal rights claimed. Without any doubt, there has been a false representation of a matter of fact, whether by words or by conduct, by false and/or misleading allegations, or by concealment of that which should have been disclosed, which deceives and is intended to deceive and/or to cause legal injury. Facts and events related to Project AUA's activities have been submitted and called as evidence of reference (Meetings-discussions and legal tips from attorneys).

Submitted by:

Aspr Surd
(Project AUA)

"You Should Not Give Up the Fight"

To know whether or not to pursue a specific agenda in related activity objectives means another meeting, another trip to Italy, a lot of broken promises, one more phone call for suggestions and recommendations, and once again awaiting another election for the mayor of Avezzano. The same facts and events that happened in the last four decades are reoccurring at the present time. In Avezzano there is another election for the office of the mayor, and it is suggested we wait until after this election before arranging for another meeting with city hall of Avezzano officials. However, the key contact person reaffirmed one more time what has been said so many times: "Law #43-1956, foreign capital investment in Italy, must be enforced, and you should not give up the fight against the city hall of Avezzano, considering the illicit wrongdoings and damages caused to the undertaken activities." It seems that some light is coming out to shine on those "obscure forces" that have placed obstacles against the development of Campus facilities at the pre-purchased, rezoned land, as per local government deliberation and contractual agreement.

It is not new to report once again that after all these years, not only frustration but extreme disappointment exists in the actions of lawyers and their courts in the matter in which decisions are made in reference to the undertaken litigations and related legal claims. Apparently lawyers and their courts do not reflect the kind of justice at the standard of law expected at any courtroom level; no recognition has been shown that a lesson has been learned that the history of a country might repeat itself. Just as any concerned citizen in a specific community does not give up the fight to end the corruption of their elected public officials, similarly those concerned with the Campus project development must not give up their fight until justice is done. It is quite clear at this point that the city hall of Avezzano has secretly tried all kind of subterfuge and spent untold dollars and lire of taxpayers' money to cover up their wrongdoings, before finally giving up and recognizing Project AUA's claims.

This new election in Avezzano should make clear whether the new mayor and administrators will be allowed to continue spending untold amounts of taxpayers' money before the demands of those concerned citizens are accepted. On the other side, the promotion and reorganization of Project AUA's plans requires more time, personal efforts, and much more capital investment than was previously anticipated. In addition, and without any doubt, there will be even much more critical pressures and further business risks. It is obvious that commitments must be shared by those who supported and still support Project AUA's endeavors and oppose city hall's strange behavior and wrongdoings. Those concerned citizens will be persistent, and the fight won't be given up until justice is done and the truth comes to light.

There are assurances, at least, that this new election for the mayor and administrators of Avezzano city hall will bring also some new communityexpectations for the leadership of a new political force that should prompt some serious thoughts and, hopefully, dedication to work out the solution for the Campus program development together.

It must be kept in mind that after the early presentation about the Campus of International Character, the city of Avezzano's council members unanimously favored bypassing political and other kinds of community party line decisions to endorse the undertaken promotional and organizational efforts, which were, and still are, tied to the exclusive rights to develop the selected site at the identified location (Refer to city of Avezzano's deliberations). A source from the city hall of Avezzano and from other concerned citizens in the community have stated very openly: "The projected Campus program development was almost ready to roll, until the newspaper *Il Tempo*, in the local page, started to boycott the initiative's personal efforts. There was very strong public support for this project, and now after so many years of legal disputes, it must be decided what to do for urban planning in the rezoned Campus." It is still alive. However, public opinion and resentment about the entire matter exists; for example: "I do not think the city of Avezzano, and perhaps the entire country of Italy, can be allowed to lose more time. Can we, as conscientious citizens of this community, afford to lose the potential attached to the

Campus of International Character program?" Also, one of the city councilman has said many times, about the Campus issue that there is overwhelming support for Project AUA's total control of the land in the "Zona Barbazzano" and the development of the proposed parking-garage as presented and agreed upon.

It must be pointed out that these remarks came after the interlocutor was introduced directly to the "Financial-Economic Plans" submitted to the competent government authorities. The project plans, which have been shown and reviewed several times, privately and publicly, with mayors, councilmen, provincial government officials, and other concerns, still offer the possibility for building the campus facilities, such as: dormitories for students and visitors; class-rooms; gymnasium; swimming pool; administration building, library, athletic fields, and parking garages for endowment purposes. However, the Project AUA efforts ended due to the local courts, after almost a decade of promotional activities. Strange as it could be, the city hall of Avezzano backed out from its contractual obligation simply because the many mayors involved with this matter have refused to give Project AUA control of the land for the campus.

In spite the time spent during the Italian court decisions (a quarter of century), and in conformity with law #43-1956, the investment of foreign capital treaty between Italy and the United States, through the legal system Project AUA is still asking for everything embodied in contractual arrangements as defined and requested by the city hall of Avezzano: development rights to the rezoned Campus in the identified city-owned property. The Italian courts have ruled only on breach of contract in favor of the Project AUA, although the judgments are frivolous in many aspects. It was never officially mentioned to the concerned parties that the city hall of Avezzano's main purpose was to usurp Project AUA's program plans and Campus development materials to essentially benefit a third party. In the end, it must be said that the city hall of Avezzano's behavior is not only very strange, but the motives behind the cover-up are more than clear by now, consisting mainly of pernicious fraud and also of a congenital costume in pirating intellectual property rights that are very clear in the law and in human promotional efforts. A distressed councilman added: "All this is part of our community's history, and it will be with the local people for decades to come, and hopefully a lot is to be learned from it." But there are persistent doubts.

This is a petition for timely intervention to request further litigation proceedings for review of procedural tactics and principal merits to avoid postponements and delays by the Security Exchange Commission— Division of Enforcement, Washington, DC, as there is evidence of fraud and other attempts to obstruct laws and justice. The constitutional basis for the American University of Avezzano's petition is the belief and documented history of a public service mission, threatened already with foreign capital investment disaster, the reasons for which evidences are set forth in the Summons Memorandum intended to provide a current status report. Copies of legal documents will be provided as request and made part of this petition, with sworn testimony at the appropriate Security Exchange Commission session.

In summary, it is the hope of the undersigned to save the original, jointly approved efforts—economic-financial plans and some thirty (30) years of dedicated work—and large amount of US dollars andItalian lire already invested as per recommended law #43-1956 (capital investment in Italy). The petition to the SEC, Division of Enforcement, is to intervene in this specific case (as provided by the violation of the cited law and related international RICOstatute) as an entity competent to hear and determine the disputed violation and to perform the obligation incumbent upon judgments already rendered by the Italian courts, and to appoint arbitration for the reevaluation of specific capital inUSdollars to which to have recourse, as it deems necessary to make such a recommendation and/ or decide upon measures to be taken and to give effect to past and future judgements.

Accordingly, the undersigned, as imbued with legal power and related property rights, is also allowed to request a hearing session without postponement and/or continuance for negotiating a good faith and equitable plan for going forward and/or liquidating the original Project AUA's program with a fair and reasonable settlement. Therefore, by the implicit legal rights, the undersigned now comes forward to request said action by the SEC, Division of Enforcement, and while engaged in such law enforcement and judicial claims, to give notice to the Italian concern, the mayor pro-tempore, City Hall, Avezzano (Aq), Italy, to hold up further action on the petitioned matter until a fair and just revised judgment is issued.

This petition is respectfully submitted and dated by the signatory below.

Summons Memorandum

To: Sec Division Of Enforcement
450 Fifth Street, N.W.
Washington, D.C. 20549

Ref: Litigation American University of Avezzano. Inc. (Ohio); Hereinafter *AUA vs. City Hall of Avezzano (AQ), Italy*

To the premise that the truthfulness of the verdict's content from the low and high courts in Italy (Avezzano Tribunal and L'Aquila Court of Appeal) is in the correlative judgments against the city hall of Avezzano, Italy. The undersigned, born in Cocullo (L'Aquila), Italy, a citizen of United States and Italy, has entered in negotiation and subsequently into financial-economic investments in the original Project AUA's development documentation submitted to the city hall of Avezzano. Copy of this documentation is made available to the various government agencies and concerned parties in the United States and Italy. It is this particular Project AUA's program: a Campus of International Character, the fundamental premise to the land use (or rezoning) of the "Contrada Barbazzano" as part of the urban plan of the city of Avezzano. The land-use plan is better specified on related deliberations and the sale contract, which defines also the limits of the "Variante al Piano Regolatore," also adapted and approved by means of a public decree issued by the Office of the Provincial Prefect, based on the evaluation of Project AUA's documentation.

It must be underlined that when the projected Campus of International Character was first proposed and related documentation was submitted to the city hall of Avezzano, at the same time certain clarification was requested in written agreements related to a letter of intent and capital security already invested for Project AUA's activities. Law #43-1956, Investment in Italy—Treaty between Italy and the United States, dated Feb.7, 1956, was recommended to provide the most safety and guarantee for Project AUA's investment. This law is very clear, and public officials in Avezzano's city hall can not knowingly approve documents, such as deliberations, that are false or misleading and can not recklessly disregard those agreements that call into question a municipality's ability to fulfill specific obligations. Joint open meetings and those recommendations were made available before and until the summons of litigation was introduced at Avezzano Tribunal. There is evidence of illicit behavior by Avezzano's city hall officials in connection with the Campus of International Character land property dealings. This kind of behavior is a simple fraud in the book of international law. There is also evidence that during the course of land negotiations and Project AUA start-up activities, mayors and city officials made false and misleading statements and/or failed to disclose important information related to the land transaction and, hence, the related financial investment.

In such optic, to the premise that specific agreements have derived from said Project AUA's documentation, which personal ownership pertaining to the undersigned, and equally all legal rights that are connected to real estate and other property values. At the time this Summons Memorandum is forwarded, the original Project AUA documentation is still in possession of the city hall of Avezzano; according to the property rights claimed and statute laws in force, hence is made petition to the SEC Division of Enforcement to vindicate and protect the above mentioned legal rights. Evidence from this documentation file detail shady actions by specific officials of the Avezzano city hall, reckless behavior, also making false statements, discovery of wrongdoing might reveal crimes such as: theft and alteration of Project AUA's master plan and legal documents; confiscation of intellectual property rights; fraudulent behavior of public officials; and conflict of interest.

There are no doubts that specific evidence will show that those specific city officials had knowledge of the risks but failed to take appropriate steps to disclose them, and, therefore this is fraud. In fact, a municipal government that seeks access to foreign capital, as per recommended law 43-1956, can not mistake the basic documents to investors, either local or foreign. Indeed, new discovery is concerned that when the Avezzano city hall officials asked for payment and cashed a check for land as per agreement, it was never revealed that it might not be able to deliver title to the land and that were already conflicts of interest among city officials.

Background—(Project AUA's "Status quo" Report to Government Agencies files; Italian and US Embassy files; Italian courts documentation, and related verdicts): Government agency files (in both Italy and the United States), their connected Embassy consulates, and the Italian courts contain certain essential memoranda and documents indicating progressive steps and problems of Project AUA. These documentation files were jointly developed by Project AUA and the city hall of Avezzano, at all times promoted and implemented by the undersigned. Specific files will also include many notes and documents generated during Project AUA's development phases, meetings, visits, and/or otherwise.

The land title to Project AUA's campus site was never delivered, and the undersigned was forced to file a summons at the local tribunal of Avezzano, where endless flows of documentation are the results of seeking action or reasons for not acting from the city hall of Avezzano's authorities. Certain powers of attorney were delegated to lawyers to seek answers and new positions for discussion, but these efforts also came to nothing. The undersigned, especially, made several trips and incurred costly expenses, facing the wholly unexplained campaign to discredit Project AUA's efforts and to avoid the main issue of the matter—the delivery of the land title.

At this point, the project's main concern arrived at the reluctant conclusion that, for completely unknown reasons, Avezzano city hall had elected to block the endeavor. Meanwhile substantial work was done on implemented program and related activities relevant to general citizen's health education and environmental maintenance. Furthermore, financial investment was utilized for administration, promotion, real estate negotiation, project design and planning, dues and fees, cost of services, and other miscellaneous fees, as defined in detail and in summary in the submitted financial statements.

Decision and Action: The undersigned for some time has harbored the (perhaps) remote hope of an equitable solution to the Campus site controversy from the Italian courts' judgments. Meantime, it was forced by the empowered legal rights and obligations, to continue litigation against the city hall of Avezzano more than twenty (20) years (as documented by the court verdicts), to track and to challenge reported wrong information. One main reason was to expose enormous financial losses due to the city hall of Avezzano's wrongdoing. Because of the various crimes and implications the city's officials were made aware of, it is realistically recognized that a settlement of the dispute would probably involve disposition of the title to the Campus land claims. Since delay tactics and postponements have exhausted all funds for paying legal fees and related case expenditures, this imminent petition of action through the SEC Division of Enforcement is appropriated and imperative.

Thus, it is purporting to hear this petition in the public interest to prevent further obstruction of justice. During subsequent Italian court hearings, there has always been openness to inform concerned parties, specific government authorities, and others of the evidence already charged that the city of Avezzano's wrongdoing and cover-up tactics, unethical conduct, fraudulent attitude, and alleged criminal practices against Project AUA would have impinged all development efforts. There have been also charges that the city hall of Avezzano, in its attitude and in furtherance of a preplanned personal conspiracy, would have caused enormous damages to Project AUA and its promotional activities, as well as collateral activities, such as violations of RICO statute laws and personal damages to the already acquired privileges which have been lost without being afforded the due process of law. Therefore, the undersigned, vested by legal rights and power of attorney, is petitioning the SEC Division of Enforcement to review the findings from the Italian courts (Case 336/86), and to determine a just and equitable reevaluation of Project AUA's costs and related damages from other criminal violations.

The L'Aquila Court of Appeal ruling (Case 336/86), American Univeristy of Avezzano vs. City Hall of Avezzano, establishes to reevaluate the amount of 35 million according to the "ISTAT," although the financial statement submitted to the courts and other concerned parties are in US dollars. It must be stated that financial statements submitted to the authorities in the United States and Italy have been manipulated to have directed the court's ruling to an erroneous conclusion. However, new evidence far from the court's conclusion shows a turn-up of incalculable consequences. Disclosure of submitted financial statement documents still remain a crucial and fundamental aspect of the ruling. Vindication of all rights of ownership tied to Project AUA materials submitted to the city hall of Avezzano must be claimed and retained by the undersigned. The evidence from legal documentation also allows action for restitution of Project AUA's original materials, which are related to the intellectual property of the Campus of International Character, whether the city hall of Avezzano is still in possession or not. In case the city hall of Avezzano is no longer the possessor of said original materials through its own fault, then it is asked categorically to recover such material at its own expenses on behalf of the undersigned.

There is new evidence against the city hall of Avezzano's officers on charges that they have engaged in fraud by failing to fully disclose relevant financial information to Project AUA investor(s). This covers everything from failing to disclose kickbacks and bribes against specific city officials, to failing to state that the city hall of Avezzano cashed a check for land payment, after the land for the Campus was already altered. Considering the disclosure provisions of the Financial Investment Law, a very solid application for the arbitration resolution is necessary first, and/or evidence for new legal actions against the city hall of Avezzano. Again, it is no surprise that previously reported personal investigations and the trip-memo "Connubio tra Corrotti e Corruttori" could be verified by the SEC Division of Enforcement as former prominent locals "masterminded" or devised a kickback scheme, and these individuals must go on trial for criminal charges to be filed in United States under RICO statute violations.

Another aspect of this matter to be pursued is the anti-fraud statutes that bring criminal violations to the due process of law. It must be underlined that because of the fraud and kickbacks culture of the time, the projected Campus development plans suffered, which threatened the project's tax-exempt status and meant the loss of work, time, capital investment, and efforts connected with the project.

Because of law #43-1956, Financial Investment Treaty between Italy and the United States, the SEC is in a better position to arbitrate and reach a settlement with the Avezzano city hall finance officers. An agreement through arbitration must include paying Project AUA a total of 50 million US dollars to be endorsed by the SEC and Italian Ministry of Treasurer to settle claims that the city hall of Avezzano officials breached the land sale contract and altered connected project documentation. Hence, the SEC by means of a law suit to be filed in federal court in the United States, is able to freeze the corresponding funds deposited in accordance to the cited law.

The city hall of Avezzano, under a court order from United States, must agree to turn over Project AUA's original documentation to the undersigned for the arbitration process. The vindication claim to the original Project AUA documentation can be exercised also against any other possessor(s) for crimes related to intellectual property laws. This claim does not affect the statute of time limitation (*prescrizione*), because detention does not give access to adverse possession, nor to the property rights.

The action of vindication against the city hall of Avezzano, in the person of the mayor pro-tempore, is requested to be exercised according with law. In the event of failure to return such original Project AUA material, such legal action for the release and delivery of such property right is also requested. The above mentioned illegal acts by the city hall of Avezzanno and its persistent and continuing wrongdoing, together with the financial damages to Project AUA's activities have caused injury to the personal and professional reputations of the undersigned and to general business, as well.

Dear Sir:

Thank you for your letter of March 3, 1998.

Your letter is important to us. Even though we receive a large volume of letters, one of our investor assistance specialists will review your letter as quickly as possible and try to contact you within thirty days.

While you wait for our reply, we encourage you to read the enclosed flyer that explains how our office handles complaints or inquiries from investors and what you can expect from us in the weeks ahead. The flyer also contains important information about your legal rights and the deadlines you may face if you need to take legal action.

To keep track of your letter, we have assigned it the unique number that is listed in the top right corner of this letter. This number will help us locate your file quickly if questions should arise.

Thank you for your patience. We hope that our services will prove helpful to you.

After decades, things got much worse than better. History repeats itself, as evidenced by the attachment.

The Avezzano Public Hospital
Built on Parcel of Land Paid for by Project AUA

Before another trip to Italy, this article together with a schematic was given to prepare and to understand the Avezzano changing environment. Not only the road to the hospital, but a parking lot has been taken from Project AUA's proposed building structures and related facilities for the Campus. The hospital in question has been built and stands as a monument to the "obscure forces" which directly and indirectly opposed the campus realization.

The drive from Rome to the factory takes about an hour, the road winding up through hills that gradually become greener and more dramatic. You pass a dozen or so small villages perched on the top of steep hills, often completely dominated by the parish church. The road becomes steeper, the hills grow larger, and then quite suddenly there are the mountains, gray and rocky at the top, still with a big cap of snow.

Avezzano is in the middle of the Apennines, the mountainous spine that runs down the center of Italy. The location gives the chip factory a breathtaking view. It is built on the flat bed of a lake that was drained in the nineteenth century; the buildings are surrounded by mountains looming on every side. The canteen has one wall entirely composed of windows, from which perhaps a dozen peaks and the wide sky can be seen. This is not the sort of place where one expects to find a modern factory.

Texas Instruments, the American electronics giant that built the factory, says it chose the location for practical reasons: it is close to universities producing potential staff and to two other TI establishments. There is enough clean water to supply the factory with the sixty-three liters per second it needs for washing the silicon during the manufacturing stages. And the Italian government provided loans and grants amounting to more than half the total $1.2 billion cost of the project.

This vast investment was needed not to simply produce memory chips, but also more modern ones. Silicon chips benefit from economies of scale in two ways. The more bits the chip can store, the cheaper the memory is per bit. But bigger memories are more difficult to make, hence the need for more up-to-date equipment in a more modern factory. Avezzano is making chips with four million bits now, but in just a few years' time it will make sixteen-million-bit chips.

The second economy comes from the silicon itself. To make a chip, you begin with an ingot of silicon. It is a single crystal, grown from molten silicon into a long, sausage-shaped single crystal. The ingot is sawn into slices less than a millimeter thick. Several memory circuits are formed on one surface of a slice, and then the slice is cut up into chips. The fatter the sausage, the larger the slices and the more memories they can hold, cutting the price of each memory.

But the machines that handle the slices are made for a particular size of slice, and they have to be replaced or adapted to cope with bigger slices. Avezzano uses six-inch slices but has been designed so that it is relatively easy to adapt to eight inches.

However, there has been trouble in this specialized paradise: Avezzano is also the site of the worst earthquake known to have hit Italy. A recurrence could spell disaster for a sensitive factory. The individual transistors in the chips are minuscule and very vulnerable to movement while they're being made. Parts of them can be as small as 0.8 micrometers across, or 2 percent of the width of a human hair, and even the slightest movement of the chip during a stage of manufacture can be fatal. Specks of dust are equally damaging to these minute features.

Italy's worst earthquake was, in fact, 3,000 years ago, but the designers of the factory still went to extraordinary lengths to protect it against future quakes. The buildings should withstand the severest earthquake likely in a hundred years.

In any case, the Mafia is probably more of a threat in Italy these days than earthquakes. But the minister for public affairs, was having none of it. "I stress the social tranquility of this area," he declared, through an interpreter, during the opening ceremony. "There is no crime. And today, this is an exception." He continued happily: "There is no Mafia in this area. We have one of the lowest crime rates in Italy. I thank the police and the magistrates." The British journalists in the audience were delighted, not having expected to hear about anything as exciting as the Mafia at the opening of a factory.

They seemed even more impressed by the next part of the ceremony. "Why have we done all this?" said the managing director of TI in Italy, posing the ultimate question. "There are two forces behind our efforts: science and religion. For the layman, the replies to man's questions come from science. For a believer, replies to all the questions about life and work are far different because he trusts in God. We at Texas Instruments believe man's life must be made up of science and religion. The ceremony today represents a meeting between technology and faith." With that, the Bishop of Avezzano blessed the meeting hall, then the whole factory. He scattered holy water over the rostrum, and the factory was officially open. May God protect it from any Mafia and the restless earth.

Notes and Information Related to Public Health Coverage and Hospitals at Avezzano and in the Italian Regions in General.

The hospital built near the site defined for the Campus of International Character in Avezzano, Italy, as in many other hospitals in the entire country, represent the symbol of their community, which is now under investigation for certain privileged relationships between the public medical professionals and their private clinics. All over Italy, it is well know that in the majority of public hospitals that after weeks a recovered patient is usually forgotten in the structural and organizational labyrinth of the medical service bureaucracy. It is common to learn that a diagnostic examination consists only of the same words: "Another medical examination with more accuracy is needed; Particular medical tests are needed but they cannot be performed here. However, given the agreement with the regional medicare and medicaid insurance coverage, there are better possibilities to have these tests done in a private clinic; Here is a better place to be taken care of."

A private clinic in Italy, without any doubt, is a better place to recover, and certainly it becomes a positive experience. There, pretty nurses abound, full of courtesy, giving the most attention, and the place is spotless. At a private clinic, a patient is suddenly in a different kind of world. Even the medical doctors there become completely different human beings, showing the outmost dedication and concern. But, strangely enough, this human is often the same medical doctor with nasty manners who is met at the crowded public hospital, always full of noise, with sloppy nurses, roaming through those rooms that look more like a dormitory for the landing troops of World War One than anything else. Although regional medicare and medicaid insurance coverage is made available, and even if the private clinic cost is much higher than the public hospital, in the name of good health, it is provided.

In Avezzano, as well as in other parts of Italy, for instance, in the last few months there have been inquiries into hospitals and the public health insurance system that have produced files of information, very shameful, that seem to get bigger and bigger every day. This investigation into Italian medicare and medicaid and the perverse relationship between the public hospital and private clinic at the present is merely a spark of a bigger fire. In Italy, a strange development of wealthy private clinic centers coupled with the progressive empoverishment of the public health system does coexist. This is not all new, and it is very well reported by the mass media. It is very well known, also, that the Italian public medicare and medicaid insurance system is, as it always has been, the bastion of the center of power in the community. It makes it quite easy to understand why the local public hospital of Avezzano could have illegally built a road on the rezoned property developed and paid for by Project AUA. This and other issues were the main reasons why the city hall of Avezzano was not able to deliver the title for the Campus land as per written agreement and negotiations (See: Material related to litigation against the city hall of Avezzano).

To be able to understand the entire matter, the most important aspect of this investigation involves asking a question: How do public hospitals in Italy hire their medical doctors and staff? In order to answer this question, it is necessary to go a little further and to mention something that could lead to a whole new derangement mine of information: the technique usually used for the competitive public employment exams. Often, stories are told of how medical doctors and other personnel have been hired by public hospitals and the trickery used by means of the so-called "frozen ball" lottery contest.

For instance, how is one candidate preferred to somebody else? The mechanism is the following: there are several doctors who have more or less the same credentials for the same position as head of the hospital department. A decision is already made that the job position must be given to a specific doctor. However, the selection must be done by the ball extraction method, similar to a lottery. The balls, which represent each specific candidate for that job, are placed inside a box. A blindfolded person is called to extract the ball with the name of the winner candidate.

How is it possible to rig such a thing? In fact, the evening before the raffle, the ball that must be extracted is placed inside a freezer. The person who is in charge of selecting the ball, even if blindfolded, knows that the "frozen ball" must be selected. The beauty of all this is that all public exams are piloted in one way or in another. It is interesting to know how certain things are skillfully manipulated, especially in Italy, between the power of public hospitals and private clinics.

It also interesting to hear of some hot information connected with a disgusting kind of corruption that goes on and on. It seems that some insider at this point may start to talk quite openly and loudly. Perhaps this person is somebody who might also be implicated in this filthy mess of a public health system, who has a sudden attack of conscience and morality and who might push some doctors to stand out. Perhaps young doctors, who are rebelling against a system full of arrogance and thieves.

Usually in Italy, public hospital patients are admitted in the middle of the week for some kind of medical treatment. If a patient has some serious medical problems, because of weekends or a holiday there is a waiting time at least of another week before a medical doctor can make a diagnosis. As a remedy to this delay in diagnostics, the entire matter could be sped up by emergency admittance to a private clinic that is closely connected to the public hospital. This private clinic would also benefit from medicare and medicaid insurance coverage, and although it costs more, there are guarantees of better treatment.

From the acquired information, there are a multitude of cases when patients have been transferred on a regular basis from the public hospitals to the private clinics. The main reason is that at the private clinic is much quicker to take care of patients' illnesses. In contrast, at the public hospitals the process is very slow, full of negligence, and most of the time patients wait months or years to get a very serious medical opinion or surgical procedure. For instance, if there is an urgent heart surgery? A list with thousands of names is already waiting for that day or for that year to be admitted for surgery. It is not new that preoccupations and worries increase day by day, especially when all complaints addressed to competent authorities are as a normal rule ignored. Not too long ago, a study was made of these complaints in a voluminous published report. This report is pertinent information that could help to add more detailed facts to the inquiry.

Which are the competent authorities that manage the public health and the hospitals, medicare, and medicaid insurance in Italy? The State Ministry of Public Health; the Regional Administration of Hospitals and Health, and the Directors of Public Hospitals, known as USL. Italians get all kind of illnesses just thinking of them. The Ministry? Lately, this is a very famous authority, where bribe money and other illegalities headline everyday news. At this ministry, there is an investigation for corruption and other wrongdoing, similar to US RICO types of activities.

Regional medicare and medicaid? The number of those officials under investigation for wrongdoing is much higher of those who are not. As far the top local USL executives and public hospitals administrators—these persons are hired through the frozen ball technique mentioned before. Not too long ago, a patient died after a surgery was performed on the wrong person. The other patient on whom the surgery should have been performed also died because of neglect and other complications. Local newspapers reported these events, and an investigation was carried on. In spite of this and other problems, nothing has changed at the Avezzano public hospital, where the investigation is still underway.

It is also very well known that at least three-quarters of the average regional budget in Italy is allocated to medicare and medicaid purposes. About ten billion dollars, more or less, an amount ten times higher than the "hole" concealed by the renowned chemical giant Ferruzzi-Montedison, which horrifies the common citizen. That is the kind of money that the average Italian region has to allocate to directly and indirectly pay for generic and specialist medical assistance. This allocation guarantees coverage for conventional hospitals and reimbursements for those who use private clinic facilities and/or go to foreign hospitals, such as US medical institutions.

This budget is divided into eight parts: forty million dollars for partial reimbursement to patients who are cared for in nonconventional clinics and six hundred million dollars for private clinics. Why are things so wrong in the Italian public hospitals and health programs? A few calculations reveal the answer: University institutions and clinics where medical professionals are trained receive from the region an average of almost seven million dollars. Another five hundred million go to the conventional hospitals and health centers. These figures alone are enough to understand the basic mechanism that allows a kind of "perverted relationship" between public and private hospitals.

In Italy, it is enough to open a private clinic or to build a health center and make it qualify for medicare and medicaid insurance coverage; and then when some sophisticated equipment is acquired, the big play is done. The whole thing is done with very low-risk capital. That's why medical doctors and related professionals linked with the medicare and medicaid public health insurance system in Avezzano, as well as all over Italy, usually easily become rich and famous. Without flinching, this is the country's reality of yesterday, today, and tomorrow.

Some statistics show that public hospitals in Italy, in the last few years, have lost an average of three thousand beds at the regional level. Private clinics, instead, have increased their bed availability at a rate of almost 6 percent. It must be stated that the medical doctors and support personnel at these private clinics are often exactly the same ones found at the public hospitals. At the private clinics, usually the wives and other close family relatives of the most famous and prominent doctors are the owners and workers. As is openly said, three doctors perform one service in double shifts. Without any doubts, there are also gains at double cuts, as is evident from their income and wealth.

It seems that an inquiry was carried out by popular judges, identified as sweeping clean-up efforts, and several medical doctors and accomplices are already under investigation. Apart from the famous "Tangentopoli" corruption scandals in Italy, this investigation seems to be a work developed in shadows in order to reconstruct the not-too-clean plots between the public hospitals and the private clinics. However, in some of the investigation dossiers, there are petitions from patients, complaints from their families, and letters from some alarmed doctors that have been already reported in newspapers and other media. The public is quite aware of a kind of racket that diverts patients from public hospital beds to those at private clinics. The inquiry is long and difficult, although there is evidence too delicate to divulge. In any event, there are many certainties and produced evidences which are gathered with vital elements through the consultations on legitimacy of specific legal documentation.

Submitted by,

Project AUA
Sept. 24th, 1993

Update Status of the Projected Campus of I nternational Character

(Latest Development with the City Hall of Avezzano)

In the last few years, in spite of time spent on court litigation hearings, the projected American University of Avezzano, Within a Campus of International Character, has provided very important information related to specific development activities. As part of legal property rights and campus facilities building processes, these same activities have been brought to the attention of concerned parties. It has been stated more than once that including specific program activities, new and old, and already submitted materials, there is still very relevant evidence to make a significant contribution in responding to the needs of the connected community environment. Since the time when the projected Campus program was submitted to the city hall of Avezzano and other concerned parties, local environment changes have become a constant in the process in general and a variable in academic and non-academic pursuits in particular.

It must be recognized that among these variables and constants, there are certain legal commitments and some personal efforts that cannot be ignored any longer. The commitment framework still involves a persistent and continuing personal effort to establish contacts and collaborations with other concerned parties to pursue agreement objectives. However, there are several attempts to forge new mutually beneficial program alliances with private and public concerns, including constructing a user-friendly exit on the information pathway to help seek a wealth of individual brain power to resolve crucial problems and Campus program activities. The relevance of the Campus program as a center for higher learning and performance in research and development activities is the most important aspect of tasks and objectives undertaken (See specific submitted material and R/D activities).

Personal efforts in specific R/D activities have tackled environmental-health issues, including the cause and effects of in-situ community waste and the recycling process, which is carried on by a specialist team at specific locations: for instance, recovery of Solid Advanced Material (SAM) from the pyrophoric catalysts; the study of the greenhouse gas effect and related "white coal" activities are carried on mainly by Laboratory International experts. One of the most important programs submitted to concerned parties for consideration is Advanced Material In Construction Application (AMICA), which is designed for environment-health training and a relevant program in violence prevention and correction, as well as other waste potentials for community and school system recovery projects.

Also, business-environment activities undertaken at specific locations are refining program breakthrough of submitted material, which have already called the attention of Government and other concerns. The conversion of these program topics should extend economic-financial ties to offer some potential incentives for attracting new business to specific communities. It is important, therefore, that each concerned party be aware of these activities and the up-front commitment for the entire Campus program. Some of the R/D activities undertaken, as well as specific topics, have already been submitted and considered for a "SBIR" solicitation program. An outline of some of these topics has been submitted for concerned parties' acknowledgement and verification. A meeting was held on May 29, 1995, to discuss a public health program for Avezzano's projected Campus and related specific topics at L'Aquila Medical School with the dean of the medical school, the Director Public Health of CWRU; and another doctor from L'Aquila Hospital. A follow-up meeting was also held at Avezzano's city hall on May 30, 1995 to submit copies of the same public health program and to make direct contact with city officials and other concerned parties.

After a Quarter Century, a Dialogue With the City Hall of Avezzano (To Find Out About Project AUA's Campus Development): After a quarter century came another meeting with Avezzano city hall officials. This should have been a public hearing of major interest regarding Project AUA's program and facilities development in "Zona Barbazzano," the rezoned Campus area after a modification in the city's green planning, "Piano Verde" (See Deliberation and other documentation). Local citizens and concerned legal advisers have often asked for assurances that these meetings and discussions should not take place behind closed doors. An effort of civic obligation and direct information on how to bring this issue before local and not local citizens, especially in a place where the "chips" seem to have lost memory, become an outcome that the participants have taken for granted.

But concerned local citizens had many times suggested that they would have ample opportunity to comment and that there would be no deals cut or secret negotiations about past and present legal documentation and agreements. Copies of files submitted for the meeting were acknowledged and spoke for themselves. Through the dialogue with city hall officials, as suggested by the mayor of Avezzano, in the presence of my attorney, representatives, and concerned citizens, everything possible should be done until the entire city council is heard on this matter. Even before many details of this specific meeting would emerge and many other questions and answers be considered, one important point must be made once and forever about the use and ownership of the entire seventy-six acres of land negotiated and purchased for the Campus program development. (Perhaps the engineer, called for the occasion, should be able to answer some of the technical questions releated to "Variante al Piano Regolatore in Contrada Barbazzano," the rezoned Campus, and *adottato con Deliberazione N. 64 dell '8 Giugno 1968, approvato con Decreto del Ministero dei LL.PP N. 992 del 18 Luglio 1969 . . . .).*

The outcome of this specific meeting is expected to feature a surprise shift in public sentiment at the knowledge that the famous "Evergreen Plot," La Pineta, was unmistakably deflected in the past. This meeting with Avezzano city hall officials and concerned citizens, however, should try to make clear and to persuade the entire population that the initial Project AUA negotiatons aimed, above all, to benefit the surrounding community. This is an opportunity to explain what benefits Project AUA's program and operations would generate, based on a conservative annual estimate. Those attending should be reminded that the Campus zone of Avezzano was approved by the city of Avezzano's council in 1969 and a parcel of land negotiated and paid for. The multi-complex facility on a seventy-six-acre site would have been one of the largest construction projects in the city of Avezzano, perhaps only second to the drainage of Fucino's lake.

Project AUA had already submitted a plan for three phases within the entire "Campus Zone" acreage to Avezzano city hall and the prefect of the province. The first-phase construction facilities would have accomodated the buildings on the seventeen acres suggested by the city hall of Avezzano, which requested payment (See Deliberation and stipulated sales contract by the notary). Another twenty-acre parcel of land would have been bought from the same city hall by means of a public domain decree for building major residential housing for students and faculty. The Campus building facilities would have also expanded to other programs of scientific and technological pursuit, such as a research and development laboratory and public health-medical information center (See: Drafted Petition to International Court of Justice).

Since the beginning of project presentations and negotiations, there were agreements of cooperation with city hall officials to participate in building the Campus' infrastructure and, in early stages of construction development, to explore the possibilities of a feasibility study for the location of a parking garage project to ease the burden on the already congested traffic in the city of Avezzano (See feasibility study and proposals on Parking-Garage). Local supporters have suggested revamping such a project; documentation could be filed in a short period of time for consideration by the city hall of Avezzano's council. This new approach to a readaption of structural Campus concept development should be made first, to gauge the reactions of local citizens and city hall officials.

Although the land paid for and the other option for the project ownership vindication is still an open legal matter, those concerned for the Campus' construction development have suggested seeking the city hall of Avezzano's reapproval for a more flexible mixed-use designation of the "Evergreen" program, which is not clearly defined about how it is to be implemented. It must be underlined, however, that one of the major technical concerns remains whether or not the access road to the public hospital is built in accordance with the city's rezoning law.

One of the main objections centers around whether the access to the public hospital and parking area has harmed the original Campus design layout (Progetto di Massima) and any burden to the project development program and learning environment, as well as the degradation of the "Campus Zone" location and its charm and healthy atmosphere. Many local supporters of the projected Campus development still prefer to see the realization of the original Project AUA design. But there should be no surprise that at this first meeting at the city hall of Avezzano in almost a quarter century, the desire to work with everyone and make everyone very happy is openly stated, in spite any conflict of interest.

In addition to the trip-memo and suggestions submitted by the dean of L'Aquila Medical School to concerned parties, meetings and discussions were held with lawyers, mayors, doctors and even a professor from the Scuola Superiore di Polizia, Rome; as well as many others.

Submitted by:

Project AUA

Trip-Memo to Italy (May-June 1995).

To:

University Principal
Universita degli Studi L'Aquila
Piazza Vincenzo Rivera 1
67100 L'Aquila   March 13, 1995

Dear Professor:

You have been referred to me by the Human Resources Director for Texas
Instruments Italia SpA in Avezanno. Because of your position, your
input is vital to our planning.

I have been working with a group of educators and administrators
here in the United States. Their intention is to establish a learning center
in Italy that would provide educators and business leaders with a place
to hold conferences and workshops on a wide variety of subjects. These
programs could supplement existing curricula of participating institutions
or be part of a continuing education series for those professionals who
require periodic updating in their fields of interest. The participants could
be drawn from Italy or from other countries, depending on identified needs
and interests. We would like to make this a truly inter-institutional project
involving a number of universities, including your own. In this way we
would supplement and enhance the participating institutions educational
activities rather than duplicate them.

A great deal of work has already been undertaken to secure a site with
easy access that would be central to the region. The chairman of the project
is a native of your region and has been involved in negotiations for property
in Avezzano. I have been put in charge of working with universities and
their faculty, as well as helping design the facility format that will permit
it to have great flexibility to meet the varied needs of the faculty using it
for their conferences and workshops.

I am planning to be in the Avezzano, Italy, area and would like to
schedule a meeting with you and any department chairmen that you feel
appropriate to discuss how we can work together in the future. I will be in
Avezzano on May 29 and would like to set aside time either in the morning

or afternoon to talk with you and anyone else who would be interested in the project. Please let me know as soon as possible your wishes in this matter, and I will set the time aside in my schedule to be with you.

Respectfully yours,

Adjunct Assistant Professor of Family Medicine and
Director, Urban Area Health Education Center
Case Western Reserve University School of Medicine

A computerized system, comprising specific classes of white coal basic material (WCBM) rock geophysics and geomechanics field instrumentation, could be developed to assess the local environment, as well as the elastic and non-elastic stability of the underground characteristics of the proposed tunnel at the Subequana Valley, Region Abruzzo, Italy, (Ref.-Study and Research Activities of white coal; The Pescara River Banks and Up-Stream Tributaries and Others). The design of the tunnel opening and the employment of advanced technology for underground mining operations according to local standard methods of stress control could also be positively integrated to the same computer system. The instrumentation component of this system should be able to determine particular data derived from devices such as: Stressmeter, Propertymeter, Creepmeter, Exstensometer, and others, both simply and effectively. In situ information and data of the complex underground components computerized instrumentation capabilities, above all, should enable to scrutinize the available information of certain critical underground features at virtually any desirable intensity.

An effective use of the total computer system and instrumentation, in fact, should be able to provide the database necessary to design the various phases of the proposed tunnel project related to the white coal activities. Monitoring and measuring the WCBM removal rates from the tunnel, including the spatial distribution should also provide high quality closure data for use in validating and perfecting the overall project planning. The computer modellings will be employed as short—and long-term program projections, which will help to contribute to the improvement of both operations and economic operability. Additional detailed information of the computer system instrumentation, together with WCBM development activities, will be provided accordingly and with confidentiality.

Ackn.—Concerns.

Projected Tunnel in the Subequana/Peligna Valley (Abruzzo Region, Italy—Advantages and Benefits)

Tunnel excavation and exploitation of the extractive material in the Subequana/Peligna Valley of the Abruzzo region, Italy, are not the first or last construction project activities to be accomplished. The Abruzzo region itself is notorious for the many tunnels built during the course of history for other many purposes. Some of these project undertakings and underground activities provide data from present to prehistoric times. In the past, as well as the present time, the underground operational activities have consisted mainly in the excavation of the outcropping material identified as white coal basic material (WCBM). Tunneling more or less horizontally into the identified mountainsides of the Subequana/Peligna Valley is a valid alternative to descending vertically into the ground, in an open pit mode. Using advanced technology for such a tunneling excavation operation is possible because of the rock geoformation, better control of rock pressure (reliable supports for the tunnel), along with drainage, ventilation, and the usage of mechanical appliances such as the bore shaft machine designed for this type of excavation. The progress of the undertakings is connected and essentially tied to an electric power co-generator, which is needed to supply alternative energy for the operation of equipment necessary for the construction of the tunnel and for related pilot plant project activities to upgrade WCBM.

Before the tunnel activities and related operations, mainly to extract and to upgrade the selected material, are undertaken, elaborate calculations are needed not only for the geological and technical aspects of the activities but also for commercial, industrial, and other connected matters, such as finance and banking, marketing feasibility, contractor and sub-contractor agreements, local government permits, maintenance, and local manpower availability. Although methods for tunneling and material extractions may differ from one another because of differences in geological conditions and location, all these activities have certain features in common. Alternative access to the WCBM is gained either by means of a horizontal tunnel driven into the identified mountainside or by the existing problematic vertical open pit quarry. The WCBM extraction is formed into grades of suitable size and shape for domestic and foreign marketing. Only after the extensive preparatory work is completed can the actual tunneling activities commence in-situ.

WCBM underground extraction is characterized by its "dip" (inclination of strata in relation to the horizontal: the angle of dip is measured in the direction of maximum slope) and its "strike" (the horizontal direction at right angles to the dip). These two directions very largely determine the extent of the preliminary and preparatory operations (access of bore shaft machinery, subdivision into project design, sections, working contract and sub-contract), thus establishing the overall features of the tunnel's final viability. The support of the rock strata for the bore shaft and the tunnel concrete lining will depend not only on the condition of the rock geoformation but also on the life service of the tunnel construction. Thus, the main tunnel haulage road may last as long as the mountain itself, if from the outset it is provided with stronger and more durable concrete and construction materials other than headings, which have to perform their function for a relatively short time. For the WCBM tunnel extraction, a systematic project plan should be implemented and adhered to by concerned parties. Although this project plan might entail a certain amount of tunneling through unproductive rock (low grade or unclassified WCBM), the advantages of working according to a strict agreement of understanding with local government authorities is that the straight tunnel is built to connect the two adjacent valleys.

Extensive work in-situ and laboratory research and development (R/D) on WCBM activities have been addressed in other forums and related material disclosures submitted elsewhere. Although these activities are the main concern of the entire undertaking, other factors are taken into consideration for determinants of tunnel planning at the specific location. These factors are decisive for tackling related project problems, which are mainly linked to: A)—WCBM production costs that reflect specific charges for start-up, R/D, and project planning activities, as well as interest on the capital investment; B)—Transfer costs, which include the costs of transporting incoming project equipment, logistics, personnel, and outgoing shipments of raw material. An examination of comparative production costs is required, as well as separate but parallel consideration for different WCBM procurements; C)—Cost of local fuels and a co-generator of electric power, which is needed for tunneling, and further pilot plant development projects; D)—In-situ water resources and geographic factors; E)—Existing facilities, transportation, rates, and market potential; and F)—Compliance with environment-health laws established for public benefits.

In addition to these basic factors, local business performance; economic advantages and benefits to connected communities in particular and the region in general; together with possible local policies that are tied to industrial-commercial development are also examined and taken into account, as well as other tangible and intangible considerations. The influence of energy resources on the identified location, in general, is directly linked to that of WCBM process cost analysis, even though certain distinctive features are relatively connected to fuels and energy power considerations. These features are particularly striking in the transmission of electricity, where geographical variations in rates are based less upon the combined costs of generation and transmission than upon the nature of the load and the rate policies. Also, study of the supply and cost of labor require examination of individual factors to determine the quantity of labor available in the considered community, its uniformity or diversity, background of industrial or mechanical experience, existing wage scales, and general efficiency, such as adequate housing, local transportation, schools, churches, recreational facilities, and other community conditions.

Land contour, atmospheric temperatures, humidity, precipitation, waterways, and type of geoformation data are other factors are also considered. Extensive water supply is particularly needed for the WCBM extraction process, washing, humidification, and cooling. The water used by the project activity is not obtained from public water systems but rather from an indicated water well, where an abundant supply is available in-situ. The amount and type of water are carefully estimated to be available during all seasons, in view of both the immediate and potential requirements of specific proposed projects. The temperature of the water is a determinant and plays a dominant role in the entire project planning. Again, the exact location of the "Madonna della Pietra Bona" tunnel site is fundamentally dependent on the subsurface features, mainly the geoformation and strength of the underlying strata to support the tunnel lining weight, equipment excavation, and preventing excessive vibration of machinery. These are very important elements, which are taken into primary consideration for an assessment of the project evaluation. Most of the necessary work of collecting the basic data for the evaluation assessment, at this stage of the project activity, is found to be appropriately relevant, already accomplished with a private capital investment (Ref. Investment of Foreign Capital into Italy-Treaty between Italy and United States; Law #43-1956).

A broad survey and feasibility study of the location, in effect, does not remove the need for a much more intensive R/D activity of the resources from specific areas and of needs for future planning. Thus, in analyzing these data from the studies, R/D, and various location factors, the following orientative tabulation applies:

COST ITEM (Tunnel)	Total Expenditure	Percentage of total WCBM value
- MATERIALS, SUPPLIES, EQUIPMENT	$ 42,000,000	37
- WAGES AND LABOR INSURANCE	" 15,000,00	15
- FUELS AND OTHER ENERGY SOURCES	" 10,000,00	11
- CO-GENERATOR, ELECTRICITY PURCHASE.	" 7,000,00	6
- SALARIES AND CONTRACTORS SERVICES	" 6,000,000	4
-OTHER MISCELLANEOUS, INCLUDING PROFESSIONAL SERVICES, SUCH AS FEES, TAXES, PROFIT, INTEREST, ETCETERA	" 20,000,000	27
TOTAL PROJECT VALUE	$ 100,000,000	100

This orientative tabulation of anticipated items can be useful as a basis for provisional elimination of unimportant factors and for further analysis of important ones. However, it cannot stand by itself as a complete statement of relative weight of factors, because it ignores the differences in savings potential of several cost components. To conclude from the above cost projection, for instance, that materials, supplies, and equipment are rather more important than wages in determining the specific tunnel location (and/or future project planning) and that electric power rates are considerably less than half important as fuel prices is misleading, to say the least, since it implies other available alternatives in saving for WCBM cost procurement (öölitic formations). In actual fact, some of the itemized expenditures may be highly variable according to time, place, and business dealings and others not so. It is impossible to state at this point that one item is more important than another, until all factors are taken into account.

A comparative evaluation of the tunnel site, apart from intangible considerations, depends on: A)—The comparative amounts of capital investment necessary for the location finally considered, and B)—The probable operating costs respectively attributed to specific undertaken project activities. The relative importance of these two elements are tied strictly to financial circumstances (Ref. Cost Reevaluation and capital investment as per Law # 43-1956) and operating policies, as well as commitments by concerned parties. In any event, it is logical to include in the operating costs of the tunnel construction a reasonable rate of allowance for interest on the necessary capital investment. The elements that are included in the cost group are tabulated on each prospectus of the related project financial-economic plan.

Summary of Proposed Tunnel "Madonna Della Pietra Bona" and Adjacent Project Pilot Process Facilities For WCBM

Viewed as a whole, the project activities related to the "Madonna Della Pietra Bona" Tunnel, in the Subequana/ Peligna Valley, Abruzzo Region, Italy, certainly comprises a large number of interlinked operations. The whole is known and described in the "Underground Stability" methodologies investigation, including specific required patents which need careful advance planning, with adequate allowance for compensation and latitude at critical points in the system. There is a disposit of unqualified WCBM, a residue of valueless material that is encountered in lode or veins, and all this might present a difficult problem, mainly because of the manpower and costs that are involved in the underground extraction. In the tunnel operation alone, extraction wages account for something like 40 to 70 percent of the total prime cost of the qualified WCBM. It is therefore essential to utilize labor as carefully and efficiently as possible. At the same time, the tunnel operation must, perhaps more than any other project activity, concern itself with matters of safety to protect the workers from accident and injury and to ensure smooth operation of the undertaking.

Besides the underground activities (bore shaft) and WCBM tunneling extraction, the operation also includes extensive semi-surface installations, including buildings and other structures accomodating the WCBM excavation dressing and dispatch facilities, such as the boiler and power-generating plant, winding gear, lamps and lighting equipment, dressing rooms and washrooms, store areas, administrative offices, et cetera; et cetera. In addition, workshops must be fully equipped to carry out a wide variety of repairs to machinery and to store spare parts and tools that are liable to suffer damage in the rough working conditions of the WCBM underground excavation process. Hence, ventilation is imperative in the tunnel construction and serves three main purposes: to provide fresh air for respiration by the underground workers, to dilute any noxious gases that may be formed underground (including fumes from equipment), and to vent the natural heat of the rock.

It is also important to make a study connected not only to the underground tunnel ventilation, but above all that concerning "Pie' de Vent" air current and its environment. Planning for the tunnel ventilation system in reference to the surface "Monte Ventola" environment includes the preparation of the so-called "airflow-sheet diagram," comprising data on air-flow conditions. These diagrams are prepared for each section of the tunnel and for the surface area as a whole, and the data is to be checked against measurements of the actual present and future airflowin situ. For reasons of safety, in fact, the main airflow will be split up into the largest possible number of circulating currents, and it is essential to prevent short circuits; circumstances causing the airflow to bypass certain parts of the tunnel. Parts that are not accessible to natural ventilation have to be provided with auxiliary ventilation. It is important, therefore, to consider an air-compressor a priority on the list of equipment for the project design (Feasibility Study for Underground Air Storage Design and Alternative Co-generator).

Because of the high proportion of worker wages in the production costs, mechanization and advanced process technology are necessary in the tunnel activities. On the other hand, because of the often difficult conditions in which the product, via WCBM underground extraction, is obtained, the scope of mechanization of the operation process is not limited only to the bore shaft machine but is mainly related to specific methodologies defined for underground WCBM extraction stability in the tunnel. Coordination of the various mechanical handling appliances is ensured by a control center operating with automatic interlocking optical and acoustic signaling systems in conjunction with measuring and monitoring equipment; overall control is to be assisted by remote readings at the surface mobile laboratory facilities of measured quantities, electronic data processing by computers, and a variety of other up-to-date aids. A very elaborate and important device for the tunnel WCBM extraction is the fully mechanized remote-controlled hydraulic chock, which will be used to provide temporary support in situations where stability is very important, particularly at working face.

The laboratory and the Pilot Process Plant (PPP) facilities are designed to be located adjacent to the tunnel's Castel di Ieri/Goriano Sicoli location, so that only the processed WCBM, free of waste matter such as recovered CO2, can be sold and transported. In general the WCBM preparation is started with excavation, crushing, and grinding. The degree of comminution (size reduction) that is applied may depend on the size of WCBM lumps selectivity and on the requirements for the subsequent treatment to be applied. Sizing and classifying—i.e., grading the comminuted WCBM according to particle size—are important operations in the first step of the qualification process. To relieve the crushing and grinding machines of unnecessary load, particles that have been sufficiently reduced in size are removed by screening. Sizing of relatively coarse particles can most efficiently be performed by screening, and screens of many kinds are used for the purpose.

Depending on the WCBM treatment that is considered, the roasting process (Storta) and/or defined underground retort methodologies are controlled by desired temperature, that is transformed into its oxide (dead roasting); alternatively, only a proportion of selected WCBM is oxided, while the rest will remain combined with the CO2 by partial roasting. Commercially, there are many different types and varieties of roasting furnaces. The WCBM for roasting is introduced into the top of the combustion chamber, with a stream of preheated air. Gases are swirled in the chamber, so that the larger particles settle in the hopper bottom while the gases (CO2) flow to the top. The WCBM is fed into the Storta (open-hearth furnace) by a belt conveyor; although other methods are taken into consideration for the underground retort. When the Storta and the underground retort are charged or prepared, the WCBM is heated up to 1700 C, at which temperature oxidation takes place according to the standard reaction: WCBM + heat = UpgradeWCBM + CO2 + 40 Kcal.

Thanks for the attention and consideration.

Memorandum of Meetings and Discussions (Trip to Italy; Feb. 7-19, 2000)

Several meetings were held to discuss the geological aspect of the proposed activities related to the "Madonna della Pietra Bona" Tunnel (TMPB) and the pilot plant process (PPP) for the conversion of white coal basic material (WCBM) extraction. It was agreed among the participants to the meetings, especially from the conference with the Abruzzo Region "LL.PP." that a geological study of specific locations should be a top priority of the TMPB project activities. Collaboration from other experts, perhaps from CWRU's Geology Department in Cleveland, should be involved in carrying out such geological studies. Suggestions and recommendations are provided for consideration and also for an evaluation of the entire undertaking.

A geophysic study including microseismic monitoring is suggested, together with other activities to determine the underground stability of the TMPB location. It consists of recording information and analyzing the microseismic data generated in situin situ in order to determine whether the WCBM geoformation is stable or becoming unstable. Mainly in the case of an unstable geoformation, it is very important that microseismic monitoring can be used to evaluate the effectiveness of any remedial action that should be taken to prevent or control WCBM rock failure. Portable multi-geophone systems, as well as fixed versions, are available for both microseismic and acoustic-emission monitoring. It is a priority to establish in place one of the most sophisticated microseismic monitoring systems, such as the arrival-time source-location, in geotechnical field. It is apparent that a large number of events can occur daily if the TMPB underground activities are even moderately microseismically active.

While a great deal of time and money is required to gather some of this geotechnical data, even more time and effort is needed to assess information to determine the cause of a problem. It is understood and agreed to establish "credibility"; meaningful analysis and interpretation of the data should include the site geology, WCBM rock properties, loading conditions, TMPB excavation geometry and sequence, and any other field measurements that are necessary. Visits to problem areas must be made on a continuing basis, and related observations from the geological study concerns should be considered, as they are closer to the problem and have a good feeling for how the WCBM rock and/or underground activity is behaving. It is also recognized that rock excavation is a major environmental hazard at the location's "open pit" quarry. The resulting loss of anticipated WCBM production and related expenses of troubleshooting and repair must be considered carefully to avoid any operational problems. Personal suggestions and recommendations are made available for reference. Thank you for your attention.

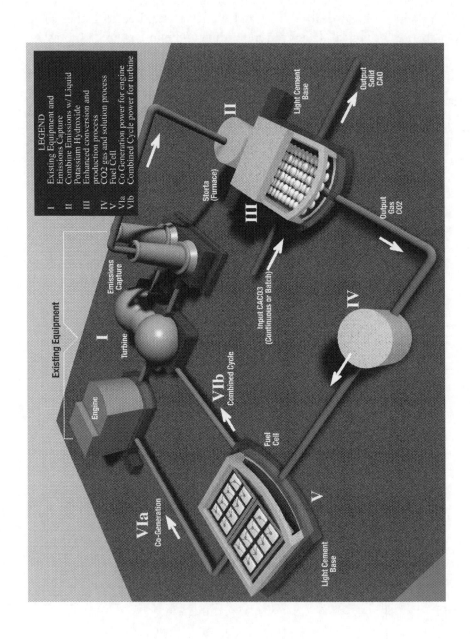